PARMENIDES

Studies in Continental Thought

Martin Heidegger

PARMENIDES

Translated by
André Schuwer and
Richard Rojcewicz

Indiana University Press
BLOOMINGTON AND INDIANAPOLIS

Publication of this work was supported by funding
from Inter Nationes, Bonn.

This book is a publication of

Indiana University Press
601 North Morton Street
Bloomington, IN 47404-3797 USA

http://www.indiana.edu/~iupress

Telephone orders 800-842-6796
Fax orders 812-855-7931
Orders by email iuporder@indiana.edu

Published in German as *Parmenides* © 1982
by Vittorio Klostermann,
Frankfurt am Main

English translation © 1992 by Indiana University Press
First paperback edition 1998

Manufactured in the United States of America

Library of Congress Cataloging-in-Publication Data

Heidegger, Martin, 1889–1976.
    [Parmenides. English]
    Parmenides / Martin Heidegger ; translated by André Schuwer
and Richard Rojcewicz
        p.   cm. — (Studies in Continental thought)
    Translation of: Parmenides; based on a lecture course given
1942–43 at the University of Freiburg.
    Includes bibliographical references
    ISBN 0-253-32726-1 (alk. paper). — ISBN 0-253-21214-6
(pbk. : alk. paper)
    1. Parmenides.   2. Philosophy.   I. Title.   II. Series.
B3279.H48P3713   1992
182'.3—dc20   91-19431

2 3 4 5 6 03 02 01 00 99 98

Contents

v

Contents

TRANSLATORS' FOREWORD

This book is a translation of the text of Martin Heidegger's lecture course from the winter semester 1942-43 at the University of Freiburg. It was published posthumously as vol. 54 of his "Collected works" (*Gesamtausgabe*) in 1982. As the editor of the volume indicates, the course was actually entitled "Parmenides and Heraclitus," but in view of the preponderant treatment of Parmenides over Heraclitus in the lectures as delivered, the title was altered in publication.

In accord with Heidegger's firm directive, his collected works are not appearing in a critical edition but as writings *"aus letzter Hand."* That is to say, the volumes in the series come "straight from his hand" and contain a minimum of scholarly apparatus such as variant readings, commentaries, emendations, etc. "Ways, not works" (*Wege, nicht Werke*) —that is the motto Heidegger placed at the head of his *Gesamtausgabe*. The difference is surely not that ways are meandering and tentative, works polished and final. The motto is thus not a kind of apology for a lack of rigor. Heidegger had in mind something else entirely; perhaps we could say that for him a work is the work of an author but a way is a way of thought. The motto thus expresses Heidegger's desire that attention be diverted away from himself as holding such and such an opinion, originating such and such a standpoint, having such and such a place within the history of philosophy, etc. All that sort of historical-philological consideration was of minor importance to Heidegger. He wished to have certain ideas examined on their own merit, and he wished that others would engage themselves in the issues facing thought, but he had no desire to be the subject of learned debate as to what he "really" did or did not say. Naturally, Heidegger wanted his writings to be issued with due editorial care. But it was his belief that the scholarly trappings of a critical edition, though well meant, could obscure a focus on the matter of thought and lead to "Heidegger scholarship" of a most sterile kind. Hence the *Gesamtausgabe letzter Hand*.

The translations of the volumes in the collected works come under the same strictures. The reader will find here everything available to aid his or her understanding of the text that the reader of Heidegger's original German possesses, which amounts to little more than the bare text itself. In particular, neither the editor nor the translators feel compelled, or even justified, to prejudge for the reader what she or he will find within these pages. We shall limit ourselves here, then, to a few brief remarks concerning some technical aspects of the translation.

Heidegger treats language with the utmost respect, and he exploits all the possibilities his native German offers, especially for plays on words. Yet this linguistic dexterity can be exasperating for the work of translation. Very seldom can a play on words in German be carried over into English without convoluted turns of phrase. In one or two places we felt justified in taking a certain liberty with English in order to capture something of Heidegger's use of language. For instance, Heidegger's word for "beginning" is *Anfang*. Etymologically, *Anfang* derives from *an* (in, at, to) and *fangen* (to seize, take, catch). This derivation supports Heidegger's claim that the beginning of thinking is not something the primordial thinkers carry out from their own resources but something the beginning does to them; they do not themselves take up the beginning, but, quite to the contrary, they are seized and taken up *by* the beginning. Happily (though perhaps there are those who will be disconcerted by our recourse to it) the English language has another word for "beginning"—with an etymology corresponding to that of *Anfang*. That word is "inception," deriving from the Latin *in* (in, at, to) and *capere* (to seize, take, catch). We believe that our employment of "in-ception" (with a hyphen to emphasize the derivation) in the appropriate context is at least a semi-successful example of preserving both the letter and spirit of Heidegger's language. The reader should be advised, however, that we are well aware of Heidegger's warning, in the very book at hand, against just such a procedure: e.g., in his proscription of translation as a mere copying of "word-forms." And in fact very rarely did we find it possible to translate by matching word-forms. Two examples might be illustrative in this regard: the words *Übersetzung* and *Entbergung*.

Entbergung is a coinage on Heidegger's part. It means, essentially, "disclosure" and becomes Heidegger's preferred translation of the Greek ἀλήθεια (aletheia, "truth"). For Heidegger, as is well known, ἀλήθεια has a rich essence, and he attempts to capture something of that richness by emphasizing in turn the two components of the word *Entbergung*. Thus he maintains that truth is both an Ent*bergung* and an *Ent*bergung. A translation that slavishly followed the word-form would say that truth is a *dis*closure and a dis*closure*. But this would fail to capture the change in sense that occurs when the accent is placed on the *Bergung*, for the word by itself means "salvage," "recovery," "shelter." Yet to declare simply that ἀλήθεια signifies both disclosure and shelter would surely seem to be combining two unrelated items. The translation of *Ent*bergung then has to retain the ideas both of closure (to show the connection with "disclosure") and shelter (to indicate the sense of *Bergung*). Depending on the context, our translation of *Ent*-bergung has varied somewhat, but for the most part we have had recourse to the circumlocution "sheltering en-closure."

Übersetzung would ordinarily be rendered "translation." Again Heidegger plays on the components of the word and distinguishes between Über*setzung* and *Über*setzung. And, once again, a translation that merely copied the form, *trans*lation versus trans*lation*, would miss the point, even though the derivation of these English and German words is practically the same: they both mean "to carry over." By emphasizing the prefix, in German the sense changes in a way that cannot be captured in English by following the same strategy. For Über*setzung* no longer refers to the linguistic act of translation but has a more basic concrete sense of literally "carrying over." We have thus rendered Über*setzung* as "transporting." Heidegger's claim that every act of translating is founded upon a transporting (of ourselves into a new realm of meaning) should then be understandable.

Finally, the text, as one might expect in a book on ancient philosophy, is heavily flavored with Greek and Latin. It is giving away no secret that Heidegger decried the Latinizing of things Greek, and one of the central themes of the present volume is the impoverishment in the understanding of Being concomitant with such "transporting." It seemed to us, therefore, that it would be altogether inappropriate, although perhaps making for easier reading, to Romanize the Greek script in a book so adamantly opposed to Latinization. To the reader unfamiliar with Greek, certain passages might appear rather formidable, then. Nevertheless, almost every word Heidegger employs in a classical language is also translated by him, and in those few instances where that is not the case we have included a translation in a footnote, hoping our version does not violate Heidegger's own style of translation, determined as it is by his highly individual and original interpretation of the ancients.

For the rest, the book's format and content very closely match the source text. The German pagination is indicated in the running heads, and all footnotes are Heidegger's, or the editor's, except for those few translators' notes marked "Tr."

A.S.
R.R.
Simon Silverman Phenomenology Center
Duquesne University

PARMENIDES

Introduction

Preparatory Meditation on the Name and the Word *ΑΛΗΘΕΙΑ* and Its Counter-Essence. Two Directives from the Translating Word *ΑΛΗΘΕΙΑ*.

a) Ordinary acquaintance and essential knowing. Renunciation of the prevalent interpretation of the "didactic poem" by heeding the claim of the beginning.

Παρμενίδης καὶ Ἡράκλειτος, Parmenides and Heraclitus—these are the names of the two thinkers, contemporaries in the decades between 540 and 460, who at the outset of Western thought uniquely belong together in thinking the true. To think the true means to experience the true in its essence and, in such essential experience, to know the truth of what is true.

Chronologically, 2,500 years have elapsed since the outset of Western thought. But the passing of the years and centuries has never affected what was thought in the thinking of these two thinkers. And this resistance to all-consuming time is by no means due to the simple conservation of the thought these thinkers had to think—i.e., a conservation somewhere, at some supratemporal place, as the so-called "eternal." On the contrary, what is thought in this thinking is precisely the historical, the genuinely historical, preceding and thereby anticipating all successive history. We call what thus precedes and determines all history the beginning. Because it does not reside back in a past but lies in advance of what is to come, the beginning again and again turns out to be precisely a gift to an epoch.

In essential history the beginning comes last. Naturally, to a way of thinking acquainted only with the form of calculation, the proposition "The beginning is the last" is nonsense. To be sure, at first, at the outset, the beginning appears veiled in a peculiar way. Whence stems the re-

1

markable fact that the beginning is easily taken for the imperfect, the unfinished, the rough. It is also called the "primitive." And so the thinkers before Plato and Aristotle are said to be "primitive thinkers." Of course, not every thinker at the outset of Western thought is by that very fact also a thinker of the beginning, a primordial thinker. The first primordial thinker was named Anaximander.

The two others, the only others besides Anaximander, were Parmenides and Heraclitus. An impression of arbitrariness is bound to arise from our distinguishing these three thinkers as the first primordial thinkers preceding all other thinkers of the Occident. And in fact we do not possess any easily available proof that could provide an immediate foundation for our allegation. For that, we would need to acquire a genuine relation to the primordial thinkers. Such will be our goal in these lectures.

In the course of the ages of Western history, later thinking is not only distant from its outset—i.e., chronologically distant—but also, and above all, it is removed from its beginning—i.e., distant with respect to what is thought. Subsequent generations become more and more alienated from the early thinking. Finally the distance becomes so great that doubt arises as to whether or not a later age is at all capable of rethinking the earliest thoughts. To this doubt another one attaches, questioning whether such a project, supposing it is in fact possible, would be of any use. What could we hope to accomplish, wandering astray amid the almost vanished traces of a long since past thought? And these doubts as to the possibility and usefulness of the undertaking receive still further reinforcement from the circumstance that this early thinking has been transmitted to us only in fragments. Here lies the explication of the fact that the views of scholars concerning the early "philosophy" of the Greeks vary widely and that the apprehension of these philosophical thoughts is utterly uncertain.

The intention to reflect today on the thinking of Parmenides and Heraclitus is in this way surrounded by manifold doubts and objections. We shall allow these doubts and objections to stand and so spare ourselves the task of rebutting them in detail. Even if we wanted to engage in a confrontation with these objections, we would still have to accomplish first of all what is unavoidable in any case, namely to think the thoughts both these thinkers have thought. And we could then not escape this one requirement that, before all else, we attend to the words of these thinkers. Perhaps if we pay sufficient attention and persevere in our thinking, we will discover the aforementioned doubts to be without foundation.

The words of Parmenides have the linguistic form of verses and strophes. They seem to be a "poem." But because the words present a "philosophical doctrine," we speak of Parmenides' "doctrinal poem" or "didactic poem." Yet this characterization of his thoughtful utterances actually arises out of an impasse. We know poetry and poems, and we also know philosophical treatises. It is easy to see, however, that in the verses of Parmenides there is hardly anything "poetical," though on the contrary we find a great deal of what is generally called "the abstract." It therefore appeared that the best way to characterize the content of the thoughtful statements in question was to take into account at once both moments, the form of the verse and the "abstract content," and so speak of a "doctrinal" or "didactic poem."

Perhaps, however, we have here neither a "poem" of "poesy" nor a "doctrine." But how the words are said and how the said is thought, that can surely be made clear only if we first know what is thought here and what had to come to speech. Here in a unique way the word is spoken and a dictum is uttered. We will therefore henceforth call the primordial word of Anaximander, of Parmenides, and of Heraclitus the dictum of these thinkers. We mean by their "dictum" the whole of their utterances, not just single propositions and enunciations. In order to give tradition its due, however, we shall still speak at first of the "didactic poem" of Parmenides.

(Since a separate edition of Parmenides' text has not been available for a long time, I had the text transcribed and copied. The transcription is arranged in such a way that the participants in the course, following the progress of the individual lectures, can insert the respective translation on the facing page.)

We will choose the most secure way to learn what is said and thought in the words of Parmenides. We will follow the text. The appended translation already contains an interpretation of the text. This interpretation, of course, needs clarification. But neither the translation nor the clarification carry much weight so long as what is thought in the word of Parmenides does not itself address us. Everything depends on our paying heed to the claim arising out of the thoughtful word. Only in this way, paying heed to the claim [*Anspruch*], do we come to know the dictum [*Spruch*]. What man heeds, what respect he gives to the heeded, how original and how constant he is in his heedfulness, that is what is decisive as regards the dignity allotted to man out of history.

To think is to heed the essential. In such heedfulness essential knowing resides. What we usually call "knowing" is being acquainted with something and its qualities. In virtue of these cognitions we "master" things. This mastering "knowledge" is given over to a being at hand, to its structure and its usefulness. Such "knowledge" seizes the being, "dominates" it, and thereby goes beyond it and constantly surpasses it. The character of essential knowing is entirely different. It concerns the being in its ground—it intends Being. Essential "knowing" does not lord it over what it knows but is solicitous toward it. For instance, to take just one example, every "science" is a cognitive mastering, an outdoing, and a surpassing, if indeed not a complete bypassing, of a being. All of which occurs in the manner of objectivization. Versus this, essential knowing, heedfulness, is a retreat in face of Being. In such retreating we see and we perceive essentially more, namely something quite different from the product of the remarkable procedure of modern science. For the latter is always a technical attack on a being and an intervention for purposes of an "orientation" toward acting, "producing," wheeling and dealing. Thoughtful heedfulness, in contrast, is attention to a claim that does not arise from the separate facts and events of reality and does not concern man in the superficiality of his everyday occupations. Only when this claim of Being, and not some objectivity or other out of the multiplicity of beings, addresses us in the word of Parmenides will the knowledge of his "propositions" have any justification. Without paying attention to this claim, whatever care we might contrive in the clarification of his thinking occurs in a void.

The order of our clarification of the individual fragments is determined by an interpretation of the leading thoughts. We base the separate clarifications on this interpretation, one which, of course, can only gradually come to light. The individual fragments are numbered in Roman numerals. We shall begin, it would seem arbitrarily, with the first fragment and specifically with verses 22–32.

I, 22–32.

22   And the goddess received me with sympathy; she took my right
       hand in her hand; then she spoke the word and addressed me
       in this way: "O man, companion of immortal charioteers,
25   arriving at our home with the steeds that convey you. Blessing
       be bestowed on you! For it is not an evil fate which has sent you
       ahead to travel on this way—and truly this way is apart from men,
       outside their (trodden) path—but, rather, rule and order. There
       is, however, a need that you experience everything, both the stable
       heart of well-enclosing unconcealment,
30   as well as the appearing in its appearance to mortals, where there
       is no relying on the unconcealed. Also this, however, you will
       learn to experience: how the appearing
32   (in the need) remains called upon to be apparent, while it shines
       through everything and (hence) in that way brings everything to
       perfection.

The thinker Parmenides tells of a goddess who greets him as he arrives at her home in the course of his travels. To the greeting, whose proper essence the goddess herself clarifies, she adds an announcement of the revelations she has in store for the thinker as he goes his way. Hence everything the thinker says in the subsequent fragments of the "didactic poem" is the word of this goddess. If, at the very beginning, we pay heed to this and preserve it well and rigorously in our memory, from then on we shall take our direction from the insight, to be acknowledged gradually, that the dictum of the thinker speaks by bringing into language the word of this goddess.

Who is the goddess? We anticipate the answer conveyed only by the "didactic poem" as a whole. The goddess is the goddess "truth." "The truth"—itself—is the goddess. Hence we shall avoid the locution that would speak of a goddess "of" the truth. For the expression "goddess of truth" evokes the idea of a goddess to whose patronage and blessing "the truth" is only entrusted. In that case, we would have two items: on the one hand "a goddess" and on the other "the truth," standing under divine protection. We could then illustrate this state of affairs in accordance with familiar examples. The Greeks worshiped, for instance, the goddess Artemis as the goddess of hunting and of animals. Hunting and animals are not the goddess Artemis herself but are what is dedicated to her and what stands under her protection. If, however, Parmenides calls the goddess "truth," then here truth itself is being experienced as a goddess. This might seem strange to us. For in the first place we would consider it extremely odd for a thinker to relate his thinking to the word of a divine being. It is distinctive of the thinkers who later, i.e., from the time of Plato, are called "philosophers" that their own meditation is the source of their thoughts. Thinkers are indeed decidedly called "thinkers" because, as is said, they think "out of" themselves and in their very thinking put themselves at stake. The thinker answers questions he himself has raised. Thinkers do not proclaim "revelations" from a god. They do not report the inspirations of a goddess. They state their own insights. What then are we to make of a goddess in this "didactic poem" which brings to words the thoughts of a thinking whose purity and rigor have never recurred since? But even if Parmenides' thinking did arise out of a ground as yet hidden to us and therefore rightfully stood in a relation to the goddess "truth," we would nonetheless still be lacking the immediate appearance of a divine figure such as we are familiar with in the Greek world. Athena, Aphrodite, Artemis, and Demeter appear as unequivocally delineated "divine persons." The goddess "truth," on the other hand, is largely "abstract." One could even maintain that we have to do here with no "mythical experience" of this goddess but that a thinker out of his own initiative is "personifying" the universal concept "truth" in the indeterminate figure of a goddess. In fact we very often come across this device of "hypostatizing" universal concepts as divinities, especially in later antiquity.

Perhaps the thinker Parmenides is using a similar device in order to give more fullness and color to his otherwise all too "abstract" thoughts. In addition, if we consider that the start of Western thought is accomplished with the Greeks, according to the prevalent view, by a dissociation of "logos" (reason) from "mythos," then it seems entirely understandable that in the first "primitive" attempts at such thinking there might still be preserved remnants of "mythical" representation. By means of such reflections, the presence of a goddess in a "philosophically didactic poem" might be adequately explained. And from this explanation it follows that the reference to the goddess and she herself can now be dismissed as poetical and pseudo-mythical decorations, since indeed what matters is only to come to know the "philosophical system" of the thinker.

That is the merest sketch of a widely-held position concerning the appearance of the goddess in the didactic poem of Parmenides. Although it is advocated in all sorts of treatises, it nevertheless remains a singular error. If this position originated only in the presumption of successive generations to know everything better, or if it were merely the product of historiographical comparison, calculating back and forth between the appearances of former and later times, then we could dispense with such explanations. The difficulty is that in them a mode of thought is speaking which, over two millennia, has solidified itself in the West and is in a certain respect even an aberrant consequence of the very thinking expressed in Parmenides' "didactic poem." We ourselves move within the long tradition of this mode of thinking, and we take it therefore as the "natural" one.

Supposing, however, that the thinking of Parmenides and of Heraclitus is essentially of an other kind, then what is required of us is a renunciation of the prevailing views, a renunciation that has nothing to do with the mere refutation of scholarly misinterpretations of the two thinkers. Actually, the renunciation touches us personally and affects us in an ever new manner and ever more decisively. Only superficially does this renunciation seem to be a "negative" attitude. In truth it accomplishes the first step, whereby we pledge our heedfulness to the claim of the beginning, a beginning which, in spite of the historiographically represented temporal remoteness, is closer to us than what we are wont to consider the nearest.

Recapitulation

1) Outset and beginning. Ordinary thinking and the thinking begun by the beginning. Retreating in face of Being. The few and simple texts. Reference to "translating."

We are attempting to follow the path of thought of two thinkers, Parmenides and Heraclitus. Both belong, historiographically calculated, to the early period of Western thought. With regard to this early thinking in the Occident, among the Greeks, we are distinguishing between *outset* and *beginning*. Outset refers to the coming forth of this thinking at a definite "time." Thinking does not mean here the course of psychologically represented acts of thought but the historical process in which a thinker arises, says his word, and so provides to truth a place within a historical humanity. As for time, it signifies here less the point of time calculated according to year and day than it means "age," the situation of human things and man's dwelling place therein. "Outset" has to do with the debut and the emergence of thinking. But we are using "beginning" in a quite different sense. The "beginning" is what, in this early thinking, is to be thought and what is thought. Here we are still leaving unclarified the essence of this thought. But supposing that the thinking of a thinker is distinct from the knowledge of the "sciences" and from every kind of practical cognition in all respects, then we have to say that the relation of thinking to its thought is essentially other than the relation of ordinary "technical-practical" and "moral-practical" thinking to what it thinks.

Ordinary thinking, whether scientific or prescientific or unscientific, thinks beings, and does so in every case according to their individual regions, separate strata, and circumscribed aspects. This thinking is an acquaintance with beings, a knowledge that masters and dominates beings in various ways. In distinction from the mastering of beings, the thinking of thinkers is the *thinking of Being*. Their thinking is a *retreating in face of Being*. We name what is thought in the thinking of the thinkers the beginning. Which hence now means: Being is the beginning. Nevertheless, not every thinker, who has to think Being, thinks the beginning. Not every thinker, not even every one at the outset of Western thought, is a primordial thinker, i.e., a thinker who expressly thinks the beginning.

Anaximander, Parmenides, and Heraclitus are the only primordial thinkers. They are this, however, not because they open up Western thought and initiate it. Already before them there were thinkers. They are primordial thinkers because they think the beginning. The beginning is what is thought in their thinking. This sounds as if "the beginning" were something like an "object" the thinkers take up for themselves in order to think it through. But we have already said in general about the thinking of thinkers that it is a retreating in face of Being. If, within truly thoughtful thinking, the primordial thinking is the highest one, then there must occur here a retreating of a special kind. For these thinkers do not "take up" the beginning in the way a scientist "attacks" something. Neither do these thinkers come up with the beginning as a self-produced construction of thought. The beginning is not something dependent on the favor of these thinkers, where they are active in such and such a way, but, rather, the reverse: the beginning is that which begins something with these thinkers—by laying a claim on them in such a way that from them is demanded an extreme retreating in the face of Being. The thinkers are begun by the beginning, "in-cepted" [*An-gefangenen*] by the in-ception [*An-fang*]; they are taken up by it and are gathered into it.

It is already a wrong-headed idea that leads us to speak of the "work" of these thinkers. But if for the moment, and for the lack of a better expression, we do talk that way, then we must note that their "work," even if it had been preserved for us intact, would be quite small in "bulk" compared with the "work" of Plato or Aristotle and especially in comparison with the "work" of a modern thinker. Plato and Aristotle and subsequent thinkers have thought far "more," have traversed more regions and strata of thinking, and have questioned out of a richer knowledge of things and man. And yet all these thinkers think "less" than the primordial thinkers.

The problematic circumstance that a modern thinker needs a book of 400 or more pages in order to express something of what he has to say is an unerring sign that modern thinking stands outside the realm of the primordial thinking. In this connection we might recall Kant's *Critique of Pure Reason* and Hegel's *Phenomenology of Spirit*. Such signs make us realize that for a long time now the world has been out of joint and man is on the path of error. We must, however, also bear in mind that the book grounding modern philosophy, Descartes's *Meditationes de prima philosophia* comprises little more than a hundred pages and that decisive treatises of Leibniz require only a few sheets of letter-writing paper. These facts, apparently only extrinsic, point out that in these treatises, very concentrated and simple as regards their internal construction, a transformation of thinking is enacted, one which, to be sure, does not arrive at the beginning but which once more approaches its perimeter. Because we have been forced, for a long time now, to procure our knowledge by a process of selection from the excess of what is spoken and written, we have lost the capacity to hear the *few simple things* said in the words of the primordial thinkers.

The difficulty in understanding, the reason it takes such pains to follow their path of thought, does not reside in the presumed difficulty of the "text" but resides only in the unwillingness and incapacity of our existence. With regard to the beginning there is no process of selection. All we can do is either set ourselves on the way toward the beginning or shun it. We shall attempt here to prepare for the first possibility.

We concentrate all our endeavors, therefore, toward becoming attentive for once to the word of the primordial thinkers. We begin with a reference to the word of Parmenides. It is handed down to us in fragments, some larger, some smaller. The whole into which the fragments fit is still clearly enough recognizable and expresses in verse form the thoughts of a thinker. Hence it expresses a philosophical "doctrine." Therefore we speak of the "doctrinal" or "didactic poem" of Parmenides.

The fragments are counted in Roman numerals (VIII, 45 means: eighth fragment, verse 45). We will present a translation of various fragments before clarifying them. This translation expresses in our language the Greek word. Our language is familiar to us. Nevertheless, knowing the translation does not at all guarantee an understanding of the words of the thinker. Therefore we stressed in the first lecture: "The appended translation already contains an interpretation of the text. This interpretation, of course, needs clarification."

We must attend to this carefully: the translation does indeed contain the interpretation, but this interpretation does not come to light merely by hearing the translation. Precisely because the translation speaks in the words of our language, the danger of misinterpretation is in fact heightened. For, now, versus the Greek words, the words of the translation can easily be accepted according to the everyday meanings so familiar to us—without our having to pay attention to the fact that each translating word receives its content out of the thinker's whole thought. If, for example, the word "way" occurs in the translation, or the word "heart," that does not at all mean a decision has been made as to what "way" and "heart" mean there. Nor is it decided whether we are even capable of thinking the essence of "way" and the essence of "heart" as truly intended there or in Parmenides' sense at all. Of course, it cannot be denied that everyone knows "in general" what "way" and "heart" mean. But only a translation thoroughly guided by an interpretation is, within certain limits, capable of speaking for itself.

We are beginning with an elucidation of the first fragment of the so-called "didactic poem" and specifically with its concluding part, verses 22–32. The translation runs:

22   And the goddess received me with sympathy; she took my right
       hand in her hand; then she spoke the word and addressed me
       in this way: "O man, companion of immortal charioteers,
25   arriving at our house with the steeds that convey you. Blessing
       be bestowed on you: For it is not an evil fate which has sent you
       ahead to travel on this way—and truly this way is apart from men,
       outside their (trodden) path—but, rather, rule and order. There
       is, however, a need that you experience everything, both the stable
       heart of well-enclosing unconcealment,
30   as well as the appearing in its appearance to mortals, where there
       is no relying on the unconcealed. Also this, however, you will
       learn to experience: how the appearing
32   (in the need) remains called upon to be apparent, while it shines

through everything and (hence) in that way brings everything to perfection.

Parmenides is telling us about a goddess. The appearance of a "divine being" in the train of thought of a thinker strikes us as odd—because, on the one hand, in general a thinker is not supposed to proclaim the message of a divine revelation but is to assert on his own what he himself has questioned. And even when the thinker thinks about "the divine," as occurs in all "metaphysics," this thinking τὸ θεῖον (the divine) is, as Aristotle said, a thinking from "reason" and not a reiteration of propositions from the "belief" of a cult or a church. The appearance of a goddess in the didactic poem of Parmenides is, however, particularly disconcerting because it is the goddess "truth." For "the truth," just like "beauty," "freedom," or "justice," counts for us as something "universal," something extracted from the singular and the actual, from what is at any particular moment true, just, or beautiful, and is therefore represented "abstractly," in a mere concept. To make of "the truth" a goddess amounts to turning the mere notion of something, namely the concept of the essence of truth, into a "personality."

b) Two directives from the translating word ἀλήθεια. The conflictual character of unconcealedness. Preliminary clarification of the essence of ἀλήθεια and of concealedness. Transporting and translating [Übersetzen—Übersetzen].

If we hear in an initial and vague way of the goddess "truth" in the "didactic poem" and infer that here the "abstract notion" "truth" is being "personified" in a divine figure, then we are posing therewith as ones who believe they know both what "the truth" is as well as what is the essence properly belonging to the divinity of the Greek gods.

But in fact we do not know anything about either. Even if we could suppose we were instructed about the essence of truth as the Greeks thought it by taking the doctrines of Plato and Aristotle as a norm, we would already be on a false track that will never, on its own, lead back to what the early thinkers experienced when they gave a name to that which we signify by "truth." If we asked ourselves off the top of our heads what precisely we think when we use the word "truth," we would very quickly run into a tangled manifold of "views" or, perhaps, a general perplexity. What of course is more important than counting the divergent interpretations of truth and of its essence is the insight, bound to arise on such an occasion, that we have up to now never seriously and carefully reflected on what exactly it is we call "the truth." In the meantime, however, we always and constantly desire "the truth." Every age of history seeks "the true."

But how seldom and how little does man understand the essence of the true, i.e., truth. Even if we people of today found ourselves in the happy condition of knowing the essence of truth, that would still not guarantee our being capable of thinking what in the early thought of the Greeks was experienced as the essence of truth. For not only the essence of truth, but also the essence of everything essential, has in every case its own wealth, from which an age in history may only draw a small amount as its own portion.

If we say in anticipation and without proof that the goddess Ἀλήθεια appears in the "didactic poem" of Parmenides not just for the sake of "poetic" embellishment but rather that the "essence" "truth" holds sway throughout the words of the thinker, then we need to clarify in advance the essence of ἀλήθεια.

The attempt to attain by means of thinking the proximity of the essence of ἀλήθεια, in order to be solicited by it, shall require of us, who are still more distant from this essence than the Greeks themselves already were, vast detours and remote prospects. Such things, however, would be necessary even for us to be able to think only a little of the word of Anaximander, Heraclitus, or Parmenides in such a way that we are thinking out of that dimension in which there shows itself what for these thinkers is the to-be-thought and what remains for the future, although in a veiled way, the to-be-thought. And every endeavor to think ἀ-λήθεια in a somewhat suitable manner, even if only from afar, is an idle affair as long as we do not venture to think the λήθη to which, presumably, ἀλήθεια refers back.

What the Greeks name ἀλήθεια we ordinarily "translate" with the word "truth." If we translate the Greek word "literally," however, then it says "unconcealedness." It seems as if the "literal translation" consisted simply in patterning our word to correspond with the Greek word. While this is the beginning of literal translation, it is also in fact its end. The work of translation does not exhaust itself in such imitative building of "word-forms," which then often sound artificial and ugly. If we merely replace the Greek ἀλήθεια with our "unconcealedness," we are not yet actually translating. That occurs only when the translating word "unconcealedness" transports us into the domain of experience and the mode of experience out of which the Greeks or, in the case at hand, the primordial thinker Parmenides say the word ἀλήθεια. It is therefore an idle play with "word-forms" if we render ἀλήθεια by "unconcealedness," as has become fashionable recently, but at the same time attribute to the word "unconcealedness," now meant to replace the word "truth," a significance which we have merely gleaned from the ordinary later use of the word "truth" or which offers itself as the outcome of later thinking.

What is named "unconcealedness" ["*Unverborgenheit*"], what we have to think in the name ’Aλήθεια in order for our thought to be fitting, is not yet experienced thereby, let alone secured in rigorous thinking. It could be that the specially formed word "dis-closure" ["*Entbergung*"] comes closer to the essence of the Greek άλήθεια than the expression "unconcealedness," which nevertheless, for several reasons, is at first appropriate to serve as the guiding word for a meditation on the essence of άλήθεια. It should be kept in mind that in the following we will be speaking of "unconcealedness" and "concealment" but that the obvious expression "unconcealment" ["*Unverbergung*"] is avoided, although it is the "most literal" translation.[1]

Every attempt at a "literal" translation of such foundational words as "truth," "Being," "semblance," etc. immediately arrives within the radius of an intention reaching essentially beyond the clever fabrication of literally matched words. We could appreciate this sooner and in a more serious way if we reflected on what it is to "translate." At first we conceive of this process in an external and technico-philological way. It is said that "translating" is the transposing of one language into another, of the foreign language into the mother tongue or vice versa. What we fail to recognize, however, is that we are also already constantly translating our own language, our native tongue, into its genuine word. To speak and to say is in itself a translation, the essence of which can by no means be divided without remainder into those situations where the translating and translated words belong to different languages. In every dialogue and in every soliloquy an original translating holds sway. We do not here have in mind primarily the operation of substituting one turn of phrase for another in the same language or the use of "paraphrase." Such a change in the choice of words is a consequence deriving from the fact that what is to be said has already been transported for us into another truth and clarity—or perhaps obscurity. This transporting can occur without a change in the linguistic expression. The poetry of a poet or the treatise of a thinker stands within its own proper unique word. It compels us to perceive this word again and again as if we were hearing it for the first time. These newborn words transpose us in every case to a new shore. So-called translation and paraphrase are always subsequent and follow upon the transporting of our whole being into the realm of a transformed truth. Only if we are already appropriated by this transporting are we in the care of the word. Only on the basis of a respect for language grounded in this

---

1. See pp. 132ff.

way can we assume the generally lighter and more limited task of translating a foreign word into our own language.

But the more difficult task is always the translation of one's own language into its ownmost word. That is why, e.g., the translation of the word of a German thinker into the German language is especially difficult—because there reigns here the tenacious prejudice to the effect that we who speak German would understand the German word without further ado, since it belongs, after all, to our own language, whereas, on the contrary, to translate a Greek word we must in the first place learn that foreign tongue. We cannot discuss here in a more penetrating way to what extent and why every discourse and every saying is an original translation within one's own language and precisely what "to translate" means here. In the course of our introductory lectures on ἀλήθεια there will perhaps at times be an opportunity to experience something of these matters.

In order for us to be in a position to transport ourselves into the realm of the Greek word ἀλήθεια and so be able to speak this word henceforth in a thoughtful way, we must first become alert to and follow the directive provided by the translating word "unconcealedness." The directive shows as it were the direction of the transporting. The directive leads, if we limit ourselves to its main features, into a *fourfold*.

On the one hand, the word "un-concealedness" directs us to something like "concealedness." What, as regards "un-concealedness," is previously concealed, who does the concealing and how it takes place, when and where and for whom concealment exists, all that remains undetermined. Not only now and for us who are trying to reflect on ἀλήθεια under the guidance of its translation as "unconcealedness," but also and precisely among the Greeks, that which is intimated about concealedness remains undetermined and even unquestioned. The Greeks experience genuinely and express in word only unconcealedness. Nevertheless, the directive toward concealedness and concealing provides us now with a clearer realm of experience. In some way or other we surely do know the likes of concealing and concealedness. We know it as veiling, as masking, and as covering, but also in the forms of conserving, preserving, holding back, entrusting, and appropriating. We also know concealedness in the multiple forms of closing off and closedness. From these modes of concealedness and concealing, "unconcealedness" immediately gains clearer features. The realm of the "concealed-unconcealed" is, if we do not deceive ourselves, more immediately familiar and accessible than what is expressed in the banal titles *veritas* and "truth." Strictly speaking, the word "truth" does not give us anything to think and still less anything to represent "intuitively." We must immediately call for help from a borrowed "definition" of truth in order to give significance to the word. A special consideration is first needed if we are to introduce ourselves into the realm of meaning of the word "truth." "Unconcealedness," though, is different in appealing to us immediately, even if also here we first probe uncertainly for what is properly meant.

Second, the word "unconcealedness" indicates that something like a suspension or cancellation of concealedness belongs to the Greek experience of the essence of truth. The prefix "un-" corresponds to the Greek ἀ-, which grammar calls "α privativum." What kind of *privatio*, deprivation, and taking away is at stake in a privative word-formation depends in each case on what it is that is exposed to the deprivation and impairment. "Un-concealedness" can mean concealedness is taken away, cancelled, evicted, or banned, where taking away, cancelling, evicting, and banning are essentially distinct. "Un-concealedness" can also mean concealedness is not allowed at all, that, although possible and a constant menace, it does not exist and may not arise. From this multiplicity of meanings of the prefix "un" it is easy to see that already in this respect un-concealedness is difficult to determine. And yet it is precisely here that a basic feature of the essence of un-concealedness comes to the fore, which we must expressly hold in view in order to experience the primordial Greek essence of "truth." This opposition resides in un-concealedness itself. In the essence of truth as un-concealedness there holds sway some sort of conflict with concealedness and concealment.

Recapitulation

2) The question of the name of the goddess and how to translate it. The essence of truth as opposed to concealedness, according to the first two directives. Un-*concealedness* and *Un*-concealedness.

The first passage we are clarifying belongs to Fragment I and begins with verse 22: καί με θεὰ πρόφων ὑπεδέξατο, . . . "And the goddess received me with sympathy . . ."

The goddess appearing here is the goddess Ἀλήθεια. We ordinarily translate: the goddess "truth." This goddess greets the thinker upon his arrival at her home and reveals to him what he has to experience henceforth; it will be for this thinker the to-be-thought and will remain from now on in the history of truth what is primordially to be thought. We can easily discern, if only in broad outlines, that the essence of this goddess "truth" decides everything about the thinker and the to-be-thought. Therefore, prior to the formal clarification of the individual fragments and verses, we must attempt to illuminate the essence of "truth." With this purpose we ask: What does the name of the goddess mean? That is, what is the meaning of the Greek word ἀλήθεια, which we translate as "truth"? Here we are "dealing," apparently, with a word. Because word and language have become for us a conveyance and a tool for communication, one among others, to speak of "dealing with words" produces at once a fatal impression. It is as if, instead of mounting a motorcycle, we would remain standing before it and make a speech about it with the intention of learning in this way how to ride it. But a word is not a tool, even to one who maintains language is only a conveyance or a means of communication, such that it would be a matter of indifference whether we say "University" ["Universität"] and thereby still think of something or whether we ramble on about the "U" ["Uni"]. Perhaps one studies today only at a "U."

To be sure, neither are we "dealing" here with mere "word-forms" ["Wörter"]. In science, of course, one can deal with word-forms as one would treat the history of the evolution of earthworms. Ἀ-λήθεια means, "literally" ["wörtlich"] translated, "un-concealedness." By attending to the "literal," we seem to take the word seriously. Nevertheless we are disrespecting words [Worte] so long as we only take an interest in the form of the words. The "literal" translation must not simply copy the form and thereby "enrich" the translating language with "new," unusual, and often unwieldy locutions, but it must go beyond the form and reach the words themselves. Erudition about the form does not guarantee a knowledge of the words. These latter say what is properly to be said: the dictum. Of course, if we listen to the literal in such a way that before all else, and therefore constantly, we heed the word and think out of the word, then the high repute of the "literal" is justified—but only then.

We must hear the literally taken word in such a way that we heed its directives in their pointing to the dictum. In such heeding we then hearken to what the word is trying to say. We exercise attentiveness. We begin to think.

Let us now attempt to pursue the directives provided by the literal translating word "unconcealedness," so that we might thereby hear the Greek word ἀλήθεια more clearly and thus surmise something of the essence of "truth" as experienced by the Greeks. The word "unconcealedness" provides a fourfold directive.

The first two directives can be indicated and fixed by changing the emphasis in the word "unconcealedness": un-*concealedness* and *un-*concealedness. Un-*concealedness* points immediately to "concealedness." Where there is concealedness, a concealing must occur or must have occurred. Concealing can exist in many modes: as covering and masking, as conserving and putting aside, as closing off and original preserving—just as with a source that wells up only as long as it is already preserving. But what it is the Greeks experience and think when they allude to a "concealedness" in every "unconcealedness" is not immediately evident. It can be grasped only by a special consideration. And that in turn requires a prior knowledge of the modes of concealing in general. Only thus can "concealedness," as the Greeks thought of it, and its circumscribed essential realm be distinguished adequately. But before we reach that far, the Greek word ἀλήθεια has already obtained a certain proximity by means of its translation as "unconcealedness"; for the experiential domain of "concealing" and "not concealing," "concealed" and "unconcealed," is at once more clear and more familiar than any meaning we would attribute to our ordinary word "truth" by means of an adventitious reflection. The "meaning" and "definition" of "truth" gained in that way would have to be expressly noted by us each time. And we would be at risk of fastening upon only one of the many random definitions possible from various philosophical standpoints. Now concealment, on the contrary, is something we are acquainted with—because the things themselves and their connections hide themselves from us and for us, or because we ourselves bring about concealments, perform and allow them, or because both a concealing of "things" and a concealing of this concealing occur in an interplay through us.

The translating word *un*-concealedness directs us, secondly, to the striking fact that the Greeks think in the essence of truth something like the taking away, cancellation, or annihilation of concealment. Corresponding to this negation of concealment, truth for the Greeks is, as it were, something "negative." Thereby an odd state of affairs comes to light, to which our ordinary negation-less word "truth" (as well as *veritas* and *verité*) bars every way. What the prefixes "*ἀ-*" and "un-" in the words *ἀ-λήθεια* and "un-concealedness" properly mean is at first as little decided and founded as is the meaning of the "concealedness" that is removed and "negated." What we can see clearly here is only this: the essence of truth as unconcealedness stands in some sort of opposition to concealment. Indeed it appears unconcealedness is involved with concealedness in a "conflict," the essence of which itself remains in dispute.

Part One

The Third Directive from the Translating Word *ΑΛΗΘΕΙΑ*: The Realm of the Opposition between *ΑΛΗΘΕΙΑ* and *ΛΗΘΗ* in the History of Being.

§2. *First meditation on the transformation of the essence of truth and of its counter-essence.*

a) The conflictual character of un-concealedness. The third directive: truth in oppositional relations. The resonance of ἀλήθεια in subjectivity. Reference to Hegel and Schelling. Directive toward the oppositions between concealedness and unconcealedness, falsity and truth.

"Truth" is never "in itself," available by itself, but instead must be gained by struggle. Unconcealedness is wrested from concealment, in a conflict with it. Unconcealedness is not simply gained through conflict in the general sense that among humans truth is something to be sought out and to be struggled for. Rather, the sought and struggled for, regardless of the conflict in man over it, is in its very essence a conflict: "unconcealedness." It is unclear who is struggling here and how those involved are struggling. It is important, however, to think for once this conflictual essence of truth, an essence which has been shining for 2,500 years in the faintest of all lights. The task is to experience properly the conflict occurring within the essence of truth.

To be sure, the essence of the conflict is at first itself controversial. Presumably, "conflict" here means something other than mere quarrel and fight, other than blind discord, other than "war," and other than "competition" as well. Perhaps these are only variations and initial appellations of the conflict, the primordial essence of which we may surmise in the essence of truth in the sense of ἀλήθεια and which we will come to know one day. Perhaps the word of Heraclitus, so often misused and always truncated, Πόλεμος πάντων . . . πατήρ ἐστι, as

rendered "War is the father of all things . . . ," has in common with
Greek thinking only the empty verbal sound.

But how are we to know anything definite of the essence of πόλεμος
(which, according to the dictionary, does indeed literally mean "war"),
and how are we even to surmise the essence of the "polemical" named
here, as long as we know nothing of a conflict indigenous to the very
essence of truth? And how could we know the primordial conflictual
character of the conflict in the essence of truth as long as we did not
experience its essence as unconcealedness and knew ἀλήθεια at most
as a word-sound buzzing in the air? The conflictual essence of truth
has already been alien to us and to Western thought for a long time.
For us, "truth" means the opposite: that which is beyond all conflict
and therefore must be nonconflictual.

Accordingly, we do not understand to what extent the essence of
truth itself is, in itself, a conflict. If, however, in the primordial thinking
of the Greeks the conflictual essence of truth was experienced, then
it cannot astonish us to hear, in the dicta of this primordial thinking,
precisely the word "conflict." The interpretation of the Greek world
by Jacob Burckhardt and Nietzsche has taught us to recognize the "agonal principle" and to see in the "competitive match" an essential "im-
pulse" in the "life" of this people. But we must then go on to ask
where the principle of the "agon" is grounded and whence the essence
of "life" and of man receives its determination so that it is "agonal."
"Competitiveness" can only arise where the conflictual is experienced
before all else as what is essential. But to maintain that the agonal
essence of Greek humanity rests on a corresponding predisposition of
the people would be an "explanation" no less thoughtless than saying
the essence of thinking is grounded on the capacity to think.

We have noted so far that, on the one hand, unconcealedness belongs
to the realm where concealment and concealing occur. On the other
hand, *un*-concealedness makes manifest a conflictual essence; i.e., it
is unconcealing when in it something comes to pass that is in conflict
with concealment.

"Unconcealedness" provides a third directive, according to which
truth, on the basis of its conflictual essence, stands within "oppositional" relations.[1] For the usual theory of truth, the opposite to truth
is merely "untruth" in the sense of falsity. Something is either true
or false. To be sure, in the age of the first completion of Western metaphysics, in the philosophy of Schelling and Hegel, thinking reaches the
insight that something can at the same time, though in different respects, be true as well as false. Also, in the form of "negativity," something discordant appears here within the essence of truth. But to infer

---

1. See below, pp. 117-119.

that what we have said about the conflictual essence of truth coincides with the doctrines of Schelling and Hegel, or could be understood in hindsight with the help of their metaphysics, would be even more disastrous than the sheer ignorance of these relationships. For the main feature of the essence of truth in the modern metaphysics of Schelling and Hegel is never ἀλήθεια in the sense of unconcealedness but is certainty in the sense of *certitudo*, which, since Descartes, stamps the essence of *veritas*. Anything resembling the self-certitude of the self-conscious subject is alien to the Greeks. But, conversely, a resonance of the Greek essence of ἀλήθεια still pervades the essence of the modern "subjectivity of the spirit," which, correctly understood, has nothing to do with "subjectivism." But the beginning appeals only to what is of the beginning, and no resonance rivals the original sounding. The two do not coincide. Nevertheless both are the same, even when they appear to diverge to the point of being irreconcilable. This holds in what follows for the fourth directive, which may be able to provide to an attentive thinking the Greek understanding of ἀλήθεια.

This recollection of the history of the essence of truth in Western thought, necessary here, though to be sure very elementary, suggests concomitantly that we would be prey to coarse falsifications if we interpreted the thinking of Parmenides and Heraclitus with the help of modern "dialectics," claiming that in the primordial thinking of the Greeks the "oppositional" and even the basic opposition of Being and Nothing "plays a role." Instead of the facile, and apparently philosophical, procedure of borrowing from Schelling and Hegel for help in interpreting Greek philosophy, we have to exercise attentiveness and follow the directives truth in the essential form of unconcealedness can afford us. Of course, as an immediate reaction to this, we are tempted to remark that we today can grasp the primordial thinking of the Greeks only by interpreting it on the basis of our own representations. Thereby the question arises as to whether the thinking of Schelling and Hegel, their whole work, does not possess an incomparably higher rank than the thinking of today. Would it occur to any person of insight to deny that? We must also concede that the beginning will show itself, if it shows itself at all, only with our contribution. But the question remains as to what sort of contribution this is; whence, and how, is it to be determined? Similarly, it might very well seem that our endeavor to think, the beginning is but an attempt, out of our present and for it, to come to grips with the past historiographically. It would be equally useless, and in fact an aberration, if we were trying to draw up an account about something requiring a more essential effort and preparation, namely the foundation and development of a metaphysical basic thesis in the course of the tradition of Western thinking instead of simply attempting to heed the beginning. Yet who could deny that in this attempt we are constantly exposed to the danger of pressing forward, along with our contemporaries, in an undue fashion? Nevertheless, we shall attempt to heed the directives furnished by the essence of unconcealedness, an essence hardly ever thought and always difficult to think.

Unconcealedness suggests an "opposition" to concealedness. The ordinary opposition to truth is untruth in the sense of falsity. We find this opposition already very early in the thinking and speaking of the West and also in its poetry. After what we have remarked up to now about truth as unconcealedness, we obviously have to be wary of interpreting later notions of the false and falsity into earlier "representations." On the other hand, we can adequately think the early meanings of "the false" as opposed to the true only if we have previously reflected on the true in its truth, i.e., on unconcealedness. But, by the same token, unconcealedness (ἀλήθεια) itself can be grasped adequately only from its counter-essence, the untruth, and therefore from falsity, i.e., within that domain of essential experience opened up along with ἀλήθεια. From this it is clear that we can never think "the true" and "the false," "truth" and "falsity," as separate from each other in essence, and even less could we think truth as "unconcealedness" in such a way, for here the oppositional relation to concealment is manifest immediately in the very name. Therefore, if falsity, in the early way of thinking, already appears as one of the opposites to truth, i.e., to unconcealedness, then this essence of falsity as opposed to unconcealedness must be a type of concealedness. If unconcealedness gives the essence of truth its character, then we must attempt to understand falsity as a concealment.

b) The question of the counter-essence of ἀληθές. The absence of ληθές; the ψεῦδος. The veiling of basic meanings. The counter-word λαθόν; λανθάνομαι thought in the Greek way. Forgetting as experienced on the basis of concealment. Homer, Iliad, XVIII, 46; X, 22; Odyssey, VIII, 93.

Pursuing this directive, we will begin by asking what is the word for the counter-essence to ἀλήθεια. Τὸ ἀληθές is translated as "the true." This means "the unconcealed," in accordance with our interpretation of ἀλήθεια as unconcealedness. As long as it remains unclear, however, in what sense "unconcealedness" is to be thought, the translation of ἀληθές by "unconcealed" also stands under an essential reservation. The opposite of the "unconcealed," the concealed, can easily be found, in name at least, if we simply revoke the α-privativum, annul the cancellation of the concealed, and let it, "the concealed," remain. Terminologically, the crossing out of the α leads to ληθές. But nowhere do we actually find this word as the name for the false. Instead, the Greeks call the false τὸ ψεῦδος. This word has another stem entirely and another root and accordingly another basic meaning, not directly ascertainable. In the root "λαϑ" resides "concealing." That is not what ψεῦδος means, at least not immediately. We are tempted to point out that also in our language the counter-word to "truth," namely, "falsity," is an entirely different word. But perhaps the Greek counterwords ἀλήϑεια—ψεῦδος are closer to each other than our corresponding words "truth" and "falsity." It could be that ψεῦδος can be thought appropriately only in reference to ἀλήϑεια, but it could just as well be, precisely because ψεῦδος is the ordinary counter-word to ἀλήϑεια, that it will suggest how ἀλήϑεια itself is to be experienced.

In the attempt to trace the basic meanings of words and word-forms we are often guided, of course, by inadequate ideas of language in general, which then contribute to the current misjudgments about the very inquiry into basic meanings. We are wrong to think that the word-forms of a language originally possessed the pure basic meaning, which then got lost with the passage of time and became distorted. The basic and root meaning, on this view, remains quite hidden and only appears in the so-called "derivations." But this theory already leads us astray, for it presupposes that there would exist somewhere the "pure basic meaning" in itself, from which then other meanings would be "derived." These erroneous ideas, reigning supreme in linguistics even today, originate in the circumstance that the first reflection on language, Greek grammatics, was developed under the guiding lines of "logic," i.e., the theory of declarative assertions, propositional theory. Accordingly, propositions are composed out of words, and the latter denote "concepts." These indicate what is represented "in general" in the word. This "general" of the concept is then considered to be the "basic meaning." And the "derivations" are particularizations of the general.

Even though our thoughtful inquiry is aiming here at a basic meaning, we are nevertheless guided by an entirely different conception of the word and of language. To claim we are involved in a so-called "word-philosophy," which sorts out everything from mere verbal meanings, is admittedly very convenient, but it is also such a superficial view it does not even deserve to be labeled false. What we are calling the basic meaning of words is their beginning, which does not appear at first, but at last, and even then never as a detached formation, a specimen we could represent as something for itself. The so-called basic meaning holds sway in a veiled manner in all the modes of saying the respective word.

The counter-word to "unconcealing" (true), ἀληϑές, has quite an unrelated sound: ψεῦδος. We translate τὸ ψεῦδος as "the false," without exactly knowing what "false" means here and how it is to be thought—above all in the Greek sense. In any case it would now finally appear to be the time to consider once and for all that the counter-word to ἀληϑές is not what seems to lie closest, ληϑές or λαϑές or some similar-sounding word, but ψεῦδος. This remark, however, does not completely reveal the enigmatic character of the opposition in question. The word ψεῦδος as the word for the "false" is in fact connected to something we do not find with respect to the word ἀληϑές, namely a privative meaning formed on the same stem: το ἀψευδές—the un-false. But that is exactly what is "without falsity" and hence is the true. At the outset of book Σ (18) of the Iliad, Homer tells us of the lament of Achilles and his mother Thetis over his fallen friend Patroclos. The Nereides, the goddesses of waterways, grieve with Thetis; among these goddesses is mentioned in Σ 46 ἡ ’Αψευδής—the goddess "without falsity." Now we have only to write this name ἡ ’Αψευδής under the name ἡ ’Αλήϑεια in order to receive an important clue. If for the Greeks the counter-essence to unconcealedness is falsity and accordingly truth is unfalsity, then concealedness must be determined on the basis of falsity. If, in addition to this, concealedness permeates the essence of unconcealedness, then the enigma arises that in the Greek sense the essence of truth receives its character from the essence of falsity. This, however, might very well appear to be a singular mistake if we consider that the "positive" never springs forth from the negative, but, at most, conversely, the latter might stem from the former. Yet we know in the meantime that the Greek name for the essence of truth expresses precisely this enigma, according to which concealedness and the conflict with it are decisive for that essence. And it is precisely therefore that we could surely expect that in the counter-word to unconcealedness, concealedness would be named with an appropriate clarity. But instead of that we hear of ψεῦδος. The counter-words to ἀλήϑεια arising from the stem λαϑ seem to be missing.

But this is only seemingly so, above all because we translate a familiar Greek word of the stem λαϑ, to which ἀλήϑεια belongs, namely λανϑάνομαι, in such a way that the essential is obliterated. According to the dictionary, λανϑάνομαι means "to forget." Everyone understands what that means. Everyone experiences "forgetting" daily. But what is it? What do the Greeks think when they signify by the word λανϑάνεσϑαι what we call "to forget"?

First of all we need a clarification of λανϑάνειν. Λανϑάνω means "I am concealed." The aorist participle of this verb is λαϑών, λαϑόν. Here we find the counter-word to ἀληϑές we have been looking for. Λαϑόν is the being that is concealed; λάϑρᾳ means "in a concealed way," "secretly." Λαϑόν means what is concealed, what keeps itself concealed. Nevertheless λαϑόν, the being that is concealed, is not the counter-word to ἀληϑές, the "unconcealed"—that is, insofar as the counter-word to the unconcealed means falsity. For the concealed is not ipso facto the false. But presumably, on the other hand, τὸ ψεῦδος, the false, always remains in essence *a kind* of concealedness and concealing. Perhaps we must indeed understand τὸ ψεῦδος under the guidance of "concealing" and "being concealed," and especially if the words of the stem "concealing" and "concealed" have within Greek thought and speech a dominating semantic power. And in fact they do. It is just that in the Latin and in all Romance languages, as well as in our own Germanic style of speaking and thinking, it is utterly obliterated. Before we can clarify the essence of ψεῦδος as it is thought by the Greeks, we have to acknowledge that and to what extent λανθάνειν, "being concealed," is for the Greeks an essential feature of all appearance of beings. Λανθάνω means "I am hidden." Homer (Odyssey, Θ [8]) has the singer Demodokos, after the festive meal in the palace of the king of the Phaeacians, tell of the hard lot that befell the Greeks before Troy. Because of his sorrow in remembering these times, Odysseus covers his head with his mantle. Θ, 93:

ἔνθ' ἄλλους μὲν πάντας ἐλάνθανε δάκρυα λείβων,
'Αλκίνοος δέ μιν οἶος ἐπεφράσατ' ἠδ' ἐνόησεν
ἥμενος ἄγχ' αὐτοῦ,

"But then he (Odysseus) shed tears, without the others noticing it,
Alkinoos alone was aware of his sorrow . . ."

The German translation of Voss apparently comes closer to the Greek word because in a certain way it integrates the word ἐλάνθανε from verse 93:

"To all other guests he concealed his flowing tears."

But ἐλάνθανε does not mean transitively "he concealed"; λανθάνω does not mean "I conceal," but rather "I am concealed." 'Ελάνθανε, said of Odysseus, means "He (Odysseus) was concealed." "Literally," and thought in the Greek way, Homer says: "but then in relation to all others he was concealed as the one shedding tears." It is, according to our way of speaking and thinking, linguistically more correct to translate, "Odysseus, unnoticed by the others, shed tears." Greek thinking is reversed, indeed to such an extent that "concealing" in the sense of "being concealed" is precisely the ruling word. The Greeks say: Odysseus was concealed to the others as the one shedding tears.

In another place, from the Iliad X (22), verse 277, we find a similar incident. In the duel with Hector, Achilles missed with his first lance because Hector ducked out of the way. The lance stuck in the ground:

ἀνὰ δ' ἥρπασε Παλλὰς 'Αϑήνη,
ἂψ δ' 'Αχιλῆϊ δίδου, λάϑε δ'"Εκτορα, ποιμένα λαῶν.

Voss translates:

"the goddess seized it (the lance) and immediately gave it back to the
Peleidian, unnoticed by the warlike Hector."

This is "well" thought and said in our German language: unnoticed
by Hector, Athena gave Achilles back his lance. Thought, however, in
the Greek way, it means: Athena was concealed to Hector in her giving
back of the lance. We see once more how "concealedness" makes up
the basic feature of the behavior of the goddess, which basic feature
of concealment first bestows on her particular action the character of
its "Being." But perhaps the exact reversal of our way of experiencing,
thinking, and speaking in relation to the Greek way appears most clear-
cut in the example of the well-known Epicurean proverb: λάϑε βιώσας.
We translate in "correct" German: "Live unnoticed." But the Greeks
say: "Be concealed in the way you conduct your life." Here concealment
determines the character of the presence of man among men. The "concealed" and the "unconcealed" are characters of the very being itself
and not characteristics of the noticing or apprehending. Nevertheless,
perceiving and saying have indeed for the Greeks, too, the basic feature
of "truth" or "untruth."

It may be clear from these few remarks how decisively the domain
and the occurrence of concealing and concealedness hold sway, for the
Greeks, over beings and over human comportment toward beings. If
now, after this comment and in its light, we once more consider the
most common Greek word of the stem λαϑ, namely λανϑάνομαι, then
it is plain that the usual and indeed "correct" translation by our German
word "to forget" renders nothing at all of the Greek way of thinking.

Thought in the Greek fashion, λανϑάνομαι says: I am concealed from
myself in relation to something which would otherwise be unconcealed
to me. This is thereby, for its part, concealed, just as I am in my relation
to it. The being sinks away into concealment in such a manner that
with this concealment of the being I remain concealed from myself.
Moreover, this concealment is itself concealed. Something similar does
indeed occur when we forget this or that. In forgetting not only does
something slip from us, but the forgetting slips into a concealment of
such a kind that we ourselves fall into concealedness precisely in our
relation to the forgotten. Therefore the Greeks say more precisely ἐπιλανϑάνομαι, in order to capture the concealedness in which man is
involved, especially with respect to the concealment's relation to what
is withheld from man because of it. A more uncanny way to think

the essence of forgetting in one single word can hardly be imagined.

The way Greek speech in general uses λανθάνειν (being concealed) as a "ruling" word, as well as the interpretation of the essence of forgetting precisely through this event of concealing, already show clearly enough that in the "existence" of the Greeks, i.e., in their dwelling in the midst of beings as such, the essence of concealment holds sway essentially. From this we can already surmise more readily why they experience and think truth in the sense of "unconcealedness." But in view of this dominating event of concealment, should not the essence of the most common opposite to truth, i.e., the essence of falsity, i.e., τὸ ψεῦδος, also be determined on the basis of concealing, even though in the sound of the word ψεῦδος the stem λαθ- cannot be heard?

We become assured in this surmise when we consider that the false and untrue, e.g., an incorrect judgment, is a kind of not knowing, in which the "true" state of affairs is withheld from us, not in exactly the same way as "forgetting," which the Greeks do experience on the basis of concealment, though indeed in a corresponding way. Now whether Greek thinking also conceives the essence of ψεῦδος on the basis of concealment can only be shown by paying heed to the immediate self-expression of the Greek experience and, at the start, not at all by entering into what the Greek thinkers themselves explicitly say about ψεῦδος.

Recapitulation

Τὸ ψεῦδος as the opposite of *ἀληθές*. The relationship between the stems of the words *ἀλήθεια* and *λανθάνω*. Reference to Homer, Odyssey, VIII, 93. The withdrawal of forgetting.

We are trying to become attentive to the dictum of Parmenides of Elea, a thinker who conceived and uttered that dictum around the time the temple of Poseidon was constructed in Poseidonia, later Paestum, not far from Elea. The dictum of this thinker expresses the word of the goddess 'Ἀλήθεια, a name we usually translate as "truth." The essence of the goddess "truth" is present throughout the entire edifice of the dictum, in each of its verses, but above all and purely in the guiding statement, which is precisely silent on the name 'Ἀλήθεια. Therefore, prior to the elucidation of the individual fragments, and on behalf of them, we must learn something of the essence of this goddess; on the other hand, only by thinking through the entire "didactic poem" will there appear for us the essence of this ἀλήθεια in its primordial form and character.

We consider at first the name of the goddess ’Aλήθεια, that is, unconcealedness. Of course, the mere fact of learning that "ἀλήθεια" is the
way the Greek language expresses "truth" does not tell us anything
about the essence of truth, as little as we learn something about horses
by knowing the Latin expression "equus." But if we translate ἀλήθεια
by "unconcealedness," and thereby transport ourselves into this word's
directives, then we are no longer constrained within linguistic significa-
tions but stand before an essential nexus that engages our thinking
down to its very foundations. We are pursuing the four directives provided by the name ’Aλήθεια as translated "unconcealedness." In this
way we hope to experience something of the primordial essence of
truth in Greek thought.

First, un-*concealedness* refers to concealment. Concealment hence permeates the primordial essence of truth.

Secondly, *un*-concealedness indicates that truth is wrenched from
concealment and is in conflict with it. The primordial essence of truth
is conflictual. What "conflict" means here remains a question.

Thirdly, un-concealedness, in accordance with the just-mentioned
characterizations, refers to a realm of "oppositions" in which "truth"
stands. Since it is on the basis of the "oppositional" essence of unconcealedness that its conflictual essence first becomes visible, we have
to consider more closely the question of the "opposition" in which truth
stands. Western thinking accounts untruth the sole opposite to truth.
"Untruth" is identified with "falsity," which, understood as incorrectness, forms the evident and obtrusive counterpart to "correctness." The
opposition holding sway at the beginning is known to us under the
names ἀλήθεια καὶ ψεῦδος, veritas et falsitas, truth and falsity. We interpret the latter opposition as correctness and incorrectness; but truth
as "correctness" is not of the same essence as truth in the sense of
"unconcealedness." The opposition of correctness and incorrectness,
validity and invalidity, may very well exhaust the oppositional essence
of truth for later thinking and above all for modern thinking. But that
decides nothing at all concerning the possible oppositions to "unconcealedness" as thought by the Greeks.

We must therefore ask how the primordial thinking of the Greeks
sees the opposition to "unconcealedness." Reflecting on this, we encounter the surprising fact that τὸ ψεῦδος immediately presents itself
as the opposite of ἀλήθεια and ἀληθές; we translate correctly: "the
false." The opposite of unconcealedness is therefore not concealedness
but indeed falsity. The word ψεῦδος is of another stem and does not
immediately say anything about concealing. Which is odd, especially
since we claim and maintain that the primordial essence of truth is
"unconcealedness"; for, in that case, the opposition corresponding to
it, i.e., contradicting it, must involve something like "concealedness."

But that is not what we find at first. For just as soon as the word
ἀληθές is spoken, so is its counter-word, τὸ ψεῦδος. One might then
be tempted to conclude finally that the essence of truth is in no way
determined on the basis of unconcealedness and concealment. But perhaps this is an overly hasty conclusion. We stand too uncritically under
the prejudice of the opposition between truth and falsity taken for
granted a long time ago, and we do not take offense at the plurality
of names signifying it, which we constantly and without much thought
use as formulas to discriminate our judgments and decrees. Perhaps
we are not simply being premature when we conclude that, due to
the priority of ψεῦδος, the origin of the essence of truth cannot be
unconcealedness and concealment. Perhaps there is in fact no room
at all for "conclusions" here; instead, this is a domain requiring us
to open our eyes and to see—to see with clear vision. In such "foresight"
we see that in the experience and speech of the Greeks the counter-
word to ἀληθές, and more generally, the word from which this privative
formation is derived, is not missing at all. Ἀλήθεια is tied to the verbal
stem λαθ-, which means "concealing." To the stem λαθ- pertains the
verb λανθάνω, "I am concealed"; the aorist participle, λαθών, λαθόν,
means "being concealed." Yet at first this is only the observation of
a linguistic fact. What is decisive is to see which relations among beings
are expressed by the word λανθάνω. They are of such a kind that we
are hardly capable of repeating them, and instead, by our way of translating the Greek word, we cover them over completely.

Homer says of Odysseus in Θ (VIII), 93: ἐλάνθανε δάκρυα λείβων.
We translate in "correct" German: "He (Odysseus) shed tears, unnoticed
by the others present." In Greek experience the word of Homer says:
"He (Odysseus) was in concealment as the one shedding tears." Correspondingly, we translate the famous Epicurean admonition λάθε
βιώσας as "Live unnoticed"; thought in the Greek way, it says, "Be
in concealment as one conducting his life." It could be observed with
regard to these examples that we have here a really interesting linguistic
fact, that compared to our German modes of expression the Greek language expresses itself in a reverse manner. But what we see here is
more than just "interesting." It is decisive—namely, for an understanding of the primordial essence of truth, whose Greek name, ἀλήθεια,
is related to the word λανθάνω, the use of which is now starting to
dawn upon us. For precisely the way λανθάνω, in the examples just
referred to, is the ruling word tells us that what is named in this word,
the "concealed," has a priority in the experience of beings, and, specifically, as a character of beings themselves it is a possible "object" of
experience. In the case of the weeping Odysseus, the Greeks do not
consider that the others present, as human "subjects" in their subjective
comportment, fail to notice the crying of Odysseus, but they do think

that round about this man and his existence there lies a concealment causing the others present to be, as it were, cut off from him. What is essential is not the apprehension on the part of the others but that there exists a concealment of Odysseus, now keeping the ones who are present far from him. That a being, in this case the weeping Odysseus, can be experienced and grasped depends on whether concealment or unconcealment comes to pass.

In the light of these remarks we will now also consider, more carefully than is usual, an ordinary word of the stem λαϑ-, namely λανϑάνομαι or ἐπιλανϑάνομαι. We translate the word, again correctly, "to forget." But what does "forget" mean? Modern man, who organizes everything in such a way that he can forget it as quickly as possible, should surely know what forgetting is. But he does not know. He has forgotten the essence of forgetting, supposing he ever did give a thought to it, i.e., extend his thought into the essential realm of forgetting. This indifference with regard to "forgetting" does not at all depend on the hastiness of his "way of life." What is happening here proceeds from the very essence of forgetting, which withdraws itself and hides.

Therefore it could be that an invisible cloud of forgetting itself, the oblivion of Being, hangs over the whole sphere of the earth and its humanity, a cloud in which is forgotten not this or that being but Being itself, a cloud no airplane could ever breach even if capable of the most formidable altitude. Accordingly, it could also be that at an appropriate time an experience precisely of this oblivion of Being might arise—arise as a need, and so be necessary. It could be that with a view to this forgottenness of Being a remembering might awaken, one thinking of Being itself and nothing else, considering Being itself in its truth, and thinking the truth of Being and not only, as in all metaphysics, beings with respect to their Being. For this there would be required, before all else, an experience of the essence of forgetting, of that which is concealed in the essence of ἀλήϑεια.[1]

The Greeks experienced forgetting as a coming to pass of concealment.

§3. *Clarification of the transformation of* ἀλήϑεια *and of the transformation of its counter-essence* (**veritas, certitudo, rectitudo, iustitia, truth, justice**—λήϑη, ψεῦδος, falsum, *incorrectness, falsity*)

---

1. *Being and Time* is the first attempt to think Being itself out of the basic experience of the oblivion of Being. I.e., it is an attempt to prepare this thinking, to pave the way for it, even at the risk of remaining on a "path leading nowhere" ["*Holzweg*"].

a) The intrinsically different meanings of ψεῦδος and "false." The
essential domain of the counter-word ψεῦδος as letting-appear
while covering up. Reference to Homer, Iliad, B 348ff. Dissembling
concealment: the basic meaning of ψεῦδος. Τὸ ἀψευδές: the
"dis-hiding," and the ἀληθές. Reference to Hesiod, Theogony,
Verse 233f. The ambiguity of ἀληθές.

In order to clarify the essential relations the Greeks see in the essence
of ψεῦδος, we should first consider briefly how we understand "the
false."[1]

"The false" means for us, on the one hand, as in the case of "false
money" or a "false Rembrandt," a falsified thing. Here the false is the
non-genuine. An assertion, however, can also be "false." In that case,
the false is the untrue in the sense of incorrect. We also tend to conceive
an incorrect assertion as an erroneous one, to the extent incorrectness
as error is opposed to correctness as truth. Nevertheless, not every false
assertion is an erroneous one. For example, if someone in court makes
a "false statement," he does not himself have to be in error. In fact,
he precisely cannot be in error; he must rather know the "true state
of affairs" in order to be able to make a false statement. Here the false
is not the erroneous but the deceiving, the misleading. Consequently,
on the one hand the false is the spurious thing; on the other hand,
it may be an incorrect assertion; the latter, again, can be a wrong one,
that is, an erroneous assertion, or it can be a misleading one. We also,
however, call a man "false"; we say, "The police have made a false
arrest." Here the false is neither the falsified, nor the erring, nor the
misleading, but the "wrong" man—not "identical" with the one being
sought. This "false" man, as in fact he is, i.e., the wrong man, can,
however, be entirely "without falsity." He does not at all have to be
a "false" man in the sense of one who is, by cunning, generally inclined
toward deception in his behavior and attitudes. Finally, the term "false,"
in the sense of the wily, is also applied to animals. All cats are false.
The feline is the false; hence German speaks of false gold and silver
as "cats' gold" and "cats' silver."

So it is clear that the false does not always have the same meaning.
Nevertheless we surmise that the various senses of the false are some-
how related to one same basic essence. But what this latter is remains
undetermined.

Likewise the Greek ψεῦδος, which we readily translate with the word
"false," means many different things. We notice that immediately if,
e.g., we want to clarify what a pseudonym is. This foreign word is

---

1. Concerning the word "false," *falsum*, see pp. 35-38.

composed of ὄνομα ("name"), and ψεῦδος or, to be more exact, ψευδές. Literally translated, a "pseudonym" is a "false name." Is it really so? Not at all. If an impostor assumes a noble name and travels under this "false name," he is not then bearing a "pseudonym." The noble name is indeed supposed to conceal who its bearer is "in truth." Nevertheless, the "false name" of the impostor is no mere cover name. Such a name is used for military operations, for example the "operation Michael" on the Western front in the previous war. This name simply covers something that is in no way to appear. On the contrary, however, the assumed name of an impostor not only covers up his "true nature"; in addition, while covering, it also has to let the bearer of the name appear in "grandeur," a grandeur which to be sure does not belong to him, as little as does the name. In contradistinction, the "pseudonym" is neither simply a false name nor a cover name, nor even a name that is simply misleading. The "pseudonym," i.e., the essentially fitting name, is indeed supposed to cover up an author; yet in a certain way it also has to let him come into the open, and in fact not as one he in truth is not (the case of the impostor), but as the one he really is. Thus Kierkegaard published in 1843, in Copenhagen, this work: *Fear and Trembling. The Dialectical Lyric of Johannes de Silentio.* This "Lord Silence" intended to intimate hereby something essential about himself and his literary activity. Similarly the "pseudonyms" of Kierkegaard's two books *Philosophical Fragments* (1844) and *Training in Christianity* (1850) stand in an essential relation. The first bears the name of the author Johannes Climacus; the other is published by Anti-Climacus.

The meaning of ψεῦδος in "pseudonym" eludes us if we translate it as "false." We have here a covering that at the same time unveils something recondite and does so in a specifically recondite way, whereas a "false name," e.g., that of the impostor, is also not simply incorrect, but it covers up while making visible something pertaining only to the facade and to the most unrecondite.

Under the force of the essential relations named by the Greek word ψεῦδος, we have already spoken, almost "automatically," of "covering," and "veiling," but at the same time also of "letting-appear." Ψεῦδος pertains to the essential realm of covering, hence it is a kind of concealing. The covering involved in ψεῦδος, however, is always at the same moment an unveiling, a showing, and a bringing into appearance. Now it is time, however, to leave the word to the Greeks themselves, so we may have a witness testifying that, and to what extent, ψεῦδος belongs to the essential realm of concealing and unconcealedness. Let us cite two places, the one from Homer, the other from Hesiod. These places ["*Stellen*"] are not mere authorities ["*Belegstellen*"], which by the simple accumulation of a large number would gain demonstrative power; for it is not a matter here of demonstrating and arguing, but of a pointing out that opens our eyes. What is decisive here is not the sheer number of the places, in the quotation of which generally one place is left in darkness as much as the others, in the expectation that the one unclear place would clarify the others and then that the darkness of all the places taken together would result in clarity. What is decisive is the transparency of the essential in one single place. To be sure, it might be necessary to refer to several of these places, if it is necessary to make the same thing visible under different aspects. For now, it only matters to acknowledge that ψεῦδος belongs in the essential domain of appearing, and letting-appear, and of unconcealedness.

The quotation from Homer is taken from the second book of the Iliad (B 348ff.). Here the poet has Nestor say that for the Greeks there is no hope of returning home from the battlefield of Troy:

> πρὶν καὶ Διὸς αἰγιόχοιο.
> γνώμεναι εἴ τε ψεῦδος ὑπόσχεσις, εἴ τε καὶ οὐκί.

Voss translates:

> (as) "previously, from the lightning-thrower we knew whether he was out to deceive us or not."

The reference is to Zeus, and the event called to mind took place the day the Greeks in Argos boarded their ships to go to Troy.

> ἀστράπτων ἐπιδέξι᾽, ἐναίσιμα σήματα φαίνων.

Voss translates:

> "On the right his lightning flashed, a sign portending good fortune."

Literally translated, the verse says, "Zeus, slinging his lightning bolts to the right and letting appear propitious signs." In the first passage quoted these signs are called ὑπόσχεσις. The best translation would be our word "reservation," but this is fixed too much in a certain direction of meaning because of the Latin word *reservatio*. Ὑπόσχεσις means a holding out and holding forth, a showing which holds forth and at the same time holds something back, and hence does not show. It belongs to the essence of the σῆμα, the sign, that it itself shines (shows itself) and in this appearing also indicates something else: the sign, in appearing itself, lets something else appear. The lightning bolts going to the right are a portent. Since they are on the right, they let something propitious appear, though to be sure in such a way that they, as signs, still hold back and veil the outlook of the upcoming course of the campaign against Troy. And now, according to the word of Nestor, it is time to determine whether or not the portent from Zeus is ψεῦδος or not. When is it ψεῦδος? If the bolts going to the right, as signs of propitious destiny, conceal the actual disaster still withheld from the Greeks though already allotted to them. Ψεῦδος applies, as Homer says simply, to Zeus σήματα φαίνων, to Zeus in the way of his letting signs appear. He always lets something appear in the signs. He holds out something unconcealed. At the same time, however, the sign conceals, and indeed as sign, always only denoting and referring, but never openly displaying what it refers to in the same way it itself, as self-showing, appears. Such a sign is in every case a concealing that shows. But the question remains whether this type of concealment only holds back (i.e., holds back the glimpse into destiny) or whether it is a show-ing whose concealing aspect dissembles what is to come. In that case, the holding forth on the part of the showing which appears, and thereby the sign itself, are ψεῦδος. The concealing is a dissembling. The guiding basic meaning of ψεῦδος resides in dissembling (obstructing or disguis-ing). Thereby we must take this word in its literal sense, which is still familiar to us. "Dissembling" does not yet mean here self-disguising as the deceptive character of a person; it is not, in modern terms, a comportment of the "subject," but is rather an "objective" event occur-ring in the realm of beings. We say a house in the neighborhood is obstructing the view of the mountains. Dissembling as ob-structing is first of all a concealing in the manner of covering up. We cover up, e.g., a door that is not supposed to be seen in the room, and disguise it by placing a cupboard in front of it. In this way an appearing sign, a gesture, a name, a word, can also disguise something. The cupboard placed before the door not only presents itself as this thing and not only disguises the door by covering over—i.e., concealing—the wall which at this place has an opening, but, rather, the cupboard can be disguising to the point that it pretends there is no door at all in the wall. The cupboard disguises the door, and by being placed before it, it distorts the "actual" state of the wall. Our language contains the beau-tiful word "to hide" [*verhehlen*]; the originally simple "concealing" is called veiling [*verhüllen*]. "Hiding" refers to concealing and concealed-ness; to "hide nothing," to make "no secret" out of something, signifies there is no mystery to it, nothing concealed. To the same word stem as "hiding" belongs our word "hole," the hideaway, the hidden place that can itself contain something and conceal it. Our German language, which is more and more delivered over to corruption, once even had the word "dis-hide" [*enthehlen*]: to bring something out of hiddenness, to take it out of concealedness, dis-close it— ἀλήθεια: dis-closure. For years I have used "disclose" [*entbergen*] as the counter-word to "concealing closure" [*verbergen*]. The ordinary sophisticated reader of newspapers obviously will consider such words an artificial mishandling of language, which "philosophers" "think up" for the sake of their stilted ways of "abstract" thought.

Ψεῦδος is a dissembling concealment, "hiding" in the stricter sense. The essential relation between "the false," as the opposite of the true, and concealing as the opposite of disclosure (the occurrence of unconcealedness) now becomes clear. And in this light the Greeks' opposition of ἀληθές and ψεῦδος no longer seems odd. Ψευδές in the sense of dissembling concealment, i.e., hiding, permits the corresponding privative formation τὸ ἀ-ψευδές, i.e., the non-hiding, the *dis-hiding*. The essence of ἀψευδές must therefore be determined in reference to ἀληθές, "the unconcealed." Hesiod bears witness to this. In his Theogony (Verse 233f.) the poet relates that Πόντος as πρεσβύτατον παίδων, the oldest and most venerable of his sons, testified: Νηρέα δ᾽ ἀψευδέα καὶ ἀληθέα—Nereus, the one who does not dissemble, who hides nothing—καὶ ἀληθέα: i.e., precisely the one who "does not conceal." The καί does not simply add the ἀληθής to the ἀψευδής; and neither is ἀληθής just a repetition of ἀψευδής, as if the same thing were being said twice. The sense here is rather that the non-hiding is grounded in the non-concealing. Nereus is without falsity precisely by reason of his relation to unconcealedness. The ψεῦδος receives its essence from the region of concealment. The non-hiding is the non-concealing: ἀληθές.

But here an objection arises, one we do not want to take too lightly: τὸ ἀληθές indeed means "the unconcealed" and in no way means, if we adhere strictly to the word, the "non-concealing." Nevertheless that is how we have to understand ἀληθές. The Greeks knew the λόγος ἀληθής, i.e., the true assertion, the one which is not concealing but disconcealing. Λόγος ἀληθής does not mean, as might seem from the form of the words, the disclos*ed* assertion but, instead, the disclos*ing*, true assertion, which as such can very well be concealed and does not have to be unconcealed. The same holds a fortiori with ἀλήθεια. It expresses "unconcealedness," the unconcealed, but also means "unhiddenness" or disclosure in the sense of non-hiding or non-concealing.

For a long time now, of course, thinking, and especially modern thinking, has found no difficulty here. The matter is said to be quite simple. Ἀληθές in the sense of "unconcealed" applies to the "objects" that appear to us, and ἀληθές in the sense of "non-concealing" applies to assertions and knowledge about "objects," thus to the comportment of the "subject" toward objects. This solution sounds convincing. But it rests on the presupposition that in the realm of ἀλήθεια and ἀληθές,

i.e., for the Greeks, there would be something like the distinction between "object" and "subject" and the so-called subject-object relation.
But it is precisely the essence of ἀλήθεια that makes it impossible for
something like the subject-object relation to arise. Hence it would con-
fuse everything and stand matters upside down if we attempted to clarify the apparent equivocity of ἀληθές and ἀλήθεια with the help of
the subject-object distinction.

But ἀληθές is in fact ambiguous, and indeed in a manner almost
unbearable to a Greek ear, since ἀληθές means precisely the unconcealed and remains distinct from the "non-concealing." But what is
distinct does not have to be separated; perhaps it belongs to a unity.
The one, which is thus two-fold, would then be ambiguous. To the
unconcealed belongs disclosure. What discloses is related to the disclosed and the unconcealed. Ἀληθές and the corresponding ἀλήθεια
are ambiguous. How does this ambiguity arise? Upon what is it
grounded, if indeed it exists at all? Or do we have here merely the
semblance of ambiguity? Up to now only this has become clear: if
ἀληθές is ambiguous insofar as it means both "disclosing" and "the
disclosed," then it is inappropriate to claim ἀληθές means the "unconcealed." If in fact the disclosed is only what it is on the basis of a disclosing, then precisely the sense of "disclosing" is the original meaning
of ἀληθές. And insofar as ἀληθές is properly said of ἔπος and λέγειν,
then it appears on the whole that ἀλήθεια is originally characteristic
of the word, of speech, and of asserting. Nevertheless, for the Greeks,
and still in Aristotle, ἀλήθεια is a character of beings and not a characteristic of the perceiving of beings and of assertions about them. What
then is originally disclosing (ἀληθές): speech (λέγειν), or beings (ὄν),
or neither one?

Before we answer these questions, which aim at the heart of the
matter of the essence of ἀλήθεια, we must first take the measure of
this essential realm in its broad extent. That means we have to consider
the essence of concealment still more profoundly. The false in the sense
of ψεῦδος as dissemblance is a concealing. But then is every concealing
necessarily a dissembling? Is every concealedness in itself already "falsity"? In order to make a decision here, the essential realm of concealment must first come closer to us.

Before we take a far-sighted look into the domain of the essence
of concealment, however, we must first present the elucidation we have
held back up to now because it could only be understood after the
clarification of the essence of ψεῦδος for the Greeks. So we must clarify
what the word "false" denotes, and a brief illumination needs to be
given of the significance of the priority of the false within the essential
determination of the "untrue."

Recapitulation

1) The so-called correct translation of ψεῦδος by "false." The manifold meanings of "false" and ψεῦδος. The dissembling and hiding of ψεῦδος in the region of the essence of concealment and unveiledness. Reference to Homer and Hesiod.

We are inquiring into the opposite of "truth" with the intention of clarifying the essence of the goddess 'Αλήθεια. Everyone knows this opposite. "Falsity" is what is opposed to truth. This opposite is, as we say, so "natural" that we encounter it everywhere and constantly move within it. Therefore a "philosophy" is not required in order to bring to light the opposition between the "true and false." The early Greeks already knew the opposition τὸ ἀληθές—τὸ ψεῦδος. We translate correctly: the true and the false. The translation is "correct" to this extent, that the Greek words τὸ ἀληθὲς καὶ τὸ ψεῦδος do not mean "the good and the bad," which is in Greek τὸ ἀγαθὸν καὶ τὸ κακόν. Yet the Greek word τὸ ἀληθές does not mean "the true" but "the unconcealed." The counter-word to ἀληθές in Greek, namely ψεῦδος, does not, however, contain immediately in its form or in its stem anything of "concealedness." But we "really" should expect that, precisely because from the earliest Greek times τὸ ψεῦδος occurs univocally and decisively, and hence everywhere, as the opposite to ἀληθές. But, and this is what is really remarkable here, we in fact do not expect of ψεῦδος, as the evident opposite of ἀληθές, the unconcealed, a relation to the sphere of meaning of concealing and non-concealing. Why not? On the one hand because it has already been a long time since ἀληθές was still thought of as the "unconcealed," i.e., because we no longer experience unconcealedness and cannot experience it. Instead, we understand ἀληθές as the *verum* and *certum*, as the "true" and the "certain," maintaining that what is "understood" is, as it were, self-evidently "true" and "certain." On the other hand, the truly uncanny riddle of the Greek opposition of ἀληθές and ψεῦδος is not a problem at all since it has equally become customary, long ago, to understand ψεῦδος as "the false." Of course we recognize, already in this brief reflection, that what we so straightforwardly and "massively" call the "false" bears in its essence a special richness.

The false is, in one case, the falsified thing, i.e., the spurious ("false money," a "false Rembrandt"). The false is, secondly, an assertion: false in the sense of incorrect, or as we also say, erroneous. But a "false statement," e.g., made in court, does not ipso facto have to be erroneous. He who in such circumstances speaks "falsely" may precisely not be in error about the state of affairs if he is to be able to say what is not the case. This sort of "false statement" is not erroneous but is, rather, misleading. We also call a person "false." We say, "The police made a false arrest," and here "false" means "wrong." Yet the falsely arrested, the wrong man, does not have to be a "false man" in the sense of one who behaves in a cunning way and who poses everywhere as someone he is not. And, in the sense of the wily, we also call animals "false." All cats are false. The feline is "the" false; hence the origin of speaking, as Germans do, of "cats' gold" and "cats' silver."

The Greek ψεῦδος has many meanings, just as does our word "false." This becomes apparent if we attempt to elucidate the foreign word "pseudonym." Literally translated, this ψεῦδος-ὄνομα is a "false name." A pseudonym, however, is no "false name," for it is in fact appropriate to the one bearing it. The term "false name" applies, rather, to an impostor, e.g., "Count So-and-so." This name is indeed supposed to cover up its bearer, although the name used by the impostor is again not a mere "cover name" like the sort of names used in military operations ("Operation Michael") or in espionage. The name of the impostor is, of course, supposed to cover, but at the same time it is to let the one who bears the name appear in *grandeur* and to provide for his "stepping out" under the corresponding title. To be sure, what the covering name lets appear at the same time, the grandeur, is here only "semblance." In contradistinction to the impostor's name, the genuine "pseudonym" actually manifests something of the "true being" of its bearer. The "pseudonym" also covers up, but in such a way that it indicates simultaneously the recondite, concealed essence of the author and his literary task. The genuine pseudonym does not simply make the author unknown; it is meant, rather, to call attention to his concealed essence. By using a pseudonym the author expresses even more about himself than he does when he employs his "correct" name. Kierkegaard's pseudonyms ("Johannes de Silentio," "Joh. Climacus," "Anti-climacus") bring out this essence of the pseudonym and consequently the essence of ψεῦδος. Ψεῦδος involves a covering that simultaneously unveils. "False" gold looks like gold, shows itself as gold, and in doing so—though of course only by doing so—it hides what it is in truth: non-gold. The essence of ψεῦδος finds its determination in the domain of concealing, unveiling, and letting-appear.

The objection can always be raised against this understanding of ψεῦδος that it is but our "interpretation." Therefore we need to know how the Greeks themselves experienced ψεῦδος. Two places from early Greek poetry are indicative. The one is from Homer's Iliad, the other from Hesiod's Theogony. The passage from the Iliad (B, 348ff.) deals with the question of whether or not Zeus's sign, lightning bolts flashing on the right, is ψεῦδος, i.e., whether he is unveiling or concealing the "true" destiny alloted to the Greeks. "To be ψεῦδος" or "to be not ψεῦδος" presupposes here that Zeus lets something or other appear in the first place. In fact Homer speaks of Zeus φαίνων, Zeus who lets something appear. But "to let appear" is indeed to unveil. How then can he conceal? Zeus must let something come into appearance; however, such a thing, while it shows itself, at the same time only foreshadows or portends, and hence does not completely unveil but simultaneously shrouds. This is the manner of the showing of signs: σήματα. It is therefore that Zeus is called in this passage Ζεῦς σήματα φαίνων—the one who lets signs appear. A "sign" is that which, in appearing and pointing out, thereby lets something else appear—though in such a way that it does not relegate this to the manifest (where the sign itself appears) but precisely holds it back, i.e., veils. This self-appearance and self-disclosure, which also veils something by holding it back, is precisely what showing is. Only where there holds sway a letting appear and, hence, a disclosing, does there exist the free play for the possibility of ψεῦδος, i.e., the showing that also covers and holds back. The essence of ψεῦδος resides in an exhibiting that conceals, or, we could say, it resides in a dissembling.

We must nevertheless think this "dissembling" (obstructing, disguising) as both a process and a state of affairs. A neighboring house "obstructs" the self-showing of the mountain; a cupboard put in front of the door "disguises" the wall at that place and presents it thereby as a wall that is not broken up. The cupboard disguises—on the one hand by covering up the hole in the wall, and also, at the same time, by making appear and presenting an unbroken wall. The disguising is a hiding. This old German word (Verhehlen) derives from hehlen (hide, secrete), which means "to conceal." "Hiddenness" is concealment. We now use "dissembling" and "hiding"—and indeed in a "negative" sense—for the most part only with reference to human behavior, which we understand as "subjective" in opposition to "objective" events. "Dissembling" is for us "self-dissembling," and this becomes, in relation to others, "deceiving." Similarly, "hiding" also is used in a subjective sense: not to hide something to oneself, not to fool oneself, i.e., not to delude oneself, not to dissemble to oneself: to be "without a hidden secret," without concealment, and without veiling digression, i.e., in the case of an action or a communication. Originally, however, "hiding" meant any kind of "concealing"; the older German language knew even the word—which has since been lost—"dis-hide" [enthehlen]: to take out of concealedness. For many years I have used in my lectures the word "dis-close" [Entbergen]. In case there should come a time when we are again capable of experiencing dis-closure and unconcealedness (ἀλήθεια), we might also find again the lost word "dis-hiding" and appropriate it anew. "Hiding" [Hehlen] is, moreover, closely related to "hole" [*Höhle*], a hideaway that conceals something while it itself remains unconcealed.

Since τὸ ψεῦδος, according to the testimony of Homer, belongs to the essential realm of hiding, i.e., concealing and disconcealing, the Greek opposition of the otherwise unrelated words ἀληθές and ψεῦδος no longer seems odd. The Greeks think in ψεῦδος a concealing, and we must not forget that ψεῦδος is used of "signs," e.g. lightning; thus ψεῦδος does not merely characterize human behavior. Of course it is often used of ἔπος, μῦθος, and λέγειν, of the word and of speech. But even "the word" is for the Greeks primordially not just a formation produced by the "human subject." Because the Greeks think in ψεῦδος concealing as an event, therefore even ψεῦδος, veiling, can now become a point of departure for the formation of a counter-word which means the "non-false," and hence the "true," and for which the ordinary word for "true," namely τὸ ἀληθές, is not needed. The opposite of "hiding" is "dis-hiding." The "dis" is in Greek "α"; to ψεῦδος and ψευδές is opposed ἀψευδές, the not-hiding. Hesiod gives simple, univocal information concerning this word and its basic meaning (Theogony, verse 233). Nereus, the oldest and most venerable son of the God of the sea Πόντος, is called ἀψευδέα καὶ ἀληθέα, "the one who does not dissemble"; καί does not mean here simply "and," but it denotes an explaining "because." Nereus is "the one who does not dissemble," *because* he is the ἀληθής—*because* he is the not-concealing. Ψευδής is determined on the basis of "-ληθῆς." Τὸ ἀληθές now means, "literally" translated, before all else "the unconcealed," "the disclosed." Something unconcealed, disclosed, e.g., a piece of rock, does not have to be "disclosing." Indeed in this case, the unconcealed and disclosed, the piece of rock, can never be "disclosing" at all. On the contrary, what is "disclosing" is man's speech and perception.

The Greeks denote, however, the "disclosed" as well as the "disclosing" with the same word ἀληθές, which literally means the "unconcealed." At any rate, we maintain that the translation of ἀληθές as "the unconcealed" is the only "literal" one. But now it can be seen that ἀληθές, in the double sense of "disclosed" and "disclosing," is ambiguous. We come to know this ambiguity very clearly on the detour through ψεῦδος and its counter-word ἀψευδές. We also realize that mysterious relations obtain here. In order to appreciate the essence of the ambiguity of ἀληθές and, above all, to experience its ground, we have first to traverse the realm of essence of un-concealedness and disclosure in its broad extent. That means we must first consider the essence of concealment in a more penetrating way. Ψεῦδος in the sense of dissembling is a concealing. But is then every concealing necessarily a dissembling? Is every concealedness in itself already ψεῦδος, i.e., "falsity"? And what about "concealing closure" and its various modes?

b) The un-German word "false." *Falsum, fallo, σφάλλω*. The Roman priority of "overthrowing" in the Latinization of ancient Greece through the *imperium* (command) as essential ground of *iustum*. The transporting of ψεῦδος into the Roman-imperial domain of overthrowing. The real event of history: the assault of Latinizing in the Greek-Roman domain of history and the modern view of the Greek world through Roman eyes.

"False"—what are we to say about this word? "False" derives from the Latin *falsum*. We would do well to become attentive at last, and remain attentive, to what the Brothers Grimm (German Dictionary, III, 1291), who must know, note under this word with a tone of wrath [*Ingrimm*]: "False, *falsus*, an un-German word of which there is no trace in Ulfilas." An "un-German word"—he who is not too faint-hearted will be alarmed at this observation and will never again get rid of his dismay. The word "false" [*falsch*] entered the German language in the early Christian Middle Ages through the Latin *falsum*. The stem of the Latin word *falsum* (*fallo*) is "fall" and is related to the Greek σφάλλω, i.e., to overthrow, bring to a downfall, fell, make totter. But this Greek word σφάλλω never became the *genuine* counter-word opposed to ἀληθές. I deliberately say "genuine," because the Greek σφάλλω can sometimes be translated "correctly" by "deceiving"; what is meant, however, thought in the Greek way, is "making totter," "making stagger," "letting stumble into erring." But man can be led into such tottering and falling in the midst of the beings appearing to him only if something is put in his way obstructing beings, so that he does not know what he is dealing with. First something must be held forth and set forth, and then something else entirely must be delivered, so that man can "fall for" what is presented that way and thereby fall down. Bringing to a fall in the sense of misleading first becomes possible on the basis of a putting forth, dissembling, and concealing. Following a pervasive ambiguity, σφάλλω is related to "putting something up"; thought in the Greek way, that means to place something in the unconcealed and to let what thus stands there appear as enduring, i.e., as presencing. Σφάλλω is opposed to such putting up insofar as it does not let the presencing stand in its standing-there but overthrows it, for it puts up something else in place of it and alleges that what is put up is what stands. Τὸ ἀσφαλές means the un-falling, what remains standing in its abiding and enduring, i.e., in Greek, remains in its presencing into the unconcealed. Τὸ ἀσφαλές is never the "certain" and the "secure" in the modern sense of *certitudo*.

Because the bringing to a fall, in every sense, is only a subsequent effect within the field of the essence of dissembling and concealing (which constitute the essence of ψεῦδος), therefore what is connected with "falling" and bringing to a fall cannot for the Greeks be the original and proper opposite to "unconcealedness," to ἀληϑές.

Why, however, is the *falsum*, the "bringing to a fall," essential for the Romans? What realm of experience is normative here, if the bringing to a fall attains such a priority that on the basis of its essence there is determined the counter-essence to what the Greeks experience as ἀληϑές, the "unconcealing" and the "unconcealed"?

The realm of essence decisive for the development of the Latin *falsum* is the one of the *imperium* and of the "imperial." We will take these words in their strict and original sense. *Imperium* means "command." To be sure, we now understand the word "command" in a later, Latin-romanic, sense. Originally "command" [*Befehl*] (the "h" should be written after the "l": *befelh*) meant the same as "to cover": to "commit" (command) the dead to the earth or to the fire, to entrust them to a cover. The original meaning of "command" survives in our expression, "I commend (command) thy ways to the Lord" (i.e., entrust to protection and sheltering cover). This commending is preserved in our word "recommend." Instead of "recommend," Luther always used the word "commend"—*commendare*. On its way through the French language, "commend" became *commandieren*, i.e., more precisely, the Latin *imperare*, *im-parare* = to arrange, to take measures, i.e., *prae-cipere*, to occupy in advance, and so to take possession of the occupied territory and to rule it. *Imperium* is the territory [*Gebiet*] founded on commandments [*Gebot*], in which the others are obedient [*botmäsig*]. *Imperium* is the command in the sense of commandment. Command, thus understood, is the basis of the essence of domination, not the consequence of it and certainly not just a way of exercising domination. The God of the Old Testament is a "commanding" God; His word is: "Thou shalt not," "Thou shalt." This "shalt" is written down on the tables of the law. The gods of the Greeks are not commanding gods but, rather, ones that give signs, that point. The Roman gods, quite to the contrary, are designated by the Latin word *numen*, which means "bidding" and "will" and has the character of command. The "numinous," strictly taken, does not at all touch the essence of the Greek gods, i.e., gods who dwell in the region of ἀλήϑεια. In the essential realm of the "command" belongs the Roman "law," *ius*. This word is connected with *jubeo*: to bid, to let something be done by bidding and to determine it through this doing and letting. The command is the essential ground of domination and of *iustum*, as understood in Latin, the "to-be-in-the-right" and the "to have a right." Accordingly, *iustitia* has a wholly different ground of essence than that of δίκη, which arises from ἀλήϑεια.

Command, as the essential ground of domination, includes being-superior, which is only possible as the constant surmounting of others, who are thereby the inferiors. In this surmounting there resides again the constant ability to oversee. We say that to "oversee" something means to "dominate" it. This overseeing, which includes the surmounting, involves a constant "being-on-the-watch." That is the form of acting which oversees everything but still keeps to itself: in Latin, the *actio* of the *actus*. The surmounting overseeing denotes the dominating "sight" expressed in the often quoted phrase of Caesar: *veni, vidi, vici*—I came, I *oversaw*, and I conquered. Victory is only the effect of Caesar's seeing and overseeing, whose proper character is *actio*. The essence of the *imperium* resides in the *actus* of constant "action." The imperial *actio* of the constant surmounting of others includes the sense that the others, should they rise to the same or even to a neighboring level of command, will be brought down—in Latin *fallere* (participle: *falsum*). This bringing to a fall pertains necessarily to the imperial realm. The bringing to a fall can occur in a "direct" attack and overthrowing. The other can, however, also be brought down by being "tripped up" from behind in a furtive way. The bringing to a fall is then subterfuge, "trick" [*Trick*], which word, not accidentally, comes from the "English." Subterfuge is, considered from the outside, the roundabout and therefore mediate bringing to a fall versus immediate overthrowing. Thereby the fallen are not destroyed but are in a certain way raised up again—within the limits fixed by the dominating ones. This "fixing" is in Latin *pango*, whence the word *pax*—peace. This is, imperially thought, the fixed situation of the fallen. Actually, to compass someone's downfall in the sense of subterfuge and roundabout action is not the mediate and derived, but the really genuine, imperial *actio*. The properly "great" feature of the imperial resides not in war but in the *fallere* of subterfuge as roundabout action and in the pressing-into-service for domination. The battles against the Italian cities and tribes, by means of which Rome secured its territory and expansion, make manifest the unmistakable procedure of roundabout action and encirclement through treaties with tribes lying further out. In the Latin *fallere*, to bring down, as subterfuge, there resides "deceiving"; the *falsum* is treachery and deception, "the false."

What happens when the Greek ψεῦδος is thought in the sense of the Latin *falsum*? The Greek ψεῦδος, as hiding and consequently also as "deceiving," is now no longer experienced and interpreted on the basis of concealing but instead on the basis of subterfuge. The Greek ψεῦδος, by being translated into the Latin *falsum*, is transported into the Roman-imperial domain of bringing to a downfall. Ψεῦδος, dissembling and concealing, now becomes what fells, the false. Thus it is clear that Roman experience and thinking, organizing and expanding, constructing and working, from their essential outset never moved within the region of ἀλήθεια and ψεῦδος. As a kind of historiographical constatation, it has been known for a long time now that the Romans took things over from the Greeks in many ways and that this appropriation was also a recasting. One day we must consider in what regions of essence and out of what background this Romanizing of Greece came to pass. The transformation of ψεῦδος, i.e., the appropriation of "concealing" into the sense of "bringing to a fall," extends so far that the Latin language even adopts the construction and the use of the Greek word λανθάνω, "I am concealed." This transformative adoption is favored through the Indo-germanic affinity between the Greek and Latin languages. Greek says: λανθάνει ἤχων; we correctly translate: "He comes unnoticed." But thought in the Greek way it says: "He is concealed as the one who is coming." The Roman historiographer Livy says: *fallit hostis incedens.* In our language: "The enemy approaches unnoticed." Closer to the Latin: "The enemy deceives as the one who is approaching." But what the sentence really says is: "The enemy, as the one approaching, brings to a fall." That is absurd and makes sense only if *fallere*, as bringing to a fall, is thought in the sense of subterfuge, which in turn is thought as deceiving and then as hiding. The Greek ψεῦδος was appropriated, but without an experience of the essential domain of concealment that is normative here. Similarly, Livy speaks of a man, *qui natus moriensque fefellit.* Our German language would render it: "who was born unknown and died unknown." According to the Roman way of thinking: "who at his birth and at his death brought men to a fall and misled them." But what Livy says can be made meaningful if thought in the Greek manner: "At his birth and at his death concealedness surrounded him." A newborn is unlikely, at his birth, to "trip up" his fellow men, though that is precisely what the Latin word says, and bring them to a fall, or even simply deceive them. But surely, on the contrary, he can dwell in concealedness. The Latin *fefellit* signifies another realm of essence than that of the Greek ἐλάνθανε. The Latin *falsum* is alien to the Greek ψεῦδος.

The domination of the Romans and their transformation of Hellenism are in no way limited, however, to individual institutions of the Greek world or to single attitudes and "modes of expression" of Greek humanity. Nor does the Latinization of the Greek world by the Romans amount simply to the sum of everything they have appropriated. What is decisive is that the Latinization occurs as a *transformation of the essence of truth and Being* within the essence of the Greco-Roman domain of history. This transformation is distinctive in that it remains concealed but nevertheless determines everything in advance. This transformation of the essence of truth and Being is the genuine event of history. The imperial as the mode of Being of a historical humanity is nevertheless not the basis of the essential transformation of ἀλήθεια into *veritas,* as *rectitudo,* but is its consequence, and as this consequence it is in turn a possible cause and occasion for the development of the true in the sense of the correct. To speak of the "transformation of the essence of truth" is admittedly only an expedient; for it is still to speak of truth in an objectifying way over and against the way it itself comes to presence and history "is." The transformation of the essence of truth likewise supports that domain in which the historically observable nexuses of Western history are grounded. That is why the historical state of the world we call the modern age, following historiographical chronology, is also founded on the event of the Romanizing of Greece. The "Renaissance" of the ancient world accompanying the outset of the modern period is unequivocal proof of this. A more remote, but by no means indifferent, consequence of the Romanizing of Greece and of the Roman rebirth of antiquity is the fact that we today still see the Greek world with Roman eyes—and indeed not solely within historiographical research into ancient Greece but also, and this is the only decisive thing, within the historical metaphysical dialogue of the modern world with that of the ancients. The metaphysics of Nietzsche, whom we like to consider the modern rediscoverer of ancient Greece, sees the Greek "world" exclusively in a Roman way, i.e., in a way at once modern and un-Greek. Similarly, we still think the Greek πόλις and the "political" in a totally un-Greek fashion. We think the "political" as Romans, i.e., imperially. The essence of the Greek πόλις will never be grasped within the horizon of the political as understood in the Roman way. As soon as we consider the simple unavoidable essential domains, which are for a historiographer naturally of no consequence, since they are inconspicuous and noiseless, then, but only then, do we see that our usual basic ideas, i.e., Roman, Christian, modern ones, miserably fail to grasp the primordial essence of ancient Greece.

Recapitulation

2) Reconsideration of the essence of the "false" and of the hiding and "dis-hiding" of ψεῦδος. The rule of the Roman imperial "high command" and the breadth of the distinction between ψεῦδος and *falsum*.

We are considering the essence of ψεῦδος, a word usually rendered "false." But for what purpose are we "busying" ourselves with the false, supposing we are "busy" here at all? Indeed we desire the true, and it is difficult enough to try to find it and preserve it. We want the "positive." Why then all this brain-racking over the negative? These are all legitimate questions.

But in our meditation it is not the false itself we are pursuing. We are reflecting "only" on the essence of the false. And the essence of the false is not itself something false. It is so far removed from that that the essence of the false might even participate in what is most essential to the essence of the true. It could indeed be so difficult to find the truth, and therefore we find it so rarely, because we do not know, and do not want to know, anything about the essence of the false. It could be that we are wandering about in an uncanny delusion if we believe the essence of the negative is itself something "negative." Who knows nothing of the essence of death lacks every trace of a knowledge of the essence of "life." The essence of death is not a non-essence. The essence of negativity is nothing negative, but neither is it only something "positive." The distinction between the positive and the negative does not suffice to grasp what is essential, to which the non-essence belongs. The essence of the false is not something "false."

Tὸ ψεῦδος—we usually translate "the false"—is, for Greek thought, "dissembling." Dissembling lets something it sets out and sets up appear differently than it is "in truth." In the "different than" resides the "not-such-as," which, experienced on the basis of "dis-hiding" and unconcealedness, brings about a concealment. Nevertheless, insofar as dissembling not only sets "something else" before—namely, before what is to be presented—but lets something appear otherwise than it is "in truth," dissembling also unveils and hence is a kind of disclosure. If ψεῦδος were altogether without this basic feature of hiding and "dis-hiding," and hence without the feature of concealing, then ψεῦδος could never arise as the counter-essence to ἀλήθεια, unconcealedness. "The false," in the Greek sense, has the basic feature of concealment. To keep immutably in our sight the primordial Greek experience of ψεῦδος, we need to clarify how the essence of the false is delimited beyond the Greek world and even beyond its historical time, though there too it is still understood in general in the shadow of the light of ancient Greece.

The word "false" is an un-German word and derives from the Latin *falsum*, which, as participle, pertains to *fallere*. Of the same stem is our word "fell," to bring about a downfall, and the Greek σφάλλω. We translate this Greek word by "deceive," but we must not forget that "deception," understood in the Greek way, is determined by ψεῦδος, by dissembling and setting-before, by hiding. In Greek thought, the word σφάλλω, "I deceive," names a consequence of the essence of ψεῦδος. In Latin thought, the word *fallere* as "to bring to a fall" denotes the ground of the essence of ψεῦδος. What is the basis for the priority of *fallere* in the Latin formation of the counter-essence to truth? It lies in this, that the basic comportment of the Romans toward beings in general is governed by the rule of the *imperium*. *Imperium* says *im-parare*, to establish, to make arrangements: *prae-cipere*, to occupy something in advance, and by this occupation to hold command over it, and so to have the occupied as territory. *Imperium* is commandment, command.

The Roman law, *ius—iubeo*, I command—is rooted in the same essential domain of the imperial, command, and obedience. Command is the ground of the essence of domination; which is why a clearer and more proper translation of *imperium* is "high command." To be superior is part and parcel of domination. And to be superior is only possible through constantly remaining in the higher position by way of a constant surmounting of others. Here we have the genuine *actus* of imperial action. In the essence of the constant surmounting there resides, as the valley amid the mountains, the holding down and the bringing to a fall. Mere "felling" in the sense of striking down is the coarsest way, but not the genuinely essential imperial way, of bringing to a fall. The great and most inner core of the essence of essential domination consists in this, that the dominated are not kept down, nor simply despised, but, rather, that they themselves are permitted, within the territory of the command, to offer their services for the continuation of the domination. The bringing to a fall aims at keeping the overthrown standing in a certain sense, though not standing high. Imperial bringing to a fall, *fallere*, is therefore a going after and a going around that lets stand. For the Romans, the essence of deceiving, of leading into error, of dissembling, and thus of ψεῦδος, is determined by *fallere*, by felling. The erroneous becomes *falsum*.

Supposing now that this distinction between the Greek ψεῦδος and the Roman *falsum* originates in other domains and has another weight than the distinction in the style of Greek and Roman pots and pans and spear points, and supposing that here a transformation takes place in the essential ground of the historicity of all history, then we need to reflect more thoughtfully on this Roman transformation of Greece. That the Occident still today, and today more decisively than ever, thinks the Greek world in a Roman way, i.e., in a Latin, i.e., in a Christian way (as paganism), i.e., in the Romanic, modern-European, way, is an event touching the most inner center of our historical existence. The political, which as πολιτικόν arose formerly out of the essence of the Greek πόλις, has come to be understood in the Roman way. Since the time of the *Imperium*, the Greek word "political" has meant something Roman. What is Greek about it now is only its sound.

c) The imperial in the form of the curial of the curia. The connection between *verum* and "true." The un-German meaning of "true" through the Roman-Christian *verum*. *Verum*: the established right as counter-word to *falsum*. *Verum* and *a-pertum*; λαθόν and its counterpart to ἀληθές.

How then how do matters stand as regards the essence of the false, the Roman *falsum*? A closer consideration of the process by which the Romans took up Greek poetry, thought, speech, and artistic production shows that *falsum*, "bringing to a fall," has transformed ψεῦδος, "dissembling," in accord with its own spirit and in so doing has itself been changed and thereby dislodged. Such change is ever the most dangerous, but also the most enduring, form of domination. Since then, the Occident has known of ψεῦδος only in the form of *falsum*. For us, the opposite of the true is the false. But the Romans did not only lay the foundation for the priority of the false as the standard meaning of the essence of untruth in the Occident. In addition, the consolidation of this priority of the false over ψεῦδος and the stabilizing of this consolidation is a Roman accomplishment. The operating force in this accomplishment is no longer the *imperium* of the state but the *imperium* of the Church, the *sacerdotium*. The "imperial" here emerges in the form of the curial of the curia of the Roman pope. His domination is likewise grounded in command. The character of command here resides in the essence of ecclesiastical dogma. Therefore this dogma takes into account equally the "true" of the "orthodox believers" as well as the "false" of the "heretics" and the "unfaithful." The Spanish Inquisition is a form of the Roman curial *imperium*. By way of Roman civilization, both the imperial/civil and the imperial/ecclesiastical, the Greek ψεῦδος became for us in the Occident the "false." Correspondingly, the true assumed the character of the not-false. The essential realm of the imperial *fallere* determines the not-false as well as the *falsum*. The not-false, said in Roman fashion, is the *verum*.

On our path of a preparatory clarification of the essence of ἀλήθεια, and hence of the Greek experience of the essence of truth, we have now elucidated the words ἀληθές, "unconcealing" or "disclosing," ψεῦδος, "dissembling," *falsum*, "bringing to a fall," and thereby also the word "false" itself. Consequently, the main conditions have been fulfilled for us to learn how matters stand with the Latin word for ἀληθές, i.e., *verum*, and how, above all, matters stand with our word for ἀλήθεια, "truth," and with the word "true." Since "true" is the counter-word to "false," the latter stemming from the Latin *falsum*, *verum* as the Latin counter-word to *falsum* must surely belong together with *falsum* in the same essential domain and hence must also draw the "true" into this domain. Here, of course, we are presupposing that "true" and *verum* belong together. This holds insofar as our German word for "true" ["*wahr*"] was early on determined by the Latin-Christian *verum*. That process has its own depth and its great bearing, precisely because *veritas* and *verum*, in the preaching of Christianity, did not present themselves to the Germans as arbitrary Latin words. For Christian faith is proclaimed, in its totality, as "the" *veritas*, "the" *verum*, "the true," since Christ says of himself: ἐγώ εἰμι ἡ ὁδὸς καὶ ἡ ἀλήθεια καὶ ἡ ζωή (John 14, 6).

Only the sound of this phrase is Greek. That is why it could pass forthwith into the Latin language of the Vulgate: *Ego sum via, et veritas,* et vita. "I am the way and the truth and the life." Our words "truth" and "true" take their meaning from *verum* and *veritas* as these prevail in the Latin language of the Church. Whether, besides this, and prior to it, our German "true" had a root meaning proper to it, not determined by *verum* and hence by *falsum*, is controversial, because it is obscure. It is obscure because nowhere does another essence of "true" and "truth" come to light within the historicity of German history. It would not be said as decisively of the word "true" what the brothers Grimm say of "false": an un-German word. Nevertheless we must say it: "true" is an un-German word in view of the unequivocally clear fact that the basic meaning of "true" is determined by the Latin-Christian *verum*.

But what does the Latin *verum* mean? The stem *ver* is Indo-Germanic, as is the stem *fall* of σφάλλω, *fallere*, "fall." The stem *ver* appears unequivocally in our German word *wehren* ["to resist"], *die Wehr* ["defense"], *das Wehr* ["dam"]; therein lies the moment of the "against," "resistance": "the resistant"—the dam against . . . Italic-Oscic *veru*, the gate—which shuts off passage and entrance—*verostabulum*—*vestibulum*—vestibule, the space before the properly separating entrance, which stands *ver*, against, it, (*stabulum*), the space in front of the door. But the standing-against is not the only moment in the *ver*. For in that case the word *Ab-wehr* ["resistance," literally, "defense-from"] would be a mere tautology; *Wehr* ["defense"] is not already in itself and only defense-against. In "Parcifal," *ver* does not mean resistance; instead, it means to defend oneself, maintain oneself: resistance-for. Thus *ver* means to keep one's position, hold one's place. To be sure, resistance always belongs here in a certain sense, yet this resistance is one that has to derive from a steadfastness. *Ver* means to be steady, to keep steady, i.e., not to fall (no *falsum*), to remain above, to maintain oneself, to keep one's head up, to be the head, to command. Maintaining oneself, standing upright—the upright. Thus it is from the essential domain of the imperial that *verum*, as counter-word to *falsum*, received the sense of established right. Thereby from the original word *ver* a meaning has been extracted that clearly comes to the fore in the old Latin *veru* in the sense of gate and door, but also in the German *das Wehr* ["dam"], the gate that shuts and locks, the dam that seals off. The original element in *ver* and *verum* is that of closing off, covering, concealing, and sheltering, but it is not *die Wehr* ["defense"] as resistance. The corresponding Greek word of this Indo-Germanic stem is ἔρυμα—the defensive weapon, the covering, the enclosure. Ἔρυμα—to which the Roman word *verum* is immediately connected—means in Greek, however, precisely the opposite of the Greek word for "true," i.e., it is the opposite of ἀλήθεια. *Verum*, ἔρυμα—the enclosure, the covering; ἀλήθεια—the dis-covering, the dis-closing. But how else could an opposition hold sway here unless they both shared, though in a concealed way, the same essential dimension? The Roman word for "the true," *ver*, has the root meaning of closing-covering and locking up, a meaning which was, to be sure, obliterated, or at least never expressly and purely liberated. The opposite to *ver*, *verum*, as the enclosing, is the non-enclosing. This "opposes" the *verum*. "Opposing," acting against, is expressed in Latin by the prefix *op-*; to be "against" the enclosing, against the *ver*, is *op-verio* or *ap-verio*, whence the Latin *aperio*: "I open." The main sense of opening, understood in the Roman way, is "non-enclosing." In the Latin word *aperire*, "to open," the original *verum* speaks. According to the verbal structure, the participle of *aperio*, *apertum*, the un-enclosed, corresponds to the Greek ἀληθές, the unconcealed. The *pertum* canceled in *a-pertum* is the *verum*. This corresponds to the Greek λαθόν (λαθές). The original *ver-*, *verum*, means the same as the Greek λαθόν, hence precisely the opposite of ἀληθές. The Roman *verum*, strictly speaking, should then be taken as equivalent to the Greek ψεῦδος, if the latter is indeed the counter-word to ἀληθές. But the Roman *verum* not only does not coincide with ψεῦδος, it is precisely the opposite of ψεῦδος as understood in Latin, i.e., *falsum*. If we reflect on this, then mysterious ways of language and of the word show themselves in the realm where the essential possibility of the word itself, i.e., the essential possibility of the truth of its essence, is decided. With regard to the Latin name for the true, *verum*, we shall keep two incidents in mind:

1. *Verum*, *ver-*, meant originally enclosing, covering. The Latin *verum* belongs to the same realm of meaning as the Greek ἀληθές, the uncovered—precisely by signifying the exact opposite of ἀληθές: the closed off.

2. But now because *verum* is counter to *falsum*, and because the essential domain of the *imperium* is decisive for *verum* and *falsum* and their opposites, the sense of *ver-*, namely enclosure and cover, becomes basically that of covering for security against. *Ver* is now the maintaining-oneself, the being-above; *ver* becomes the opposite of falling.[1] *Verum* is the remaining constant, the upright, that which is directed to what is superior because it is directing from above. *Verum* is *rectum* (*regere*, "the regime"), the right, *iustum*. For the Romans, the realm of concealment and disconcealment does not at all come to be, although it strives in that direction in *ver*, the essential realm determining the essence of truth. Under the influence of the imperial, *verum* becomes forthwith "being-above," directive for what is right; *veritas* is then *rectitudo*, "correctness," we would say. This originally Roman stamp given to the essence of truth, which solidly establishes the all-pervading basic charac-

---

1. Reading *Fallen* for *Nicht-fallen.*—Tr.

ter of the essence of truth in the Occident, rejoins an unfolding of the
essence of truth that began already with the Greeks and that at the
same time marks the inception of Western metaphysics.

d) The transformation of the essence of ἀλήθεια since Plato. The
assumption of the "representation" of ἀλήθεια through ὁμοίωσις
(as *rectitudo* of *ratio*) into *veritas*. *Rectitudo* (*iustitia*) of ecclesiastical dogmatics and the *iustificatio* of evangelical theology. The
certum and the *usus rectus* (Descartes). Reference to Kant. The
closing of the ring of the history of the essence of truth in the
transformation of *veritas* into "justice" (Nietzsche). The incarcera-
tion of ἀλήθεια in the Roman bastion of *veritas*, *rectitudo*, and
iustitia.

Since Plato, and above all by means of Aristotle's thinking, a transformation was accomplished within the Greek essence of ἀλήθεια, one
which in a certain respect ἀλήθεια itself encouraged. Ἀληθές is first
of all the unconcealed and the disclosing. The unconcealed as such
can be disclosed for humans and by humans only if their disclosing
comportment adheres to the unconcealed and is in agreement with it.
Aristotle uses the word ἀληθεύειν for this comportment: to adhere to
the unconcealed disclosively in the saying that lets appear. This adher-
ence to and agreement with the unconcealed is in Greek ὁμοίωσις—the
disclosive correspondence expressing the unconcealed. This correspondence takes and holds the unconcealed for what it is. To take something
for something is in Greek οἴεσθαι. The λόγος, which now means assertion, is constituted by the οἴεσθαι. This disclosive correspondence still
adheres to, and is wholly achieved within, the essential space of ἀλήθεια as unconcealedness.[1] At the same time, however, the ὁμοίωσις,
i.e., the agreeing correspondence, as the mode of the execution of
ἀληθεύειν, assumes, as it were, the definitive "representation" of ἀλήθεια. This is, as the non-dissembling of beings, the assimilation of the
disclosive saying to the disclosed self-showing beings, i.e., it is ὁμοίωσις.
From then on, ἀλήθεια presents itself only in this essential form and
is taken only in that way.

Veritas as *rectitudo*, stemming from another origin, is now, however,
in a sense created to assume into itself the essence of ἀλήθεια in the
henceforth "representative" form of ὁμοίωσις. The rightness of an assertion is its adjusting itself to a right rightly instituted and firmly established [*Die Richtigkeit der Aussage ist ein Sichrichten nach dem Errichteten,
Feststehenden, Rechten*]. The Greek ὁμοίωσις as disclosive correspondence and the Latin *rectitudo* as adjustment to . . . both have the charac-

---

1. On ὀρθός and ὀρθότης, see below, p. 81.

ter of an assimilation of assertions and thinking to the state of affairs present at hand and firmly established. Assimilation is called *adaequatio*. In the early Middle Ages, following the path set by the Romans, ἀλή-θεια, presented as ὁμοίωσις, became *adaequatio*. *Veritas est adaequatio intellectus ad rem*. The entire thinking of the Occident from Plato to Nietzsche thinks in terms of this delimitation of the essence of truth as correctness. This delimitation of the essence of truth is the *metaphysical concept of truth*; more precisely, metaphysics receives its essence from the essence of truth thus determined. But because the Greek ὁμοίωσις turned into *rectitudo*, the realm of ἀλήθεια, disclosure, still present for Plato and Aristotle in ὁμοίωσις, disappeared. In *rectitudo*, in the "self-adjustment to . . . ," there also resides what the Greeks call οἴεσθαι, to take something as something and to accept it thus. But whereas for the Greeks to "take something as something" was still experienced within the essential realm of disclosedness and unconcealedness, thought in the Roman way it lies outside this essential domain. To "take something as something" is in Latin *reor*—the corresponding noun is *ratio*. In a variation of the Roman saying: *res ad triarios venit*,[1] we can say: *res ἀληθείας ad rationem venit*.[2] The essence of truth as *veritas* and *rectitudo* passes over into the *ratio* of man. The Greek ἀληθεύειν, to disclose the unconcealed, which in Aristotle still permeates the essence of τέχνη, is transformed into the calculating self-adjustment of *ratio*. This determines for the future, as a consequence of a new transformation of the essence of truth, the technological character of modern, i.e., machine, technology. And that has its origin in the originating realm out of which the imperial emerges. The imperial springs forth from the essence of truth as correctness in the sense of the directive self-adjusting guarantee of the security of domination. The "taking as true" of *ratio*, of *reor*, becomes a far-reaching and anticipatory security. *Ratio* becomes counting, calculating, calculus. *Ratio* is a self-adjustment to what is correct.

Ratio is a *facultas animi*, a power of the human mind, the *actus* of which inhabits the inner man. The *res*, the thing, lies apart from *ratio*. In *rectitudo* as *adaequatio*, *ratio* is supposed to assimilate the thing. Now what is completely lacking here is the essential space of ἀλήθεια, the unconcealedness of things and the disclosing comportment of man, a space completely covered over by debris and forgotten. The essence of truth as *veritas* and *rectitudo* is without space and without ground. *Veritas* as *rectitudo* is a quality of the mind or soul in the inner man. A question was thus bound to arise as regards truth: how is it at all

---

1. The matter has come to the final stage.—Tr.
2. Ἀλήθεια has come to reason.—Tr.

possible for an inner process of the mind or soul to be brought into agreement with the things out there? And so begin the various attempts to explain it, all within an unclarified sphere.

If we consider that for a long time the essence of man has been experienced as *animal rationale*, i.e., as the thinking animal, then it follows that *ratio* is not just one power among others but is the basic power of man. That to which man is empowered by this power is decisive with regard to his relation to the *verum* and *falsum*. In order to obtain the true as what is right and correct, man must be assured and be certain of the correct use of his basic power. The essence of truth is determined on the basis of this assurance and certitude. The true becomes the assured and certain. The *verum* becomes the *certum*. The question of truth becomes the question of whether and how man can be certain and assured about the being he himself is as well as about the beings he himself is not.

The Roman world in the form of the ecclesiastical dogmatics of the Christian faith has contributed essentially to the consolidation of the essence of truth in the sense of *rectitudo*. The same realm of Christian faith introduces and prepares the new transformation of the essence of truth, the one of *verum* into *certum*. Luther raises the question of whether and how man can be certain and assured of eternal salvation, i.e., certain of "the truth." Luther asks how man could be a "true" Christian, i.e., a just man, a man fit for what is just, a justified man. The question of the Christian *veritas* becomes, in the sense just articulated, the question of *iustitia* and *iustificatio*. As a concept of medieval theology, *iustitia* is *rectitudo rationis et voluntatis*—correctness of reason and will. *Rectitudo appetitus rationalis*, the correctness of the will, the striving for correctness, is the basic form of the will in its willing. *Iustificatio* is already, according to medieval doctrine, the *primus motus fidei*—the basic stirring of the disposition of faith.[1] The doctrine of justification, and indeed as the question of certainty of salvation, becomes the center of evangelical theology. The essence of truth in the modern period is determined on the basis of certainty, correctness, being just, justice.

The inception of the metaphysics of the modern age rests on the transformation of the essence of *veritas* into *certitudo*. The question of

---

1. Sancti Thomae Aquinatis *Opera Omnia*, VI, *Commentum in Quatuor Libros Sententiarum, Volumen Primum, Distinct. II, Quaest. I, Art. V, Expositio textus: Justitia hic sumitur pro justitia generali, quae est rectitudo animae in comparatione ad Deum et ad proximum et unius potentiae ad aliam; et dicitur justitia fidei, quia in justificatione primus motus est fidei* ... [Exposition of the text: here justice is taken as general justice, which is the correctness of the soul in comparison with God and neighbor, and of one power of the soul with the other; and it is called justice of faith because in justification occurs the first motion of faith . . .—Tr.]

truth becomes the question of the secure, assured, and self-assuring use of *ratio*. Descartes, the first thinker of modern metaphysics, inquires into the *usus rectus rationis*, i.e., *facultatis iudicandi*, the correct use of reason, i.e., of the faculty of judgment. The essence of saying and asserting had already for a long time not been the Greek λόγος, i.e., ἀποφαίνεσθαι, the letting appear of the unconcealed. The essence of saying is now the Roman *iudicium*—correct saying, i.e., attaining, with certainty, what is right. Therefore the fundamental book of modern metaphysics, Descartes's *Meditationes de prima philosophia*, includes within its reflections on metaphysics the *meditatio quarta*, which treats *de vero et falso*. Now, where all that matters is the *usus rectus rationis humanae*, falsity is conceived as *usus non rectus facultatis iudicandi*. The *usus non rectus* is *error*, fault; or better: erring and error are conceived on the basis of the *usus non rectus facultatis iudicandi*. The untrue is the false in the sense of the erroneous, i.e., in the sense of the wrong use of reason.

In the second principal book of modern metaphysics, Kant's *Critique of Pure Reason*, the *usus*, the use of reason, is in question everywhere. "Critique of pure reason" means essential delimitation of the correct and incorrect use of the human faculty of reason. The question of the "correct use" treats of the will to secure the certainty which man, on his own, standing amidst beings, must attain and wishes to attain. *Veritas* in the Christian understanding, i.e., *rectitudo animae, iustitia*, provides to the modern essence of truth its character as the certainty and assurance of the content of human comportment. The true, *verum*, is what is right, what vouches for certainty, and in that sense it is the righteous, the just.

If we experience and come to know these nexuses historically, as our history, i.e., as modern European "world"-history, will it then surprise us that in Nietzsche's thought, where the metaphysics of the Occident reaches its peak, the essence of truth is founded on certitude and "justice"? Even for Nietzsche the true is the right, that which is directed by what is real in order to adjust itself to it and make itself secure in it. The basic feature of reality is will to power. What is right must conform itself to the real, hence must express what the real says, namely the "will to power." All correctness must be adjusted in terms of the will to power. Correspondence to what the will to power utters is the just, i.e., justice. It receives its essence, at the end of Western metaphysics, from the decree of the will to power. Nietzsche very often uses the word "life" as a title for the "will to power," and he uses it in accord with the usual "biological" way of thinking of the second half of the nineteenth century. Nietzsche can therefore say: "Justice is the highest representative of life itself." This is a Christian thought, though in the mode of the antichrist. Everything "anti" thinks in the spirit of that against which it is "anti." Justice, in Nietzsche's sense, presents the will to power.

Truth is, in the West, *veritas*. The true is that which, on various grounds, is self-asserting, remains above, and comes from above; i.e., it is the command. But the "above," the "highest," and the "lord" of lordship may appear in different forms. For Christianity, "the Lord" is God. "The lord" is also "reason." "The lord" is the "world-spirit." "The lord" is "the will to power." And the will to power, as expressly determined by Nietzsche, is in essence command. In the age in which the modern period finds its completion in a historical total state of the globe, the Roman essence of truth, *veritas*, appears as *rectitudo* and *iustitia*, as "justice." This is the fundamental form of the will to power. The essence of what is "just," assigned this essence of justice, is determined by Nietzsche unequivocally in the following note from the Summer of 1883, made on the occasion of his reading of a new book by Schneider, *Der thierische Wille* [*Animal will*]: "What is just = the will, to perpetuate an actual power relation . . ."[1]

The Roman *veritas* has become the "justice" of the will to power. The circle of the history of the essence of truth, as metaphysically experienced, is now closed. Yet ἀλήθεια remains outside this circle. The province of its essence is practically obliterated within the region of the domination of Western *veritas*.

It seems as if ἀλήθεια has withdrawn itself from the history of Occidental humanity. It seems as if the Roman *veritas*, and the truth which evolves out of it as *rectitudo* and *iustitia*, correctness and justice, have commandeered the field of the essence of ἀλήθεια. Not only does it seem so, it is so. The field of the essence of ἀλήθεια is covered over with debris. But if that were all, then it would be an easy task to clear the debris and once again lay open this field. The difficulty is that it is not merely covered over with debris; there has been built on it an enormous bastion of the essence of truth determined in a manifold sense as "Roman." To the "Roman" there belongs also the "Romanic," as well as everything essentially modern determined from it, which in the meantime has expanded into world history and is no longer limited to the European. (The connection visible here between τέχνη as a way of ἀληθεύειν and modern mechanical technique cannot now be exposed in more detail.)

Moreover, the bastion reinforcing the essence of truth as *veritas*, *rectitudo*, and *iustitia* has not only thrust itself in front of ἀλήθεια, but in the walls of this bastion ἀλήθεια itself is immured, after first being reinterpreted to serve as one of the building stones, hewn expressly for it. This is the reason ἀλήθεια has been understood

---

1. WW (Grossoktav), XIII, n. 462, p. 205.

ever since on the basis of *veritas* and *rectitudo* and only on that basis.

How then can we still experience ἀλήϑεια itself in its primordial essence? And if this is denied us, how are we to see, within the confines of the domination of *veritas* and *rectitudo*, that this domain of *veritas* itself nevertheless is founded in the region of essence of ἀλήϑεια and constantly appeals to it, though without, to be sure, knowing it or being mindful of it? How, within the confines of the domination of *veritas* and *rectitudo*, can we know, or even just seek to know, that *veritas* and *rectitudo* and *iustitia* cannot de facto exhaust the primordial essence of truth and in principle can never exhaust it, since they are what they are only in the wake of ἀλήϑεια? Western metaphysics may elevate the true up to the absolute spirit of Hegel's metaphysics and may claim "the angels" and "the saints" for "the true," yet the *essence* of truth has already long since retreated from its beginning, i.e., from the *ground of its essence*. It fell out from its beginning and hence is a falling away, an apostasy.

Recapitulation

3) The sending [*das Geschicht*] of the assignment of Being: retrospective consideration of the history of the transformation of the essence of truth. The "balances" of history (Burckhardt, Nietzsche, Spengler). The historical "conferral of meaning" in the modern period.

To grasp anything at all of the self-contained essence of the primordial Greek ἀλήϑεια, we who live so much later need to have in sight that against which ἀλήϑεια sets itself off for us. Therefore a sketch of the history of the transformation of the essence of truth is unavoidable. This will not be a historiographical treatment of the history of the *concept* of truth, nor will it examine how people have apprehended truth in the course of the centuries, for this apprehension itself already rests, in its correctness and incorrectness, on the holding sway of an essence of truth. Our aim is the history of the essence itself, of truth itself.

In this appeal to history, there is guiding, if you will, a conception of the essence of history. It would be fatal if it were not so. And it would be still more fatal if it were completely unclear to us. It is no less certain that it is difficult to allude to this history and that the presentation of it will be exposed to manifold gross misinterpretations from all directions.

"History," conceived essentially, that is, thought in terms of the ground of the essence of Being itself, is the transformation of the essence of truth. It is "only" this. Here the "only" does not indicate a restriction but refers to the uniqueness of the primordial essence, from which as ground the other essential features of history spring forth as essential consequences. History "is" the transformation of the essence of truth. Historical beings receive their Being from such transformation. Amid these transformations of the essence of truth occur the inconspicuous rare moments when history pauses. These pausing moments of hidden repose are the *primordial historical* moments, for in them the essence of truth originally assigns itself, and transmits itself, to beings.

For a long time it has been maintained that where there are events, motion, and processes, where something "comes to pass," there we have history, for history has to do with what "happens," and "happening" means "coming to pass." But happening and history actually mean destiny, destining, assignment. Genuinely formulated in German, we may not speak of history [*"die" Geschichte*], in the sense of coming to pass, but of sending [*"das Geschicht"*], in the sense of the assignment of Being. Luther still uses this genuinely German word [*das Geschicht*]. The question remains as to what for man is the essentially send-able or trans-mittable [*Zu-schickbare*] and the self-transmitting. If the essence of man is founded in the fact that he is that being to whom Being itself reveals itself, then the essential trans-mittal and the essence of "sending" is the unveiling of Being. But if unveiling is the essence of truth, and if in accordance with the transformation of this essence of truth the assignment of Being is also transformed, then the essence of "history" is the transformation of the essence of truth.

In the concealed repose of this transformation, there rests and sways, holds and fluctuates, congeals and whirls, that which is established on the basis of "historiography," i.e., on the basis of the investigations and explorations of objectivized "history," as events and accomplishments, i.e., as data [*Sachen*] and deeds [*Taten*], or in short, as facts [*Tat-sachen*]. These constatations then are presented with the prodigious display of the technical gadgets of modern research, making it seem that the technique of historiography is history itself. The historiographical thus becomes identified with the historical. From this "historiographical" element, "balances" are made up, "taxations" are drawn, and "shares" and "costs" are calculated, which "man" in history must pay. It is certainly no accident that a thinker of history of the rank of Jacob Burckhardt, and precisely he, moves within the horizon of "balances," "taxations," "shares," and "costs," and gives an account of history according to the schema of "culture and barbarism." Even Nietzsche thinks in terms of this schema of the nineteenth century. Nietzsche turns the "calculating of values," i.e., the accounting, into the final form of Western metaphysical thinking.

Exclusively on the basis of Nietzsche's metaphysics and without any original metaphysical thought, at the start of the twentieth century the author O. Spengler drew up a "balance" of Western history and proclaimed "The decline of the Occident." Today, as in 1918, when the arrogant book of this title came out, an eager public snaps up only the outcome of the "balance" without ever considering on which basic ideas of history this cheap balance of decline is concocted. In fact it had already been reckoned up clearly by Nietzsche, though thought out in a different way and in other dimensions. To be sure, the guild of serious researchers computed the "errors" of the book. This had the remarkable result that since then historiography itself has been conducted more and more within the horizon of Spengler's views and schemata, even where it was naturally able to make "more correct" and "more exact" constatations. Only to an age which had already forsaken every possibility of thoughtful reflection could an author present such a book, in the execution of which a brilliant acumen, an enormous erudition, and a strong gift for categorization are matched by an unusual pretension of judgment, a rare superficiality of thinking, and a pervasive frailty of foundations. This confusing semi-scholarship and carelessness of thinking has been accompanied by the peculiar state of affairs that the same people who decry the priority of the biological thinking in Nietzsche's metaphysics find contentment in the aspects of decline in the Spenglerian vision, which is based throughout on nothing but a crude biological interpretation of history.

Modern views of history, since the nineteenth century, like to speak about "meaning-conferral." This term suggests that man, on his own, is capable of "lending" a "meaning" to history, as if man had something to lend out at all, and as if history needed such a loan, all of which indeed presupposes that history "in itself" and at first is meaningless and in every case has to wait for the favor of a meaning bestowed by man. But what man is capable of in relation to history is to pay heed to it and to take care that history does not conceal from him its meaning and refuse it to him. But, as the case of Spengler shows, man has already lost the meaning of history when he has deprived himself of the very possibility of thinking about what, in the hastiness of drawing up "historiographical" balances, he is investing in the word "meaning." "Meaning" is the truth in which a being as such rests. The "meaning" of history, however, is the *essence* of truth, in which at any time the truth of a human epoch is founded. We experience the essence of the true only on the basis of the essence of truth, which in each case lets something true be *the* true that it is. We shall attempt here and now to take some steps in reflecting on the essence of truth.

4) The event of the conversion of the essence of untruth from the Greek ψεῦδος to the Roman *falsum*. The fulfillment of the transformation of *veritas* into *certitudo* in the nineteenth century. The self-assurance of self-certainty (Nietzsche, Fichte, Hegel).

We have sketched the transformation of the essence of truth in Western history in a few strokes. The basic meanings of the opposites ἀληθές-ψεῦδος, *falsum-verum*, true-false, incorrect-correct, should now be brought closer for reflection.

In the transformation of the essence of truth from ἀλήθεια, by way of the Roman *veritas*, to the medieval *adaequatio*, *rectitudo*, and *iustitia*, and from there to the modern *certitudo*, to truth as certainty, validity, and assurance, the essence and the character of the opposition between truth and untruth are also altered. The self-evident view that falsity is the only opposite to truth is thereby formed and reinforced. The result of this transformation of the essence of truth, which has prevailed for centuries in the Occident, is the event of the conversion of the essence of untruth from the Greek ψεῦδος to the Roman *falsum*. This conversion is the presupposition for the modern characterization of the essence of falsity. That becomes *error*, error in the sense of the incorrect use of the human power of affirmation and denial. The correct use of the power of judgment is determined in reference to what assures man's self-certainty. The intention toward certainty now determines for its part the direction, the kind of sight, and the selection of what is represented as that to which the judgments of affirmation and denial are imparted.

The essence of *veritas* in the form of *certitudo* unfolds in the direction of the certainty of the content of "life." The certainty of life, i.e., its constant "advantage," rests, according to Nietzsche, upon correctness, that is, upon the essential certainty of the "will to power." This is the reality, i.e., the essence, of everything "real" and not merely of man. Correctness as the essence of the will to power, i.e., assurance and certainty as its essence, is called "justice" by Nietzsche. He is thinking here, although unwittingly, in the sense of the Western tradition of *veritas* as *iustitia*. In a note[1] from the year 1885 he writes: "*Justice*, as the function of a wide-ranging power looking beyond the small perspectives of good and evil, hence has a broader horizon of *advantage*—the intention to obtain something that is *more* than this or that person." ("More," i.e., "has more value.")

From this it is clear that the power for which those perspectives, ones marking the distinction between "good and evil," are "small" per-

---

1. Ibid., XIV, n. 158, p. 80.

spectives moves within the broader (and only for it appropriate) horizon determined by Nietzsche as the horizon of "advantage." But advantage is made secure only by taking advantage. That allocates everything to the self-assurance of power. Power can only be assured by the constant enhancement of power. Nietzsche recognized this very clearly and declared that within the realm of essence of the will to power the mere preservation of an already attained level of power already represents a decrease in the degree of power. In the essence of assurance there resides a constant back-relatedness to itself, and in this lies the required self-elevation. The self-assurance as self-certainty, in this constant back-relatedness, must become absolute. The fundamental outline of the metaphysical essence of reality as truth, and of this truth as absolute certainty, is prepared by Fichte and appears for the first time in Hegel's metaphysics of the absolute spirit. Here truth becomes the absolute self-certainty of absolute reason. In Hegel's metaphysics and in Nietzsche's, i.e., in the nineteenth century, the transformation of *veritas* into *certitudo* is completed. This completion of the Roman essence of truth is the proper and hidden historical meaning of the nineteenth century.

§4. The multiplicity of the oppositions to unconcealedness in its essential character.

a) The rich essence of concealedness. Modes of concealing: ἀπάτη, (μέθοδος),κεύθω, κρύπτω, καλύπτω. Homer, Iliad, XX, 118; Odyssey, VI, 303; III, 16; Iliad, XXIII, 244. The disclosive power of *muthos* and the question of the Greek divinities.

But *veritas* and *rectitudo* do not at all fulfill the essence of ἀλήθεια. Therefore it also holds that the essence of untruth is not necessarily *falsitas*, falsity. And even if we go back to the more primal essence of untruth, ψεῦδος, which, as hiddenness, precisely indicates the basic character of concealment and in that way presents the genuine counter-essence to unconcealedness, still the question remains open whether this counter-essence, ψεῦδος, exhausts all possible opposition to truth. In the course of our considerations, we saw in fact that the Greeks, in addition to ψεῦδος, also knew of σφάλλειν, "to mislead." But this way of hiddenness, so-called "deception," is, precisely as a mode of hiding, already founded on the latter and is not a distinctive type of counter-essence to unconcealedness. This also holds for one way of hiddenness which for the Greeks was still more common and which they denoted with the word ἀπάτη. We translate again as "deception." Literally and concretely this word says: "*ab* (from) πάτος," i.e., from the right way and path. The ordinary Greek word for "way" is ἡ ὁδός, from which derives ἡ μέθοδος, our borrowed word "method." But ἡ μέθοδος does not mean for the Greeks "method" in the sense of a procedure with the aid of which man undertakes an assault on objects with his investigations and research. Ἡ μέθοδος is to-be-on-the-way, namely on a way not thought of as a "method" man devises but a way that already exists, arising from the very things themselves, as they show themselves through and through. The Greek ἡ μέθοδος does not refer to the "procedure" of an inquiry but rather is this inquiry itself as a remaining-on-the-way. In order to discern this essence of "method" understood in the Greek manner, we must first recognize that the Greek concept of "way," ὁδός, includes an element of per-spect and pro-spect. "Way" is not "stretch" in the sense of the remoteness or distance between two points and so itself a multiplicity of points. The perspective and prospective essence of the way, which itself leads to the unconcealed, i.e., the essence of the course, is determined on the basis of unconcealedness and on the basis of a going straightaway toward the unconcealed. Ἀ-πάτη is detour, by-way, and off-way, making available another prospect and supporting it in such a manner that, as way, it might indeed be the one going "straightaway" toward the unconcealed. The by-way and the off-way let us encounter what is not shown amid the appearances on the right way. But insofar as the off-way does show something, it exchanges what it shows for what is properly to be shown by the way leading straightaway on. Through this exchange [*Vertauschung*] the off-way deceives [*täuscht*] as off-way, owing to which ἀπάτη, deception, arises in the first place. Ἀπατηθῆναι means to be led on a by-way and an off-way in such a fashion that the thing to be experienced is dissembled. Ἀπάτη, too, is a manner of concealment, namely a kind of dissembling that conceals by distorting. Every hiding and dissembling is, to be sure, a concealing, but not every concealing is a hiding in the sense of dissembling and distorting.

If, accordingly, unconcealedness might still be related to other ways of concealment, then there would result an essential relation which to our way of thinking would mean that falsity and dissembling (and consequently untruth understood in those terms) are not the only opposites to truth at all, presupposing of course that we take the essence of truth as unconcealedness, i.e., disclosiveness. But were the Greeks themselves aware of other modes of concealment besides dissemblance (ψεῦδος)? Certainly. Their way of speech attests to it. We are familiar with their ordinary words κεύθω, κρύπτω, καλύπτω: to shelter, to conceal, to veil. Iliad, XXII, 118: Troy "hides" rich treasures. Odyssey, IX, 348: the boat of Odysseus has a "cache" of precious wine. Odyssey, VI, 303: house and court give "haven" to the entering ξεῖνος. Such ways of sheltering and concealing belong to the sphere of everyday relations. They do not manifest the pre-eminent level of the essence of concealment. It is already more essential to say (Odyssey, III, 16) that the earth shelters the dead. The Iliad, XXIII, 244, speaks of Άϊδι κεύθωμαι, of being ensconced in Hades. Here the earth itself and the subterranean come into relation with sheltering and concealing. The essential connection between death and concealment is starting to appear. For the Greeks, death is not a "biological" process, any more than birth is. Birth and death take their essence from the realm of disclosiveness and concealment. Even the earth receives its essence from this same realm. The earth is the in-between, namely between the concealment of the subterranean and the luminosity, the disclosiveness, of the supraterranean (the span of heaven, ούρανός). For the Romans, on the contrary, the earth, *tellus*, *terra*, is the dry, the land as distinct from the sea; this distinction differentiates that upon which construction, settlement, and installation are possible from those places where they are impossible. *Terra* becomes *territorium*, land of settlement as realm of command. In the Roman *terra* can be heard an imperial accent, completely foreign to the Greek γαῖα and γῆ.

The Greek words κρύπτειν and κρύπτεσθαι (whence *crypta* and crypt) mean sheltering concealment. Κρύπτειν applies above all to νύξ, the night. Similarly, day and night in general manifest the events of disclosure and concealment. Since to the Greeks everything that is arises, most basically, out of the essence of concealment and unconcealedness, they therefore speak of νύξ and ούρανός, the night and the light of day, when they want to express the beginning of all that is. What is said in that way is what is primordially to be said. It is authentic legend, the primordial word. Μῦθος is the Greek for the word that expresses what is to be said before all else. The essence of μῦθος is thus determined on the basis of άλήθεια. It is μῦθος that reveals, discloses, and lets be seen; specifically, it lets be seen what shows itself in advance and in everything as that which presences in all "presence." Only where the essence of the word is grounded in άλήθεια, hence among the Greeks, only where the word so grounded as pre-eminent legend pervades all poetry and thinking, hence among the Greeks, and only where poetry and thinking are the ground of the primordial relation to the concealed, hence among the Greeks, only there do we find what bears the Greek name μῦθος, "myth." The proposition that there is only *one* myth, namely the μῦθος of the Greeks, can hardly be expressed, because it expresses something far too self-evident, just as is the case with the proposition that there is only a fiery fire. But "myth" does of course have to do with the gods. "Mythology" is about "the gods." Certainly. But if we ask what is meant here by "gods," the answer is that it refers to the "Greek gods." Yet it is not sufficient to use the single God of Christianity as the measure and then point out that the

Greeks practiced a polytheism, and indeed a polytheism of gods that are comparatively less "spiritual" and altogether of a lesser nature. As long as we make no attempt to think the Greek gods in the Greek way, i.e., on the basis of the essence of the Greek experience of Being, i.e., on the basis of ἀλήθεια, we have no right to say a word about these gods, whether in favor of them or against them.

b) The connection between μῦθος and the Greek deities. Earth, day, night, and death in relation to unconcealedness. The mysterious as one of the modes of concealment. Rejection of the negativity in falsity and in dissembling as the one and only counter-essence to the truth.

Since, in these remarks on the "didactic poem" of Parmenides, we are seeking the essence of the goddess Ἀλήθεια, sooner or later a time must come when we are forced to elucidate the connection between μῦθος and the Greek deities, for only these can be considered here. Μῦθος is legend, this word literally taken in the sense of essential primordial speech. "Night" and "light" and "earth" are a μῦθος—not "images" for concealing and unveiling, "images" which a pre-philosophical thinking does not transcend. Rather, concealment and unconcealedness are in advance experienced in such an essential way that just the simple change of night and day suffices to enhance the emergence of all essence into the preserving word, μῦθος. The mere distinction between light and darkness, which we usually ascribe to day and night, does not, taken for itself, say anything. Since the distinction as such says nothing about the essence of concealment and disclosure, it does not at all have the character of a μῦθος. The distinction between light and darkness remains "unmythical" unless first of all clearness and concealment already appear as the essence of the light and the dark and along with them that which comes into the light and recedes into the darkness appears in such a way that precisely this coming into the light and this receding into darkness make up the essence in which all presence and all absence dwell. Only if we pay heed to this will we have a measure for comprehending that the primordial thinker thinks Being itself on the basis of unconcealedness and concealment. And only if we have this measure can we assess the Greek words of concealing and sheltering in their essential relations to earth, death, light, and night.

Of course, the bastion of the prevailing essence of truth, *veritas* and truth as correctness and certitude, is occluding the primordial understanding of ἀλήθεια. This does not simply mean that culturally, in historiographical presentations of the Greek world, we no longer know and appreciate the early Greek "concept of truth," but it means something else, essentially different, something momentous, and for our history the only decisive thing: the entirety of beings has in the meantime been transformed in such a way that beings as a whole, and therefore also man, are no longer determined on the basis of the essence of ἀλήθεια. Consequently, as soon as we hear of concealment and of modes of concealing, we think immediately, and only, of modes of human activity man himself controls. We do not experience concealment and disclosure as events which "come over" beings and man. If, however, for the Greeks the essence of concealment and unconcealedness was experienced so essentially as the basic feature of Being itself, must not concealment itself then display a more primordial essence, for which concealment in the form of ψεῦδος, dissemblance, in no way suffices?

Nevertheless, to a certain extent we can still recognize and understand different modes of concealment. In fact we must do so, if we wish to recapture an ability to glimpse the one mode of concealment that for the Greeks, over and beyond ψεῦδος, has codetermined the truth, the unconcealedness and unhiddenness, of all beings.

Ordinarily, concealing is for us displacing, a kind of putting "away" or putting aside. What is no longer beside us, i.e., nearby (in Greek: παρά), is gone "away" (in Greek: ἀπό). What is gone away has disappeared, is absent; what is gone away is, in a certain manner, no more, it is destroyed. Destruction, as putting aside, is a form of concealment.

There is also, however, a kind of concealment that does not at all put aside and destroy the concealed but instead shelters and saves the concealed for what it is. This concealment does not deprive us of the thing, as in cases of dissembling and distorting, withdrawing and putting aside. This concealment preserves. It is characteristic, e.g., of what we call, in a notable sense, the rare. Usually, i.e., for the mere eagerness to calculate and to snatch up, the rare is simply what is available only at times and even then only for a few. But what is truly rare is available precisely always and for everyone, except that it dwells in a concealment harboring something utterly decisive and holding in readiness high claims on us. The proper relation to the rare is not to chase after it but to leave it at rest by acknowledging the concealment.

Perhaps there are modes of concealment that not only preserve and put away and so in a certain sense still withdraw, but that rather, in a unique way, impart and bestow what is essential. The essential type of bestowal and bequest is in each case a concealment, and indeed not only of the bestower but of what is bestowed, insofar as the bestowed does not simply surrender its treasures but only lets this come into unconcealment: namely that in it a richness is lodged which will be attained to the degree it is protected against abuse. The concealment holding sway here is close to the concealment characteristic of the secret, which may have, though not by necessity, the basic character of mystery. The essence of the latter has been foreign to man from the moment he "explained" the mysterious simply as the unexplained. The mystery thus becomes a "residue" still remaining to be explained. But since technical explaining and explicability provide the criterion for what can claim to be real, the inexplicable residue left over becomes the superfluous. In this way the mysterious is only what is left over, what is not yet accounted for and incorporated within the circuit of explicative procedures.

It would surely be simplistic and not thoughtful at all if we were saying that the little ego of some individual man were capable of elevating calculability to the rank of the measure of the reality of the real. Instead, the modern age corresponds to the metaphysical depth of the course of its history, when, in accordance with its will toward the unconditional "residuelessness" of all procedure and all organizing, it builds broad avenues through all continents and so no longer has a place free for that residue in which the mystery would still glimmer in the form of mere inexplicability. The secret in the mystery is a kind of concealment, characterized by its insignificance, in virtue of which the mystery is an open one. We readily misuse the term "open secret" or "open mystery" and apply it to the situation where there is precisely nothing secret or mysterious at all but where what is already known by everyone is not supposed to be brought into the open. The "open mystery" in the genuine and strict sense, on the contrary, occurs where the concealing of the mysterious is simply experienced as concealedness and is lodged in a historically arisen reticence. The openness of the open mystery does not consist in solving the mystery, thus destroying it, but consists in not touching the concealedness of the simple and essential and letting this concealedness alone in its appearance. The insignificance of the concealment proper to the genuine mystery is already a result of the essence of the simple, which for its part is grounded primordially.

Another kind of concealment within the mysterious is displayed by the clandestine, under the cover of which, e.g., a conspiracy simmers. There the concealment has the character of an extended yet at the same time tightly knit ambush, lying in wait for the moment of the sudden outburst. The inconspicuous is here, too. But now it takes the form of camouflage and deception. Therefore this inconspicuousness must explicitly protrude everywhere and must always be concerned with safeguarding its outward appearance.

Far away from these modes of concealment, and yet within the sphere of the same essence, resides the concealed in the sense of the merely not yet known. This concealment includes, e.g., the horizon of scientific and technical discoveries. When the concealed in this sense is brought into unconcealedness, there arise "the miracles of technology" and what is specifically "American."

These comments on the essential character of concealment and concealedness, considered fully, come down to this: we are here only broaching a realm whose fullness of essence we hardly surmise and certainly do not fathom, for we are outside the mode of experience proper to it. It would therefore also be an error to claim that the rich essence of concealedness could be gained just by counting the sundry modes of concealment, under the guidance of the various "word meanings." If we speak of "kinds" of concealment we do not mean that there would be a genus, "concealment in general," to which then, following the schema of the usual logical classification, various species and their sub-species and variations would be subordinated. The connection among the kinds of concealedness is a historical one, and the historical must be kept distinct from the "historiographical." The latter is information about and acquaintance with the historical, and indeed in a purely technical sense, i.e., it calculates by balancing the past against the present and vice versa. Everything historiographical takes direction from the historical. History, on the contrary, has no need of the historiographical. The historiographer is always just a technician, a journalist; the thinker of history is always quite distinct. Jacob Burckhardt is not a historiographer but a true thinker of history.

It has been our concern merely to show that unconcealedness does not have as its only "opposite" concealment in the sense of dissemblance and falsity but that there are other modes of concealment of a completely different order, bearing no trace of the "negativity" of falsity and distortion. With these remarks, the mystery can perhaps become more open, the mystery that in the metaphysics of the Occident falsity could attain status and priority as the only opposite to truth. For the present task of an elucidation of the essence of ἀλήθεια, our reference to the "species" of concealedness may be useful in helping us grasp sooner that mode of concealment constantly present for the Greeks but not questioned by them as to its essence, with the exception that for the Greeks already the very word denoting this concealment and its domain contains enough of its own elucidation.

Thus we come upon an astonishing thing: despite the fact that the modes of concealment having nothing in common with dissemblance, distortion, and deception pervade everything so essentially, yet they were not explicitly mentioned as modes of concealment. Perhaps it is only because they are so essential that they were not explicitly named. They appear therefore in each case already under the essential form of unconcealedness, which in a certain way retains within itself concealedness and concealment and even must do so. When we see this connection we approach the miracle of the primordial essence of ἀλήθεια.

We are not sufficiently prepared, however, to say more about it. The one thing we now have to consider is that the Greeks do speak of a concealment distinct from dissemblance and distortion and related to the concealment reticently uttered in μῦθος. The concealment now to be considered is expressed by the Greeks in their words λανθάνεσθαι, ἐπιλανθάνεσθαι.

Recapitulation

Supplementary clarification: the "way" of the arriving thinker in the "didactic poem." The connection between the essence of the goddess and the ways toward and from her home. By-way and off-way. The question of the other counter-essence to disclosedness. The essence of disclosure and concealment as expressed in word and legend. The loss of the word in its preservation of the relation of Being to man. The Roman transformation of τὸ ζῷον λόγον ἔχον into "animal" rationale. Reference to Kant, Nietzsche, Spengler. Μῦθος ἔπος λόγος.

In relation to the third directive given to us by the translation of ἀλήθεια as "unconcealedness," we are asking about the oppositional character of the opposition in which "truth" stands. The previous lecture and today's, in their interconnection, accomplish an essential step, decisive not only for an insight into the essence of the opposition between truth and untruth, but decisive also for understanding Parmenides' didactic poem. Therefore the recapitulation of the last lecture must be clarified with some supplements and the immediate requirements of our project deferred.

The opposite to "truth" is called, briefly and succinctly, "untruth." The word "untruth," and likewise the word "un-just," do not ordinarily mean for us simply a failure of justice or a lack of truth. Exactly as "in-justice" is counter to justice, against justice, so is "untruth" counter to truth. The Occident thinks this counter-essence to truth as falsity. In the sphere of this counter-essence to truth, variations of falsity emerge in the form of essential consequences of untruth, of its assertion and communication. Even for the Greeks themselves, manifold modes of dissembling and distorting belong to ψεῦδος. We call ἀπάτη "deception," because in it the appurtenance of the essence of ψεῦδος to the essential realm of ἀλήθεια becomes visible anew. We must think this word, in everything it denotes, exclusively in the Greek way. ’A-πάτη is the off-way and the by-way. For the Greeks, however, the basic feature of the way—ἡ ὁδός, ἡ μέθοδος ("method")—is that by conveying along the course, underway, it opens up a view and a perspective and hence provides the disclosure of something.

In connection with this remark on the essence of the way, we must recall the first verse we selected from Parmenides' "didactic poem," where the goddess greets the thinker arriving on a "way" and immediately reveals to him that it is his destiny to have to go along an extraordinary way ἐκτὸς πάτου, outside of, off, the path men usually tread. That means something else will show itself to the thinker on his way, a view the usual way does not offer to men. Since something extraordinary shows itself on the revealing way of the thinker, we have here a self-showing, i.e., a disclosing, in a "distinguished" sense. That is also why a larger fragment of the "didactic poem" speaks of σήματα, "signs." There exists an essential connection between the essence of the goddess ’Aλήθεια and the ways leading to her home, which are determinable on the basis of this home. "Way," as providing appearances by opening up a view and a perspective, belongs within the realm of ἀλήθεια. Conversely, ἀλήθεια and its holding sway require the ways. This essential correlation between ἀλήθεια and ὁδός later comes to be known only in a concealed manner, as far as its essential ground is concerned, i.e., in the "fact" that a "method" is necessary to obtain correct representations. The way, πάτος, πάτη, of the thinker does indeed go off the usual path of men. Yet we leave it open whether this "way off" is just a by-way. It could also be the reverse, that the usual way of man is merely a perpetual by-way ignorant of itself. A way off the path, however, does not have to be a by-way in the sense of what is "way out" and unusual. Even a by-way is again not necessarily an off-way. The latter, however, is called ἀπάτη. The views afforded by the off-way represent distortions of that which comes into view on the way leading straight to the thing. "To lead on an off-way" is to mix up the ways, it is a kind of dissembling and distorting, a kind of ψεῦδος, and hence is deception. Everything of this sort "runs" counter to unconcealedness, counter to truth, and is consequently a kind of untruth, or, put in the Greek fashion, a not-disclosing and hence a concealing.

The essence of ψεῦδος, thought as the Greeks understood it, receives elucidation from the essence of ἀλήθεια, from unconcealedness, i.e., from disclosedness. Ψεῦδος, as the counter-essence to ἀλήθεια, is then more clearly determined as dissembling concealment. ’Aλήθεια for its part emerges more determinately as disclosedness in the manner of a non-dissembling letting-appear. Unconcealedness is non-dissemblance.

The question then arises whether dissemblance and distortion, together with their essential variations, are the only possible modes of concealment. The answer must be in the negative, for other modes of concealment are possible. Here then is grounded the possibility that truth as unconcealedness and disclosure is related to still other modes of concealment, and that disclosedness, in its essence, is not fixed to non-dissemblance.

To our way of thinking, this means that the counter-essence to truth is not exhausted or fulfilled in falsity. At the same time we might wonder whether the "counter" must necessarily have the sense of the purely adverse and hostile.

Of course, for us today, because of the long and unshaken predominance of falsity as the only known and acknowledged opposite to truth, it is quite "natural" and a "platitude" to say that only falsity, if anything, may stand opposed to truth. Therefore we are inclined to seek the counter-essence to ἀλήθεια only in ψεῦδος, even when discussing the Greek view. And in fact in a certain sense the Greeks themselves encourage this tendency, because from early on they identified ἀληθές and ἀψευδές, with the result that ψεῦδος is precisely what is disclaimed by the α in ἀλήθεια. The lesson to be drawn is that even if we have taken ἀλήθεια seriously, in the sense of unconcealedness and disclosedness, and have renounced every misinterpretation of ἀλήθεια as veritas, that is still no guarantee we are experiencing ἀλήθεια in its primordial essence.

If ψεῦδος is not the one and only mode of concealment, what are the others? And how can another counter-essence to disclosedness be determined from them? The Greeks experience and express concealment in many ways, not only within the sphere of the everyday handling and considering of things, but also from the ultimate perspective of beings as a whole. Death, night, day, light, the earth, the subterranean, and the supraterranean are pervaded by disclosure and concealment and remain mired in this essence. Emergence into the unconcealed and submergence into concealment dwell primordially everywhere.

This dwelling of disclosure and concealment, in advance and everywhere and always and for every being and in all Being, is expressed in the word of the Greeks. It is what is said primordially—the legendary. Therefore the essence of the word and of legend, as experienced by the Greeks, has its ground and its eminence in the fact that word and legend let appear disclosure and concealment, the disclosed and the concealed.

The essential word is not the command, order, proclamation, promise, or "doctrine." A fortiori, the word is never the merely adventitious "expression" of "representations." The word is a way of the disclosive preservation of the unconcealment and concealment of beings, a way that belongs only to Greek antiquity and is entrusted to its essence. In the word and as word the Being of beings is given in relation to the essence of man in such a way that the Being of beings, in virtue of this relation to man, lets man's essence emerge and lets it receive the determination we call the Greek one. According to this determination, man is τὸ ζῷον λόγον ἔχον—the being that emerges from itself, emerges in such a way that in this emerging (φύσις), and for it, it has the word. In the word, the being we call man comports itself to beings as a whole, in the midst of which man himself is. *Ζῷον* means "living being." But we may not understand ζωή, "life," here either in the late Greek, nor in the Roman, nor in the modern "biological" sense, as in "zoology." The "living being" is φύσει ὄν, a being whose Being is determined by φύσις, by emergence and self-opening. To be sure, this Greek determination of the essence of man was soon transformed by the Roman interpretation: ζῷον becomes *animal*, λόγος becomes *ratio*. Man is the *animal rationale*. In modern thought *ratio*, reason, is the essence of subjectivity, i.e., of the I-hood of man. Hence for Kant man is the "beast" (*animal*) that can say "I." If we think ζῷον as "animal" or more generally as "living being," in the modern-biological sense, then we are thinking in the Roman-modern and not the Greek manner. All anthropology, the philosophical as well as the scientific-biological, understands man as the "thinking animal." In the centuries of metaphysics before Nietzsche, the essence of "life" and of "animality" was not yet understood as will to power, and man did not yet arrive at the pure self-empowering of himself to all power, and hence did not "surpass" the previous essential determination. Therefore, man of today has not yet super-passed man as he was up to now. He is not yet the super-man.

This term, in the sense of Nietzsche's metaphysics, does not mean, contrary to popular opinion, a man who has outgrown the normal size, with a gigantic bone structure, as muscular as possible, with a low forehead, etc. Instead, "super-man" is an essentially metaphysical-historical concept and signifies man hitherto, always already determined as *animal rationale*, who has passed into the essential domain of the will to power as the reality of all that is real. Therefore Nietzsche can say the man who has not yet become super-man is the "animal that has not yet been identified," i.e., the animal about whose essence a final metaphysical decision has not yet been made. Pursuant to this ultimate metaphysical determination of man, Spengler wrote in his much-read book *Der Mensch und die Technik. Beitrag zu einer Philosophie des Lebens*, (1931, p. 54): "The character of the free beast of prey, in its essential features, has been passed on from the individual to the organized people, *the animal with one soul and many hands*." Then he adds a note: "And with *one* head, not many."

Through the Roman re-interpretation of the Greek experience of the essence of man, λόγος, i.e., the word, became *ratio*. The essence of the word is thus banished from its ground and from its essential locus. *Ratio* and reason take its place. Naturally, it is recognized and noted that man has the faculty of "language." Language, however, becomes one faculty among others. Finally, the curious situation arises that a special philosophy, the "philosophy of language," becomes necessary parallel to the "philosophy of art" and the "philosophy of technology." The appearance of a "philosophy of language" is a striking sign that knowledge of the essence of the word, i.e., the possibility of an experience of the primordial essence of the word, has been lost for a long time. The word no longer preserves the relation of Being to man, but instead the word is a formation and thing of language. Language is one of man's possessions, just like eyes and ears, sensations and inclinations, thinking and willing; it is the faculty of expressing and communicating "lived experience." The word is explained on the basis of vocalization, and the latter is explained on the basis of language as a phenomenon of expression which happens to be at our disposal. Language and the word serve to assume "the true" and "truth" into the expressive form of the articulation of speech, and in this way they serve to announce them. Taken for itself, however, "truth" as "correctness" is a matter of the representation of objects. The representing takes place in the "interior," and language is the "exteriorization" of this interior. Thereby correctness is communicated in a correct assertion, and the thinking and the rational activity of man enter into the expressive realm of language, with the consequence that it is considered wholly in order that already with the early Greeks ἀλήθεια occurs predominately in connection with ἔπος and εἰπεῖν, with the word and the legendary word. But the ground for this "fact" does not reside in the character of language as "expression" but in the essence of ἀλήθεια, which, as the essence of Being itself, claims the essence of man for itself as that "being" that comports itself to beings as such.

It is not because the truth is often also enunciated, but because the essence of word and legend is grounded in the essence of truth and belongs to it, that the Greek word for "true," ἀληθές, occurs already in Homer "connected" above all with "speech." A Greek word for the word is ὁ μῦθος. Another word for "word" is ἔπος. It is not accidental that the primordial poetizing word of the Greeks, the word of Homer, is an "epic." Again, another word for "word" is λόγος. We have to think that the Greeks from early on had several words for "word." On the other hand, they do not have a word for "language." They have, of course, the word γλῶσσα, tongue. But they never think the word on the basis of the "tongue" by which the word is spoken. Thus their determination of the essence of man is not ἄνϑρωπος ζῷον γλῶσσαν ἔχον—the living being that has the tongue. Cows and mules also have a "tongue." If, however, it is the essential feature of man to have the word and to appropriate it, and if the Greeks experience and understand the human being in this way, then is it not necessary that they, when they distinguish themselves and their humanity versus others, take as a point of reference for the distinction precisely this essential feature?

The Greeks distinguish themselves from other peoples and call them βάρβαροι, ones who have a strange sort of speech which is not μῦϑος, not λόγος, not ἔπος. For the Greeks, the opposite to "barbarism" is not "culture"; it is dwelling within μῦϑος and λόγος. There has been "culture" only since the beginning of the modern period; it began the moment *veritas* became *certitudo*, when man posited himself for himself and made himself, by his own "cultivation," *cultura*, and by his own "creative work" a creator, i.e., a genius. The Greeks are not familiar with the likes of either "culture" or "genius." So it is curious that even today the best classical philologists ramble on about the "cultural genius" of the Greeks. From the standpoint of the Greeks, what is called "culture" in the modern period is an organization of the "spiritual world" produced by the willful power of man. "Culture" is the same in essence as modern technology; both are in a strict Greek sense unmythical. Thought in the Greek way, "culture" and "technology" are forms of barbarism, no less than is "nature" in Rousseau.

Μῦϑος, ἔπος, and λόγος belong together essentially. "Myth" and "logos" appear in an erroneously much-discussed opposition only because they are the same in Greek poetry and thought. In the ambiguous and confusing title "mythology," the words μῦϑος and λόγος are connected in such a way that both forfeit their primordial essence. To try to understand μῦϑος with the help of "mythology" is a procedure equivalent to drawing water with the aid of a sieve. When *we* use the expression "mythical," we shall think it in the sense just delimited: the "mythical"—the μῦϑος-ical—is the disclosure and concealment contained in the disclosing-concealing word, which is the primordial appearance of the fundamental essence of Being itself. The terms death, night, day, the earth, and the span of the sky name essential modes of disclosure and concealment.

§5. The opposite to ἀληϑές: λαϑόν, λαϑές. The event of the trans-
formation of the withdrawing concealment and the human behavior
of forgetting.

a) The prevailing of concealment in λανϑάνεσϑαι.
The concealment of the forgetter in the forgotten: oblivion.
Hesiod, Theogony, V. 226f. Λήϑη and the hidden essence
of Eris (Strife), the daughter of the night. Reference to Pindar.

In discussing the opposite of ἀληϑές (the unconcealed and the disclosing), we already remarked that the opposite would have to reside in
a λαϑές, λαϑόν, if it were to be expressed in language immediately
and appropriately. Instead of that we first encountered τὸ ψεῦδος. But
this also became clear, that for the Greeks λανϑάνειν, being-concealed,
has an unequivocal prevailing essential rank, expressed in the proper
"ruling" function of the phrase λανϑάνω ἥκων, I approach unnoticed,
or, in the Greek way: I am in hiddenness as one who is approaching.
On the basis of these apparently only "grammatical" relations, there
occurs something else, which we may formulate briefly in this way:
concealedness and unconcealedness determine beings as such. That
means: disclosedness and concealment are a basic feature of Being.

The Greeks express the prevailing of concealment above all, however,
in the word λανϑάνεσϑαι or ἐπιλανϑάνεσϑαι, which we ordinarily
translate as "forgetting" and thereby reinterpret it in such a way that
the Greek essence is lost. Our earlier meditation already showed that
in "forgetting" there occurs, for the Greeks, a concealment. The forgotten is, in the experience of the Greeks, what has sunk away into concealedness, specifically in such a fashion that the sinking away, i.e.,
the concealing, remains concealed to the very one who has forgotten.
More precisely and more in the Greek vein, the forgetter is concealed
to himself in his relation to what is happening here to that which we
then call, on account of this happening, the forgotten. The forgetter
not only forgets the forgotten, but along with that he forgets himself
as the one for whom the forgotten has disappeared. A concealment
takes place here that at once befalls the forgotten and the forgetter,
without, however, obliterating them.

This concealment displays a special radiation. For the event of such
concealment we have only the word "oblivion"—which actually names
that into which the forgotten sinks—as the occurrence excluding man
from the forgotten. In general we conceive forgetting in terms of the
behavior of a "subject," as a not-retaining, and we then speak of "forgetfulness" as that by which something "escapes" us, when, because
of one thing, we forget another. Here forgetfulness is poor attention.

In addition, there is the forgetting explained as a consequence of "memory-disturbances." Psychopathology calls this "amnesia." But the word "forgetfulness" is too weak to name the forgetting that can befall man; for forgetfulness is only the inclination toward distraction. If it happens that we forget what is essential and do not pay heed to it, lose it and strike it from our minds, then we may no longer speak of "forgetfulness" but of "oblivion." The latter is a realm something may arrive at and come to and fall into, but oblivion also befalls us and we ourselves permit it in a certain way. A more appropriate name for the event of oblivion is the obsolete word "obliviation" [*Vergessung*]: something falls into oblivion. We are always in such a hurry that we can scarcely pause a moment to inquire into "oblivion." Is oblivion, into which "something" falls and sinks, only a consequence of the fact that a number of people no longer think of this "something"? Or is the latter, that people no longer think of something, already for its part only a consequence of the fact that people themselves are thrust into an oblivion and can therefore no longer know either what they possess or what they have lost? What then is oblivion? It is not just a human product and it is not simply human negligence.

If we now think of oblivion as the concealedness belonging to a characteristic concealment, then we first approach what the Greeks name with the word λήθη. In Hesiod's Theogony (V. 226f.) we read:

Αὐτὰρ Ἔρις στυγερὴ τέκε μέν Πόνον ἀλγινόεντα
Λήθην τε Λιμόν τε καὶ Ἄλγεα δακρυόεντα

"But the (goddess) Strife, the dark one, gave birth to Trouble, the one who brings sorrow,
As well as Oblivion and Absence and Suffering, the tearful."

Λήθη, "Lethe" is the daughter of "Eris." She is mentioned together with Λιμός, mistakenly translated as "Hunger." Of course forgetting is "painful" just as "hunger" is painful and agonizing. But the effects of forgetting and of hunger on the state of the body and soul, i.e., in modern terms, the physiological and psychological, or, in short, the "biological," aspects of forgetting and hunger do not "interest" the Greeks. Therefore something else is meant when λήθη and λιμός are mentioned together. It is not their effects on man but their own essence that sustains their identity. Λήθη, oblivion, is a concealment that withdraws what is essential and alienates man from himself, i.e., from the possibility of dwelling within his own essence. Λιμός does not mean "hunger" in the sense of the desire for food; the word is connected to λείπω, to leave, to let disappear, and means absence of nourishment. Λιμός does not mean the non-satisfaction of human desires and needs, but it refers to the occurrence of the absence of a donation and distribution. Such absence is essentially characterized by falling-away, as is concealment. Let us reflect on this: something falls and thereby falls away. This falling away is a kind of being-away and being-absent. What falls away no longer returns to what is present, and yet this "away" turns, in its turning away, against what is present, and specifically in the uncanny fashion that it takes no notice of it. Here we catch sight of the hidden essence of the oppositional and the conflictual, which explains why λήθη and λιμός are said to be descended from "Eris," the goddess "Strife." If hardship and suffering are mentioned here as descendants of Strife, then precisely this origin in strife should teach us to avoid the modern misinterpretation and not attempt to understand pain and suffering "psychologically" as kinds of "lived experiences." Our usual interpretation of them in terms of lived experience is the main reason Greek tragedy is still entirely sealed off to us. Aeschylus-Sophocles on the one side, and Shakespeare on the other, are incomparable worlds. German humanism has mixed them up and has made the Greek world completely inaccessible. Goethe is disastrous.

In Hesiod's Theogony only this is said about λήθη, that it, together with λιμός, was born to Eris. Ἔρις herself is the daughter of Νύξ, which is called ὀλοή, an eponym in Homer and Hesiod often belonging to Μοῖρα. We translate ὀλοή as "ruinous." This again is "correct," and yet it is quite un-Greek, for we do not see why the night is supposed to be "ruinous." To ruin is to destroy, to annihilate, i.e., to deprive of being, i.e., for the Greeks, to take away presence. The night is ὀλοή because it lets all that is present disappear into concealment. In what respect Μοῖρα is called ὀλοή will be clarified when we consider Parmenides' expression, Μοῖρα κακή, "evil fate." What Hesiod says of λήθη is sufficient for the Greeks to grasp the essence; however, for us moderns it is too little and does not enable us to see clearly the essence of λήθη and to recognize its essential relation to ἀλήθεια. Indeed we often encounter λήθη, especially in the poets, although they do not mention it in the decisive way the thinkers speak of ἀλήθεια. Perhaps it rather corresponds to the essence of λήθη to be passed over in silence. We reflect too rarely on the fact that the same Greeks to whom the word and speech were bestowed primordially could, for that very reason, keep silent in a unique way as well. For "to keep silent" is not merely to say nothing. Without something essential to say, one cannot keep silent. Only within essential speech, and by means of it alone, can there prevail essential silence, having nothing in common with secrecy, concealment, or "mental reservations." The Greek thinkers and poets largely keep silent over λήθη. But perhaps it is not an accident that at the time of the completion of the Greek world the essence of λήθη was once more explicitly remembered in a significant context. Before we consider it in detail, let us take up a verse from

Pindar's seventh Olympic Ode, for it can clarify the Greek essence of λήθη in one important respect. Of course we must renounce listening to the poetic splendor of this Ode as a whole or even only of the part immediately concerning us.

b) Awe in Pindar, Olympic Ode VII, 48f.; 43ff.; and in Sophocles, Oedipus at Colonus, 1267. Ἀρετή (resoluteness) as the disclosedness of man, determined on the basis of ἀλήθεια and αἰδώς.

The poet is telling the μῦθος of the colonization of the celebrated island of Rhodes. The colonists came without a source of gleaming fire and therefore had to set up a sacred place and have sacrifices without fire on the high point of the city "Lindos," i.e., on its ἀκρόπολις.

> τεῦξαν δ' ἀπύροις ἱεροῖς
> ἄλσος ἐν ἀκροπόλι.[1]

It was surely not on account of arbitrary negligence that the colonists came without fire. Something must have occurred that was not due simply to them themselves, just as in general what man does and allows, what man experiences and is capable of, is determined by a properly determining essence. It is with a reference to this latter that the "myth" of the foundation of the city is introduced (*ibid.*, 43ff.):

> ἐν δ' ἀρετὰν
> ἔβαλεν καὶ χάρματ' ἀνθρώποισι Προμαθέος Αἰδώς·
> ἐπὶ μὰν βαίνειτι καὶ λάθας ἀτέκμαρτα νέφος,
> καὶ παρέλκει πραγμάτων ὀρθὰν ὁδὸν
> ἔξω φρενῶν.

"Awe thrusts up the flourishing of the essence and the joy disposing man to think ahead; but sometimes there comes over it the signless cloud of concealment, which withholds from actions the straightforward way and places them outside what is thoughtfully disclosed."

These words provide a very beautiful poetic elucidation of the essence of λήθη. Here λάθα stands in opposition to αἰδώς. We translate by "awe." But that word is not meant to denote a "subjective" feeling or a "lived experience" of the human "subject." Αἰδώς (awe) comes over man as what is determining, i.e., disposing. As is clear on the basis of the opposition to λάθα (concealment), awe determines ἀλή-θεια, the unconcealed in its unconcealedness, in which the whole essence of man stands together with all human faculties. Αἰδώς, a fundamental word of Pindar's poetry and consequently a fundamental word

---

1. "They set up a sacred grove on the acropolis with fireless sacrifices."—Tr.

of the Greeks themselves, never means, even if we understand awe as a disposition, mere bashfulness, anxiousness, or fearfulness. The easiest way to touch the essence of awe [*Scheu*] as meant here is on the basis of its counter-essence, "abhorrence" [*Abscheu*]. Awe disposes us toward thinking in advance what disposes the essence of man out of beings as a whole. Αἰδώς—thought in the Greek manner—is not a feeling man possesses but the disposition, as the disposing, which determines his essence, i.e., determines the relation of Being to man. Therefore αἰδώς, as the highest, lies in essential proximity to the highest god, Ζεύς. Thus Sophocles says (Oedip. Col., 1267):

ἀλλ' ἔστι γὰρ καὶ Ζηνὶ σύνθακος θρόνων
Αἰδὼς ἐπ' ἔργοις πᾶσι,

"But Αἰδώς, together with Zeus, holds the throne of essence, raised above all others" (beings man produces and sets up).

Being itself sustains awe, namely the awe over the "to be." In this way Being at the very beginning is protective of its own essence. Αἰδώς refers to this awe, which thrusts something upon man, ἐνέβαλεν ἀρετάν. 'Αρετή is just as essential a Greek word as is αἰδώς, and the word ἀρετά (ή) is even more untranslatable. "Virtue" has too much of a "moralistic" ring; "suitability," if thought in relation to "ability" and "performance," sounds all the more "modern" and would lead us astray. 'Αρετή means the emergence and opening up and insertion of man's fundamental essence in Being. 'Αρετή is related to φυά, Pindar's word for the essence of man as it emerges into unconcealedness. 'Αρετή and ἀρτύω are of the same stem as the Latin *ars*, which became the Roman word for τέχνη, and which we translate by "art." On the basis of the insertion, emergence, and openness of man's essence in ἀρετή, he is "resolute," open, disclosing, and disclosed toward beings. In such ἀρετά, re-soluteness, man is in the literal sense "de-cided" with regard to the Being of beings; that is, "de-cision" means to be without a scission from Being.

'Αρετά as understood by the Greeks, "resoluteness," man's disclosedness as determined by ἀλήθεια and αἰδώς, is something essentially different from the modern notion of "resoluteness," grounded on man as "subject." The essence of this resoluteness is based on the act of will of man positing himself willfully on himself and only on himself. The resoluteness of the modern Renaissance man derives from the will to will. Here belongs ἀρετή as thought in the Roman way = *virtus*, in Italian *virtu'*, whence the word "virtuosity." "Resoluteness" in the modern sense is the fixed ordination of the will upon itself and belongs metaphysically within the essence of the will to will, the present form of which is exhibited by the will to power. Resoluteness in the modern sense is metaphysically not grounded on ἀλήθεια but on the self-assurance of man as subject, i.e., on subjectivity. Resoluteness, as conceived in the modern way, is the willing of what is willed in its own will; this will drives it to willing. "Being-driven" is in Latin *fanatice*. The distinguishing characteristic of modern resoluteness is "the fanatical." As understood by the Greeks, however, resoluteness, the self-disclosing opening up toward Being, has another origin of essence, namely a different experience of Being—one based on αἰδώς, awe. Awe thrusts to man, and bestows on him, ἀρετά. Awe as the essence of Being conveys to man the disclosure of beings. But opposed to αἰδώς there holds sway λάθα, the concealment we call oblivion.

Recapitulation

1) The three titles of the essential history of the Occident. Reference to *Being and Time*. Essential thinking. Reference to Hölderlin and Pindar. The beginning of the essential relation of Being to man in word and legendary word. The Greek essence of man. Reference to Hesiod.

Beyond the modes of dissemblance and distortion, there prevails a concealment appearing in the essence of death, of the night and everything nocturnal, and of the earth and everything subterranean and supraterranean. Such concealment pervades beings as a whole, from first to last. Yet it bears in itself a mode of possible disclosure and unconcealedness of beings as such, one that in advance penetrates everything. But wherever, as well as however, beings let themselves emerge for the Greeks into unconcealedness, there Being is "put into words" in an eminent way. In view of the primordial, all-pervasive occurrence of concealment and disclosure, the word is no less original in essence than disclosure and concealment. The proper essence of the word is that it lets beings appear in their Being and preserves what appears, i.e., the unconcealed, as such. Being manifests itself primordially in the word.

If we attempt to discover, from this primordial essential relation of Being and word, the hidden essential history of the Occident, then we can name the simple events of this history with three titles. (The use of such titles is of course always precarious if one does not go beyond the mere titles.) The first beginning of the essential history of the Occident can be expressed by the title "Being and word." The "and" indicates an essential relation which Being itself (and not man, who can only reflect on it subsequently) lets emerge in order to bring its essence to truth therein. With Plato and Aristotle, who speak the beginning of metaphysics, the word becomes λόγος in the sense of assertion. In the course of the unfolding of metaphysics this is transformed into *ratio*, reason, and spirit. Western metaphysics, the history of the essence of the truth of beings as such and as a whole, the history expressed in thinking from Plato to Nietzsche, comes under the title "Being and *ratio.*" That is why, in the age of metaphysics and only in it, "the irrational" also appears and, in its wake, "lived experience." As regards the title "Being and time," "time" means here neither the calculated time of the "clock," nor "lived time" in the sense of Bergson and others. The name "time" in this title, according to its clearly expressed affiliation with Being, is the given name of a more original essence of ἀλήθεια and designates the essential ground of *ratio* and of all thinking and saying. In "Being and time," no matter how strange it must sound, "time" is the given name of the primordial ground of the word. "Being and word," the beginning of the essential history of the West, is thereby experienced more primordially. The treatise *Being and Time* only points to this event in which Being itself bestows on Western man a more primordial experience. This more original beginning can only occur as the *first beginning* to a historical people of thinkers and poets in the West. These statements have nothing in common with a swaggering missionary consciousness; quite to the contrary, they have to do with the experience of the confusions and the difficulties with which a people can only slowly fit itself into the place of the destiny of the West, a destiny that conceals a world-destiny.

Therefore we need to know that this historical people, if the word "victory" is appropriate here at all, has already been victorious and is invincible, provided it remains the people of poets and thinkers that it is in its essence, and as long as it does not fall prey to the terrible—always menacing—deviation from and mistaking of its essence.

I am not saying anything new here, as no thinker at all may be the slave of the pleasure to say the new. To find new things and to search for them is a matter of "research" and technology. Essential thinking must always say only the same, the old, the oldest, the beginning, and must say it primordially. How is this expressed by Hölderlin, who is the most German poet because he poetizes inspired by the Western history of Being itself, and who is therefore the first poet of the Germans to appear, how is it expressed in his poem entitled "The song of the German"?[1]

---

1. Hölderlin, *Werke* (Hellingrath), IV, p. 129. Even the genitive in this title is already enigmatically equivocal.

O holy heart of the people, O fatherland!
    Patiently accepting everything like the silent mother earth
        And altogether unappreciated, even if already the others
            Obtain from your depths what is best in them.
They harvest the thoughts and the spirit from you,
    They love to pick the grapes, and yet they blame
        You, unshaped wine-stalk! that you
            Err around on the soil wildly and wavering.

For the Greeks the word as μῦθος, ἔπος, ῥῆμα, and λόγος is that by which Being assigns itself to man, so that he might preserve it, in his own essence, as what is assigned to him and might, for his part, find and retain his essence as man by means of such preservation. Therefore the destiny, "to have the word," λόγον ἔχειν, is the essential characteristic of the humanity that became historical as Greek humanity.

Because legend, as the disclosing word, harbors the primordial relation of Being to man, and thereby also the relation of man to beings, legend and legendary dictum are, as beings, more than every other being that man in some way creates and sets up. The ῥῆμα, the dictum that speaks and is spoken, surpasses all ἔργματα, according to Pindar (Nem. IV, 8). Nevertheless, not just any word is superior to every other "work," but only *that* dictum standing in the favor of χάρις, so that in the word the bestowal of the grace of emergent Being appears. We of today, and in general modern "culture," can now hardly obtain even a vague idea of how for the Greeks the word and legend initiate, sustain, and fulfill the essential relation of Being to man. In particular, the ordinary and most accessible "picture" of ancient Greece would prevent us from duly reflecting on the all-sustaining relation between Being and word. For we are told that the works of architecture and sculpture of the Greeks, their temples and statues, their vases and paintings, are no less an "expression" of Greek lived experience than their thought and poetry. Accordingly, the emphasis we placed on the relation between Being and word, if not exactly "false," would in any case be one-sided. Our meditation on the essence of ἀλήθεια will return to this objection at the appropriate place.

Only where a humanity is entrusted with the essence, to have the word, λόγον ἔχειν, only there does it remain assigned to the preservation of the unconcealedness of beings. Only where this assignment holds sway and where unconcealedness appears in advance as Being itself, only there does concealment also prevail in a way that can never be the mere contrary and crude opposite to disclosure, i.e., in the modes of dissemblance, distortion, misguidance, deception, and falsification.

Because there is still a more original mode of concealment to be distinguished from all that, the Greeks named it with a word which, in distinction to ψεῦδος and ἀπάτη and σφάλλειν, immediately seizes upon the relation to the original stem: concealment as λήθη.

But now since knowledge of the essence of ἀλήθεια is co-determined by a knowledge of the essence of λήθη, and since we who live so much later are wont to interpret λήθη, understood as "forgetting," in the sense of the "lived experience" and comportment of a "subject," therefore it is necessary to recognize clearly in advance the essential connections prevalent in the relation between λήθη and ἀλήθεια.

Granted, the Greek thinkers did not speak of these essential relations as we now are forced to express them. Precisely because the Greek essence of man is fulfilled in the "to have the word," Greek man could also "have" and retain the word in that pre-eminent way we call silence. The Greeks are often silent, especially about what is essential to them. And when they do express the essential, it is in a way that even then does not break the silence. Here we are referring to the ground of the pre-eminence of the tragic word in their tragedies. This is the tragic word's essential ambiguity, not created by the poets for its dramatic "effect" but spoken to them out of the essence of Being.

Why should not the Greeks, who "have" the word in such a way, keep silent and comport themselves in a concealing way precisely where they experience the original concealment itself, λήθη? But how could they keep silent about it without sometimes speaking of it? Hesiod mentions λήθη together with λιμός, i.e., together with the absence of nourishment. Both originate in the concealing night as the provenance of their essence. Pindar names the veiling essence of λήθη in another respect and directs our regard to its hidden essence.

c) Πρᾶγμα: action. The word as the realm of the essence of the human hand. Handwriting and typewriting. Ὀρθός and *rectum*. Essential action and the way toward the unconcealed. Oblivion as concealment. Man's being "away" from unconcealedness, and the word of the signless cloud. Darkening. The withdrawal of λήθη. Reference to Pindar and Hesiod.

Pindar speaks of λαθάς ἀτέκμαρτα νέφος, i.e., the signless cloud of concealment. Thereby he indicates unequivocally the veiling essence of what we call "oblivion." The cloud, passing or standing in front of the sun, conceals the brightness of the sky, hides the light, and withdraws clarity. It brings darkening and gloom over things as well as over man, i.e., over the relation of both to one another, over that in which this relation dwells. As a consequence of the darkening, the things themselves, the aspect they present, and the regard of men viewing that aspect—in short, things and men—no longer stay and move in the originally arisen light. If the veiling cloud of oblivion ἐπιβαίνει—comes over things and man—then παρέλχει πραγμάτων ὀρϑὰν ὀδὸν / ἔξω φρενῶν—"it draws actions apart from the straightforward way, into what is outside the thoughtfully disclosed."

Here we encounter the word πρᾶγμα, customarily translated as "thing" or "fact," "matter," "issue." Πράττω means to pass through, pervade, travel back a path through what is not removed and on this way arrive at something and thereupon set it up as present (ἔργω, ἔργον belong in the same sphere of meaning).

Πρᾶγμα means originally, and still in Pindar, this setting up itself as well as what is set up; more precisely, πρᾶγμα means the original unity of both in their relation—the still unseparated and essentially inseparable unity of the setting up in the arrival at something and of what is reached in the arrival and is then present as unconcealed. Πρᾶγμα is here not yet distinguished and set apart and separated as thing and fact from πρᾶξις as presumed "activity." Πρᾶγμα is not yet narrowed down to the concept of "thing," the matter "at hand" to be dealt with, to be acted upon. Nevertheless we have translated πρᾶγμα precisely by "action" [*Handlung*]. Although "action" is not the literal translation of πρᾶγμα, yet, correctly understood, "action" does touch the originally essential essence of πρᾶγμα. Things "act" [*handeln*], insofar as the things present and at hand dwell within the reach of the "hand" [*Hand*]. The hand reaches out for them and reaches them: πράττει, the reaching arrival at something (πρᾶγμα), is essentially related to the hand.

Man himself acts [*handelt*] through the hand [*Hand*]; for the hand is, together with the word, the essential distinction of man. Only a being which, like man, "has" the word (μῦϑος, λόγος), can and must "have" "the hand." Through the hand occur both prayer and murder, greeting and thanks, oath and signal, and also the "work" of the hand, the "hand-work," and the tool. The handshake seals the covenant. The hand brings about the "work" of destruction. The hand exists as hand only where there is disclosure and concealment. No animal has a hand, and a hand never originates from a paw or a claw or talon. Even the hand of one in desperation (it least of all) is never a talon, with which a person clutches wildly. The hand sprang forth only out of the word and together with the word. Man does not "have" hands, but the hand holds the essence of man, because the word as the essential realm of the hand is the ground of the essence of man. The word as what is inscribed and what appears to the regard is the written word, i.e., script. And the word as script is handwriting.

It is not accidental that modern man writes "with" the typewriter and "dictates" [*diktiert*] (the same word as "poetize" [*Dichten*]) "into" a machine. This "history" of the kinds of writing is one of the main reasons for the increasing destruction of the word. The latter no longer comes and goes by means of the writing hand, the properly acting hand, but by means of the mechanical forces it releases. The typewriter tears writing from the essential realm of the hand, i.e., the realm of the word. The word itself turns into something "typed." Where typewriting, on the contrary, is only a transcription and serves to preserve the writing, or turns into print something already written, there it has a proper, though limited, significance. In the time of the first dominance of the typewriter, a letter written on this machine still stood for a breach of good manners. Today a hand-written letter is an antiquated and undesired thing; it disturbs speed reading. Mechanical writing deprives the hand of its rank in the realm of the written word and degrades the word to a means of communication. In addition, mechanical writing provides this "advantage," that it conceals the handwriting and thereby the character. The typewriter makes everyone look the same.

We understand "action" ($\pi\rho\tilde{\alpha}\gamma\mu\alpha$) as the unitary essential realm of the things "at hand" and of the "manipulating" acting man. To "action" thus understood there belongs by essential necessity $\dot{\eta}$ $\dot{o}\delta\dot{o}\varsigma$, the way, as the circumspective course going to and fro between what is at hand and the "manipulating" acting man. The way, $\dot{o}\delta\dot{o}\varsigma$, is called $\dot{o}\rho\vartheta\dot{\alpha}$. The Greek $\dot{o}\rho\vartheta\dot{o}\varsigma$ means "straight ahead," on and along the way, namely the way of the view and prospect toward the unconcealed. The basic meaning of $\dot{o}\rho\vartheta\dot{o}\varsigma$ is different from the Roman *rectum*, that which is directed toward what is above because it directs from above and commands and "rules" from above. The Roman *rectitudo* has also misconstrued the Greek $\dot{o}\rho\vartheta\dot{o}\tau\eta\varsigma$, which belongs to $\dot{o}\mu\text{o}\dot{\iota}\omega\sigma\iota\varsigma$, whose essence is originally attached to $\dot{\alpha}\lambda\dot{\eta}\vartheta\varepsilon\iota\alpha$. The disclosive assimilation to the unconcealed within unconcealedness is a going along, namely along the way leading straight ahead, $\dot{o}\rho\vartheta\tilde{\omega}\varsigma$, to the unconcealed. $'O\mu\text{o}\dot{\iota}\omega\sigma\iota\varsigma$ is $\dot{o}\rho\vartheta\dot{o}\tau\eta\varsigma$. $'O\rho\vartheta\dot{o}\varsigma$, thought in the Greek manner, has, primordially, nothing in common with the Roman *rectum* or with our "right." To the essential realm of $\pi\rho\tilde{\alpha}\gamma\mu\alpha$, i.e., to action essentially understood, belongs the way going straight ahead "toward the unconcealed." Insofar as the veiling cloud brings gloom, the way providing the view lacks that clarity which would lead it straight away toward the unconcealed. Therefore the cloud, within action, leads the way astray ($\pi\alpha\rho\dot{\alpha}$—beside, off), leads outside of what the thinking ahead, the reflecting, and the commemorating provide when they are guided by awe. Transposed into concealment, as such a darkening, man stands in a certain way outside of what is unconcealed.

The word "cloud" suggests an experience, and not a mere lived experience, of the essence of oblivion. But no less essential is the poetic characterization of the concealing cloud. It is called $\dot{\alpha}\tau\dot{\varepsilon}\varkappa\mu\alpha\rho\tau\alpha$. The

cloud is signless; that means it does not show itself at all. This concealment as darkening keeps itself in hiddenness. All darkening always
leaves behind a brightness, which, taken for itself, can "appear" as the
only brightness. In the fact that the cloud of forgetting concealment
conceals itself as such, the uncanny character of forgetting comes to
the fore. Forgetting itself occurs already in an oblivion. If we forget
something, we are no longer with it, but instead we are already "away,"
"drawn aside." If, in forgetting, we were still with the thing, then we
could always retain what is forgotten, and then forgetting would never
occur at all. The forgetting must already have pushed us out of our
own essential realm, so that we can no longer dwell with that which
is to fall into oblivion. The essence of the veiling concealment of oblivion is first touched by the significant word ἀτέκμαρτα, "signless," in
the sense of "not showing itself," "hiding itself." Nevertheless, we have
not yet exhausted the essence of the "signless" as experienced by the
Greeks and consequently the essence of oblivion as concealment.

Τέκμαρ is the sign, that which shows, that which, while it shows
itself, at the same time shows the condition of some being which human
comportment reaches and has to reach. Our word "trademark" [*Wahr-
zeichen*; literally: "true-sign"] would be an appropriate translation, provided we think the "true" in the Greek sense. What shows itself, the
unconcealed, the indicator, can subsequently also mean "goal." But
the essence of the "goal" for the Greeks is the limitation and demarcation of the direction and range of comportment. Thought in the modern
way, a "goal" is only the provision of an "intermediate" stage within
the limitlessness of the ever increasing successes and concerns. The limit
(πέρας), as thought by the Greeks, is, however, not that at which something stops, but that in which something originates, precisely by originating therein as being "formed" in this or that way, i.e., allowed to
rest in a form and as such to come into presence. Where demarcation
is lacking, nothing can come to presence as that which it is. Ἀτέκμαρτα
νέφος, the signless cloud, i.e., the cloud that also withholds its own
presence, is an absent concealment that does not show itself. We can
now surmise something of the essence of "oblivion." It might therefore
be appropriate to accentuate once more the principal moments we have
uncovered.

Forgetting, as a kind of concealing, is an event that comes over beings
and over man in his relation to them. Oblivion occurs within the realm
of the essence of action. Forgetting is not a "subjective lived experience," not a "subjective state" in the sense of a "lapse of memory,"
etc. The concealment here does not touch only what is past but also
what is present and, above all, what, in thinking ahead, is approaching
man and what befits his comportment by providing an assigned direction. The way of man, if awe determines it and brings it the uncon-

cealed, has such a direction. The way is then a directed ὀρθὰ ὁδός. Only if the way can proceed into the unconcealed can it go on directly to the unconcealed and be the directed way. Only if it is in this manner the directed way is it the right way. What is right has the possibility of its essence and the ground of its essence in the disclosing of unconcealedness. Since, for the Greeks, the ὀρθός—straight, along—holds sway and is present only in what is unconcealed and in what goes toward the unconcealed, hence only there is an assignment possible and a setting up and a "sup-plementing" in the sense of a determining direction without any concealing and dissembling—without an occurrence of λανθάνειν. Thus in the same place Hesiod calls Nereus ἀψευδέα καὶ ἀληθέα, not distorting and not hiding, he also says of him οὐδὲ θεμιστέων λήθεται—he does not stand in concealedness with regard to the supplementing directions.

(We will have to discuss θέμιστες and θέμις when we return to the word of Parmenides. Nothing, however, can be said at all about θέμις without a preceding meditation on the essence of θέσις, "positing," as the Greeks think it.)

Forgetting, as experienced by the Greeks, is neither a subjective state, nor is it only related to the past and the "recollection" of it, and neither is it simply a matter of thinking in the sense of "re-presentation." Concealment places the entire essence of man in hiddenness and tears him in this way from the unconcealed. Man is "away" from it. He is no longer with it. He neglects and forsakes what is assigned to him. Concealment comes over man and draws him away from the πραγμάτων ὀρθὰν ὁδόν. Forgetting is no-longer-being-there-with-it and by no means only a no-longer-remembering as the lack of a representation. We are tempted to say the Greeks conceived forgetting not only in relation to cognitive comportment but also with regard to the "practical." But when we speak this way then we already think in a non-Greek way, for concealment concerns at the very outset man's entire being-with-beings. Only because this is so does forgetting concern at once and equiprimordially "theoretical" and "practical" comportment.

On the basis of this elucidation of the essence of oblivion as concealedness, and in view of what is to follow, we can summarize in a kind of "definition" the meditation we have completed. Λήθη, oblivion, is the concealment that lets the past, the present, and the future fall into the path of a self-absenting absence. And with that it sets man himself away into concealedness in relation to this withdrawal, precisely in such a manner that this concealment for its part does not, on the whole, appear. Λήθη conceals while it withdraws. It withdraws while, withholding itself, it lets the unconcealed and its disclosure lapse into the "away" of a veiled absence.

Recapitulation

2) The correlation between being, word, gathering, hand, and writing. The irruption of the typewriter into the realm of the word and of handwriting. The consequence of technology within the transformed relation of Being to man. Bolshevism: the pre-arranged completely technically organized world. The thinking and poetry of the Greeks as regards ἀλήθεια and λήθη.

Λήθη is concealment, and precisely the one that especially comes over things and man, over the reciprocal relation between them, and that draws everything in a certain sense away from a bestowed unconcealedness in such a manner that the very concealment thereby withdraws itself. The passage we discussed from Pindar's Odes (Olympic Ode VII, 48ff.) was not only meant to point at the cloud-like and signless essence of *lethe*, but at the same time it was to indicate with equal decisiveness that this unique concealment comes over the πράγματα and, as it were, befalls them. Of course, it is important to realize πρᾶγμα means neither the thing for itself nor activity for itself (πρᾶξις). Τὰ πράγματα is here rather the word for the one originally inseparable totality of the relation between things and man. We translate πρᾶγμα as "action" [*Handlung*]. This word, however, does not mean human activity (*actio*) but the unitary way that at any time things are on hand and at hand, i.e., are related to the hand, and that man, in his comportment, i.e., in his acting by means of the hand, is posited in relation to the things.

From this it is clear how the hand in its essence secures the reciprocal relation between "beings" and man. There is a "hand" only where beings as such appear in unconcealedness and man comports himself in a disclosing way toward beings. The hand entrusts to the word the relation of Being to man and, thereby, the relation of man to beings. The hand acts [*Die Hand handelt*]. The hand holds in its care the handling, the acting, the acted, and the manipulated. Where the essential is secured in an essential way, we therefore say it is "in good hands," even if handles and manipulations are not actually necessary. The essential correlation of the hand and the word as the essential distinguishing mark of man is revealed in the fact that the hand indicates and by indicating discloses what was concealed, and thereby marks off, and while marking off forms the indicating marks into formations [*indem sie zeigt und zeigend zeichnet und zeichnend die zeigenden Zeichen zu Gebilden bildet*]. These formations are called, following the "verb" γράφειν, γράμματα. The word indicated by the hand and appearing in such marking is writing. We still call the theory of the structure of language "grammar."

Writing, from its originating essence, is hand-writing. We call the disclosive taking up and perceiving of the written word "reading" or "lection" ["*Lesen*"], i.e., col-lection, gathering—("gleaning" ["*Ähren lesen*"]), in Greek λέγειν—λόγος; and this latter, among the primordial thinkers, is the name for Being itself. Being, word, gathering, writing denote an original essential nexus, to which the indicating-writing hand belongs. In handwriting the relation of Being to man, namely the word, is inscribed in beings themselves. The origin and the way of dealing with writing is already in itself a decision about the relation of Being and of the word to man and consequently a decision about the comportment of man to beings and about the way both, man and thing, stand in unconcealedness or are withdrawn from it.

Therefore when writing was withdrawn from the origin of its essence, i.e., from the hand, and was transferred to the machine, a transformation occurred in the relation of Being to man. It is of little importance for this transformation how many people actually use the typewriter and whether there are some who shun it. It is no accident that the invention of the printing press coincides with the inception of the modern period. The word-signs become type, and the writing stroke disappears. The type is "set," the set becomes "pressed." This mechanism of setting and pressing and "printing" is the preliminary form of the typewriter. In the typewriter we find the irruption of the mechanism in the realm of the word. The typewriter leads again to the typesetting machine. The press becomes the rotary press. In rotation, the triumph of the machine comes to the fore. Indeed, at first, book printing and then machine type offer advantages and conveniences, and these then unwittingly steer preferences and needs to this kind of written communication. The typewriter veils the essence of writing and of the script. It withdraws from man the essential rank of the hand, without man's experiencing this withdrawal appropriately and recognizing that it has transformed the relation of Being to his essence.

The typewriter is a signless cloud, i.e., a withdrawing concealment in the midst of its very obtrusiveness, and through it the relation of Being to man is transformed. It is in fact signless, not showing itself as to its essence; perhaps that is why most of you, as is proven to me by your reaction, though well-intended, have not grasped what I have been trying to say.

I have not been presenting a disquisition on the typewriter itself, regarding which it could justifiably be asked what in the world that has to do with Parmenides. My theme was the modern relation (transformed by the typewriter) of the hand to writing, i.e., to the word, i.e., to the unconcealedness of Being. A meditation on unconcealedness and on Being does not merely have something to do with the didactic poem of Parmenides, it has everything to do with it. In the typewriter the machine appears, i.e., technology appears, in an almost quotidian and hence unnoticed and hence signless relation to writing, i.e., to the word, i.e., to the distinguishing essence of man. A more penetrating consideration would have to recognize here that the typewriter is not really a machine in the strict sense of machine technology, but is an "intermediate" thing, between a tool and a machine, a mechanism. Its production, however, is conditioned by machine technology.

This "machine," operated in the closest vicinity to the word, is in use; it imposes its own use. Even if we do not actually operate this machine, it demands that we regard it if only to renounce and avoid it. This situation is constantly repeated everywhere, in all relations of modern man to technology. Technology is entrenched in our history.

He who has ears to hear, i.e., to grasp the metaphysical foundations and abysses of history and to take them seriously *as* metaphysical, could already hear two decades ago the word of Lenin: Bolshevism is Soviet power + electrification. That means: Bolshevism is the "organic," i.e., organized, calculating (and as +) conclusion of the unconditional power of the party along with complete technization. The bourgeois world has not seen and in part still does not want to see today that in "Leninism," as Stalin calls this metaphysics, a metaphysical projection has been performed, on the basis of which in a certain way the metaphysical passion of today's Russians for technology first becomes intelligible, and out of which the technical world is brought into power. That the Russians, e.g., are always building more tractor factories is not *primarily* what is decisive, but, rather, it is this, that the complete technical organization of the world is already the metaphysical foundation for all plans and operations and that this foundation is experienced unconditionally and radically and is brought into working completeness. Insight into the "metaphysical" essence of technology is for us historically necessary if the essence of Western historical man is to be saved.

But technology understood as modern, i.e., as the technology of power machines, is itself already a *consequence* and not the *foundation* of a transformation of the relation of Being to man. Modern mechanical technology is the "metaphysical" instrumentarium of such a transformation, referring back to a hidden essence of technology that encompasses what the Greeks already called τέχνη. Perhaps the transformed relation of Being to man, appearing in technology, is of such a kind that Being has withdrawn itself from man and modern man has been plunged into an eminent oblivion of Being. (Consequently, man can now no longer, or in the first place cannot yet, ponder the question raised in *Being and Time* as it is raised there.)

Perhaps the much-discussed question of whether technology makes man its slave or whether man will be able to be the master of technology is already a superficial question, because no one remembers to ask what kind of man is alone capable of carrying out the "mastery" of technology. The "philosophies" of technology pretend as if "technology" and "man" were two "masses" and things simply on hand, as if the way Being itself appears and withdraws had not already decided about man and technology, i.e., about the relation between beings and man and hence about the hand and the word and the unfolding of their essence.

The question of λήθη interrogates this relation of Being to man, and therefore our elucidation of the essence of πρᾶγμα, the action of the hand, had to refer to the typewriter, assuming a thoughtful meditation is a thinking that thinks of our history (the essence of truth), in which the future comes toward us.

People are generally inclined to consider philosophy an "abstract" affair. If now, apparently all of a sudden and arbitrarily, we speak of the typewriter, that is taken to be a digression, a view attesting to the fact that people are precisely not truly disposed to ponder the "concrete" they celebrate so much, i.e., to come within the proximity of the essence of things and to remove the concealment thrust upon things by mere use and consumption. Λήθη and the typewriter—this is indeed not a digression for anyone not submerged in the oblivion of Being.

According to Pindar, αἰδώς, awe, by which Being itself cares for its essence, and through which essence it dispenses ἀλήθεια to beings and to man, has λάθα for its counter-essence. The poetical words of Pindar about λήθη attest to the fact that for the Greeks the mutual counter-essence of ἀλήθεια and λήθη was experienced originally. We might therefore expect that this essential correlation between ἀλήθεια and λήθη would also, in a correspondingly original way, be thought through by the Greeks and posed in thinking. This expectation is not fulfilled. The Greeks never did explicitly think through ἀλήθεια and λήθη with regard to their essence and the ground of their essence, since already, i.e., prior to *all* thinking and poetizing, these pervade the to-be-thought as its "essence." The Greeks think and poetize and "deal" *within* the essence of ἀλήθεια and of λήθη, but they do not think and poetize *about* this essence and they do not "deal" with it. For the Greeks it suffices to be claimed by ἀλήθεια itself and to be encompassed by it. It is a sign of the necessity ruling its essence that Greek humanity, at its inception, does not need to think about the essence of ἀλήθεια (and of λήθη). And when, at the time of the close of the Greek world, in a certain sense a thinking "about" ἀλήθεια is inaugurated, then this inauguration is precisely a sign of that imminent closing. But the history of the modern world and its generations is much different.

When ἀλήθεια and λήθη are explicitly mentioned in the thoughtful speech of the Greeks, there it has the character of primordial legend and is μῦθος.

§6. *The Greeks' final word concerning the hidden counter-essence of*
ἀλήθεια, λήθη, *(I): The concluding myth of Plato's* Politeia. *The myth
of the essence of the polis. Elucidation of the essence of the demonic. The essence of the Greek gods in the light of* ἀλήθεια.
The "view" of the uncanny.

a) The πόλις, the pole of the presence of beings as determined out
of ἀλήθεια. Reference to Sophocles. The reverberation of the
conflictual essence of ἀλήθεια in the counter-essence to πόλις:
ἄπολις. Reference to Burckhardt.

The mythical presentation in Hesiod's theogony shows the provenance
of the essence of λήθη out of ἔρις (strife) and νύξ (night). And Pindar's
ode provides the clarification of a decisive essential relation. The signless
nebulosity of λήθη refers to its concealment, which itself hides itself
and thereby withdraws. This complexity of veiling and letting disappear
manifests unequivocally enough the provenance of the essence of λήθη.
This provenance is nocturnal. The night veils. But the night does not
necessarily conceal by drawing everything into the blackness of mere
darkness. Rather, the essence of its veiling consists in this, that it relegates things and people and both in their relation to one another to
the abode of a concealment. Oblivion, too, in its nocturnal essence,
does not befall man as an individual creature so as to effectuate changes
in his mode of representation, in consequence of which a person can
no longer perceive certain objects. Above all, oblivion tears things and
man away from unconcealedness, in such a manner that the one who
forgets dwells within a realm in which beings are withdrawn and man
himself is withdrawn from beings; and even this reciprocal withdrawal,
as a relation, is withdrawn from unconcealedness.

We might expect that where oblivion is experienced in this way as
withdrawing concealment, the relation between λήθη and ἀλήθεια
would not only be mentioned immediately but would be thought explicitly and assigned to meditation prior to everything else. This expectation, which is precisely ours and in no way a Greek one, is not fulfilled.
Nevertheless, the reciprocal counter-essence between ἀλήθεια and
λήθη holds sway as the basic feature of beings as a whole, in the midst
of which Greek humanity endures its history. It is almost as if what
was always already nearby and experienced is explicitly put into words
only in the age of the completion of Greek humanity, a completion
that is not a high peak but instead a high pass of transition to the
end. The Greek world comes to completion in the thinking of Plato,
and Aristotle's thinking knows and says this completion in the most
extreme possible manner.

Assuming, therefore, that in λήϑη as the counter-essence to ἀλήϑεια the primordial opposite to "truth" holds sway, and assuming further that something of the essence of Being shows itself in the essence of this opposition, then the utterance expressing primordially ἀλήϑεια's counter-essence, λήϑη, and consequently expressing ἀλήϑεια's own essence, can only be a word corresponding to the character of this primordial utterance. And that is μῦϑος.

In the historical time of the completion of Greek thinking, i.e., in Plato, thoughtful utterance takes the form of "dialogue." It is as if, before the end of Greek thinking, this very thinking, by its own character, once more wanted to speak about itself and attest to the essential rank the word enjoys where man stands in an immediate relation to ἀλήϑεια. In Plato's dialogue "Phaedrus," in the discussion of "the beautiful" (the concluding part), we see in addition that Plato recognized very clearly the priority of the immediately spoken word over the merely written one. But where would Plato's "dialogues" be if they never had been written down themselves?

Plato's most expansive "dialogue" in terms of content and range deals with the πόλις. The Romans say *res publica*, i.e., *res populi*, i.e., that which concerns the organized and established people, what is most their "business." Ordinarily we call this Platonic dialogue about the πόλις "Plato's Republic." But the difference between the modern republic, the Roman *res publica*, and the Greek πόλις is as essential as that between the modern essence of truth, the Roman *rectitudo*, and the Greek ἀλήϑεια. Actually this relation already holds on account of the fact that the essence of the Greek πόλις is grounded in the essence of ἀλήϑεια. A simple reflection, even if our focus is elsewhere, must still lead us to suspect this connection between ἀλήϑεια and πόλις. That is, if ἀλήϑεια as unconcealedness determines all beings in their presence (and that means, for the Greeks, precisely in their Being), then certainly the πόλις too, and it above all, has to stand within the domain of this determination by ἀλήϑεια, provided the πόλις does indeed name that in which the humanity of the Greeks has the center of its Being.

What is the πόλις? The word itself puts us on the right course, provided we bring to it the all-illuminating Greek experience of the essence of Being and of truth. Πόλις is the πόλος, the pole, the place around which everything appearing to the Greeks as a being turns in a peculiar way. The pole is the place around which all beings turn and precisely in such a way that in the domain of this place beings show their turning and their condition.

The pole, as this place, lets beings appear in their Being and show the totality of their condition. The pole does not produce and does not create beings in their Being, but as pole it is the abode of the unconcealedness of beings as a whole. The πόλις is the essence of the place [*Ort*], or, as we say, it is the settlement [*Ort-schaft*] of the historical dwelling of Greek humanity. Because the πόλις lets the totality of beings come in this or that way into the unconcealedness of its condition, the πόλις is therefore essentially related to the Being of beings. Between πόλις and "Being" there is a primordial relation.

This word πόλις is, in its root, identical with the ancient Greek word for "to be," πέλειν: "to emerge, to rise up into the unconcealed" (Cf. Sophocles, *Antigone*, πολλὰ τὰ δεινὰ ... πέλει).[1] The πόλις is neither city nor state and definitely not the fatal mixture of these two inappropriate characterizations. Hence the πόλις is not the notorious "city-state" but is, rather, the settling of the place of the history of Greek humanity— neither city nor state but indeed the abode of the essence of this human- ity. This essential abode gathers originally the unity of everything which, as the unconcealed, comes to man and is dispensed to him as that to which he is assigned in his Being. The πόλις is the abode, gathered into itself, of the unconcealedness of beings. If now, however, as the word indicates, ἀλήθεια possesses a conflictual essence, which appears also in the oppositional forms of distortion and oblivion, then in the πόλις as the essential abode of man there has to hold sway all the most extreme counter-essences, and therein all excesses, to the uncon- cealed and to beings, i.e., counter-beings in the multiplicity of their counter-essence. Here lies concealed the primordial ground of that fea- ture Jacob Burckhardt presented for the first time in its full bearing and manifoldness: the frightfulness, the horribleness, the atrociousness of the Greek πόλις. Such is the rise and the fall of man in his historical abode of essence—ὑψίπολις—ἄπολις—far exceeding abodes, homeless, as Sophocles (*Antigone*) calls man. It is not by chance that man is spoken of in this way in Greek tragedy. For the possibility, and the necessity, of "tragedy" itself has its single source in the conflictual essence of ἀλή- θεια.

There is only *Greek* tragedy and no other besides it. Only the essence of Being as experienced by the Greeks has this primordial character that "the tragic" becomes a necessity there. In the introduction to his lectures on the "history of Greek culture," Jacob Burckhardt knowingly inserts a thesis he heard as a student from his teacher in classical philol- ogy at Berlin, Bockh, and it runs as follows: "the Hellenes were more unhappy than most people think." Burckhardt's presentation of the Greeks, which he often repeated in his lectures at Basel from 1872 on, was constructed entirely on this insight, or, rather, surmise. Nie- tzsche had in his possession an auditor's transcript of these lectures, and he cherished the manuscript as his most precious treasure. Thus

---

1. *Antigone*, verse 332f. ["There are ... many strange things"—Tr.]

Jacob Burckhardt himself contributed to the fact that Nietzsche still thought the essence of the Greek world and of its πόλις in a Roman way. For Burckhardt considered the Greeks with a view toward the "history of Greek culture," by which he means the "history of the Greek spirit" (Introduction, p. 3). The concepts of "spirit" and "culture," no matter how they are defined, are representations belonging to modern thought. Burckhardt gave these representations a special stamp on the basis of his discovery of the "Italian Renaissance." In this way, essentially Roman, Romanic, and modern concepts flow into Burckhardt's historical thinking. Burckhardt thinks the totality of history according to three "forces": "state," "religion," "culture." The state is, in the modern view, a power. Burckhardt agrees with the thesis of F. Chr. Schlosser, that "power is in itself evil." This thesis has often been repeated in several variations. Power is called "demonic," but no reflection is given to the essence of power, nor is it said what "demonic" is supposed to mean here. The characterization of power as "evil" and "demonic" is a metaphysical judgment on something undetermined in its metaphysical essence. But a discussion in these terms does not even reach the perimeter of the essence of the πόλις. The essence of power is foreign to the πόλις, with the consequence that the characterization of power as "evil" finds no ground there. The essence of power, as meant in modern thinking about the state, is founded in the metaphysical presupposition that the essence of truth has been transformed into certitude, i.e., into the self-certitude of the human being in his self-positing, and that this latter is based on the subjectivity of consciousness. No modern concept of "the political" will ever permit anyone to grasp the essence of the πόλις.

b) Preparation for a detour over the path of a commentary on Plato's dialogue on λήθη and the πόλις. Order: Δίκη. The mortal course of the sojourn in the polis and the presence of beings after death. Christian Platonism. Reference to Hegel.

Perhaps, however, ἀλήθεια itself casts an appropriately clarifying light on the essence of the πόλις, enabling us to see why disorder and even disaster abound in the πόλις as the essential abode of historical man. These belong to the πόλις because every unconcealment of beings stands in conflict with concealment and accordingly also with dissemblance and distortion. Now, if the essence of unconcealedness and of concealment pervades the abode of the essence of historical man, then a Greek dialogue about the πόλις, assuming it is a thoughtful dialogue, must treat of the essence of ἀλήθεια. Plato does speak about ἀλήθεια, indeed in the manner of a μῦθος, at the beginning of Book VII of his dialogue on the πόλις. This "myth" is known as Plato's "cave-allegory." Many meanings have been attributed to this "allegory," but never the simple and most obvious. What is at issue in this "allegory," as even its name suggests, is a cave, a hiding, a concealing, and also uncon- cealedness. This same Platonic dialogue on the πόλις, which contains a μῦθος about ἀλήθεια, concludes, at the end of Book X, with another μῦθος. The high point of this μῦθος is what it says about λήθη (Plato, Politeia, X, 614b2-621b7).

The myth of λήθη concluding the dialogue on the πόλις is so far- reaching and rich that already for that reason it cannot be presented here in full. Besides, any merely reportorial presentation is otiose if it is to take the place of a meticulous interpretation. But we are lacking what is essential to carry out such an interpretation: an experience of the basic character of myth in general and of its relation to Plato's metaphysics. The interpretation of the individual features of this partic- ular μῦθος would only then be set in motion. So we are forced to make a detour. We shall limn the main features in broad strokes, with the intention, however, of bringing into focus the basic character of the whole, at least according to one aspect. This coincides with the question of the standing of λήθη in the whole of the myth, i.e., to what extent this whole has to lead to the naming of λήθη. The whole of this myth is built upon, and is supported by, the entire dialogue on the πόλις. In the πόλις as the abode of the essence of historical man, the abode that discloses and conceals beings as such, man is en- compassed by everything that, in the strict sense of the word, is ordered to him but is thereby also withdrawn from him. We do not understand "ordered" here in the extrinsic sense of "added to" or "put on," but in the sense of "assigned," as that which is ordained to man, in such a way that man is delivered over to this and is ordered into it, and must abide in it, if his essence is to be in order. What is ordered to man in this way, what befits man and orders him, we name with the single word *order*, in Greek: δίκη.

In the verses we already translated from the first fragment of Parmeni- des' didactic poem, we encountered δίκη together with θέμις. If there we used "order" to translate the word δίκη (which for the Greeks im- mediately resonates with δείκνυμι, to demonstrate, to indicate, and δικεῖν, to thrust), then "disorder" comes to mind as the obvious counter-word. But the "order" meant here is not the counter-essence to just any sort of "disorder" we might imagine. We mean "order" as an indicating, demonstrating, assigning, and at the same time arranging and "thrusting" order. It is to this that man has to be ordered, and so it is precisely out of it that he can err into the path of disorder, especially when the assignment conceals itself and falls away, with- drawing man from the πόλις, tearing him away from it, so that he becomes ἄπολις. Man's emerging into order and his standing within order, δίκη, is orderliness, δικαιοσύνη. Orderliness is understood here as the unveiledness of order, its holding nothing back in secret. The dialogue on the πόλις has to deal with this essential abode with regard to what takes place in it, how man dwells in it. The theme of the *Politeia* is δικαιοσύνη. In concord with the orderliness of order or in discordance with it man can be δίκαιος, orderly, or ἄδικος, disorderly. In the meditation on the πόλις there arises finally the question of what, for dwelling in the essential abode, is ordered to the orderly and the disorderly respectively, what, so to say, remains around each person as ordering.

Now, dwelling in the πόλις is a sojourn here on earth, ἐνθάδε; this sojourn in the polis, however, is in each case a περίοδος θανατοφόρος (Cf. X, 617d7), a sight-filled path and a course traversing to the end, and then stepping beyond the assigned temporal span of the earthly sojourn. This traversing course is θανατοφόρος; it harbors death and thereby leads to death. Yet the mortal course of man through the essential place of history does not exhaust the course and the journey or, more generally, the Being, of man. According to Plato, this passage of man through a βίος, this "course of life," is not the only one, but instead, after a certain time, man returns in a new form in order to begin a new course. The historiography of religion calls this the theory of "reincarnation." But we would do well, here again, to remain awhile within the compass of Greek thinking. And in that case we would say that with the completion of the current mortal course the Being of a man is not at an end. That is, in accordance with the essence of man, even after one's own death beings remain present in some fashion. Therefore the consideration of the πόλις arrives ultimately at the question (X, 614a6):

ἃ τελευτήσαντα ἑκάτερον περιμένει·

What remains round about each one respectively (the orderly as well as the unorderly) after he has finished (the mortal passage)? What surroundings does a man have when he is away from the here of the πόλις and sojourns "there," ἐκεῖ? What surroundings does he have, where is he, before he again begins a new course?

According to our usual, that is, in the broadest sense, "Christian," modes of representation, what is being raised here is the question of the "beyond." Christianity, from early on, following the path of Judeao-Hellenic teachings, has in its own way seized upon the philosophy of Plato and has seen to it that from then until now the Platonic philosophy, held out as the high point of Greek philosophy, should appear in the light of Christian faith. Even the thinking before Plato and Socrates is understood on the basis of Plato, as is evident in the ordinary

designation of this thinking: it is "pre-Platonic" philosophy, its fragments the "fragments of the pre-Socratics." Not only does Greek philosophy appear in a Christian theological interpretation, but even within
philosophy it is presented as the first stage of Christian-occidental thinking. For the first metaphysical-historical meditations on the whole of
the thinking of the West, namely Hegel's lectures on the history of philosophy, understand Greek philosophy as the stage of immediate thinking, not yet mediated and not yet come to itself. Only this latter, certain
of itself, in the modern sense the first "true" thinking, is actual thinking.
Christianity functions here as the stage of mediation. In the wake of
Hegel, the historiographical research of the nineteenth century adheres
to all his basic concepts but at the same time, in a remarkable self-
deception, rejects his "metaphysics" and flies to "Schopenhauer" and
"Goethe"; yet even there Greek philosophy in general and the philosophy of Plato in particular are represented within the horizon of a Christian Platonism. The same holds for Nietzsche as well, whose much-
celebrated interpretation of the "pre-Platonic" philosophers is actually
Platonic, i.e., Schopenhauerian, and utterly un-Greek. But what could
be more self-evident than the conviction that the most appropriate interpretations of the philosophy of Plato are those approaching it with
the aid of Platonism? Yet this procedure is comparable to the one that
would "explain" the fresh leaf of the tree on the basis of the foliage
fallen to the ground. A Greek interpretation of the thinking of Plato
is the most difficult, not because this thinking contains in itself special
obscurities and abysses, but because the following ages, and still we
today, are inclined to rediscover immediately our own, later thinking
in this philosophy. In the context of our lectures we must forego even
naming the basic presuppositions of a Greek interpretation of Platonic
thinking. The following remarks on Plato's μῦθος of λήθη are therefore
in this regard provisional.

Recapitulation

1) Politeia: the τόπος of the essence of the πόλις. The essentially
unpolitical character of the politeia of the polis. The pole of πέλειν.
The impossibility of interpreting the polis on the basis of the
"state," Δίκη, and *iustitia*. Death: transition from "here" to "there."
Platonism.

We are meditating on the counter-essence to ἀλήθεια, truth in the sense
of unconcealedness. The *primordial* counter-essence to ἀ-λήθεια is

λήθη, i.e., the signless concealment that withdraws itself as oblivion. The last word of the Greeks that names λήθη in its essence is the μῦθος concluding Plato's dialogue on the essence of the πόλις.

A thoughtful dialogue always speaks of the Being of beings. A Platonic dialogue on the πόλις therefore cannot be a consideration of a particular πόλις existing here or there. The thinker thinks the πόλις as such; he says what the πόλις is, what is its essence. This essence, what the πόλις itself is in the totality of its proper essential relations, i.e., what it genuinely is, is called πολιτεία. A thoughtful dialogue on the πόλις is from the very outset nothing but a dialogue about the πολιτεία. That is what the title says. But this title is still not unequivocal. Just as the Greek word οὐσία is used in everyday language and means there "capital," "possessions," "goods and chattels," "estates," and just as at the same time the everyday word οὐσία is elevated to a word of thoughtful speech and then comes to mean the presence of everything present, so πολιτεία means first, in the language of everydayness, the "life" belonging to a polis and determined by it, the dealings in it, and then correspondingly means the very structure of the polis in general, from which can then be discerned something like a "constitution." This latter must not be understood as a sequence of written propositions and rules, although the word pertains so originally to the "constitution" that what is written down does not merely present a subsequent "formula" or "formulation." Plato's choice of this name πολιτεία as the title of a thoughtful dialogue on the πόλις says that his theme will be the essential structure of the πολιτεία as such and consequently the essence of the πόλις in general.

It has been discovered that the πολιτεία described by Plato has never existed "in reality" and should therefore be called a "Utopia," something that has "no place." This discovery is "correct," the only problem is it does not understand what it has discovered. In truth it is the insight that the Being of beings is "actually" nowhere within beings and is not, as it were, on hand as one of their parts. Accordingly, Being should also be a "Utopia." But in truth Being, and it alone, is precisely *the* τόπος for all beings; and Plato's *Politeia* is not a "Utopia" but exactly the opposite, namely the metaphysically determined τόπος of the essence of the πόλις. Plato's Politeia is a recollection of the essential and not a plan for the factual.

The πόλις is the essential abode of historical man, the "where," to which man as ζῷον λόγον ἔχον belongs, the "where" from which alone order is ordained to him and in which he is ordered. The πόλις is the "where," as which and in which order is revealed and concealed. The πόλις is the way the revealing and concealing of order occur such that in these occurrences historical man comes into his essence and especially into his counter-esssence. Therefore we call the πόλις, wherein the Being of man in its relation to beings as a whole has gathered itself, the essential abode of historical man. Each πολιτικόν, everything "political," is always only an effect of the πόλις, i.e., of the πολιτεία. The essence of the πόλις, i.e., the πολιτεία, is not itself determined or determinable "politically." The πόλις is just as little something "political" as space itself is something spatial. The πόλις itself is only the pole of πέλειν, the way the Being of beings, in its disclosure and concealment, disposes for itself a "where" in which the history of a human race is gathered. Because the Greeks are the utterly unpolitical people, unpolitical by essence, because their humanity is primordially and exclusively determined from Being itself, i.e., from ἀλήθεια, therefore only the Greeks could, and precisely had to, found the πόλις, found abodes for the gathering and conserving of ἀλήθεια.

The thoughtless occupation of "historiographical research" mixes together essentially different epochs and civilizations of Western history, the Greek, Roman, medieval, modern, and contemporary in a single historiographical mash, and so it attains precisely the opposite of what it is supposed to. It intends to be a historical meditation on our own historical destiny. But meditation never arises from thoughtlessness. Historiographical research never discloses history, because such research is always attended by an opinion about history, an unthought one, a so-called obvious one, which it would like to confirm by this very research and in so doing only rigidifies the unthought obviousness.

Just as impossible as is an interpretation of the πόλις on the basis of the modern state or the Roman *res publica*, so is an interpretation of δίκη on the basis of the modern concept of justice and the Roman *iustitia*. Δίκη, understood as the order which ordains, i.e., assigns, to humanity its relations and comportment, takes its essence from a relation to ἀλήθεια, but δίκη is not determined by the πόλις or on the basis of a relation to the πόλις.

Every actual πόλις occurs historically on earth ἐνθάδε—here. Man's "course of life" runs through a circuit that is locally and temporally delimited and is a path within this circuit, a περίοδος, and indeed one that is θανατοφόρος, mortal, bearing death and therefore leading to death. Death brings the present course to a close, but it is not the end of the Being of a man. Death initiates a transition from the here, ἐνθάδε, to the there, ἐκεῖ. This transition is the beginning of a journey which itself again comes to a close in a transition to a new περίοδος θανατοφόρος. The question to raise is therefore: what would a person's surroundings be, what would remain for him, after he has brought to a close the present mortal course here on earth?

In Christian thought, this is the question of the "beyond." For many reasons, the danger of a conscious or even unconscious Christian interpretation of the thought of Plato is imminent. Plato's thinking entered through Philo very early into the Hellenic interpretation, and above all through Augustine into the neoplatonic Christian understanding and interpretation, and it has remained there ever since, throughout the most diverse variations. Even those who believe they are free from Christian representations and understand Plato in terms of humanism and classicism—hence presumably as "pagan"—still think in a Christian way precisely insofar as the pagan is simply the counter-Christian. Only in terms of a Christian appraisal are the Greeks "pagans." But even completely apart from the distinction between Christian and pagan, Plato's philosophy is always thought of as Platonic in the sense of a Platonism. What could our objection be to this practice of thinking Plato "Platonically"? Is it not the only appropriate way, or at any rate more "correct" than interpreting Plato's philosophy with the help of the philosophy of Kant or Hegel? Nevertheless, the attempt to interpret Plato with the help of some sort of Platonism is certain perdition. For it is like trying to "explain" the fresh leaf of the tree by means of the foliage fallen on the ground.

c) The question of the "here" and "there." Politeia, X, 614b2, and the questionableness of this "reference" to the myth.

Plato distinguishes between ἐνθάδε and ἐκεῖ; we say prudently: the here and the there, and we are right to leave aside the notions of "heaven," "hell," "limbo," "purgatory." But this is by no means sufficient, for the "there" of the Greeks is not only different in form and content but also "exists" in general in a different mode: namely, as a mode of the Greek experience of Being. As long as we do not reflect on this in an essentially fitting way, even the ἐκεῖ, the "there," of the Greeks will be a closed book. We will find ourselves helpless before the so-called underworld, "Hades," and the "shades" dwelling "there." We will then concoct some sort of "ghost psychology" and not raise first the simple question: why are there shades there? Is the shadowy character of Being in Hades connected with the essence of the Greek experience of beings and their unconcealedness? Now assuming we do not remain bound to the particular and do not inquire as historiographers of religion, then which figures dwell in the Greek "beyond" in place of "angels" and "devils"? But even if we are prepared to acknowledge that in the beyond as experienced by the Greeks not only are beings different, but also, prior to that, Being itself, and even if we have some inkling that the Greek distinction between what is here and what is there rests on an other experience of Being, yet we still cannot escape the most impelling question: how can a thinker of Plato's rank claim to know anything at all about the "there"?

This question of ours, apparently so smart, comes, of course, too late. For it is with a μῦθος that Plato answers the question of what surrounds those who have completed the mortal course here, i.e., the question of what remains in the there. At the end of the dialogue on the πολιτεία Plato has Socrates tell a story. People have often been puzzled by the occurrence of myths in the Platonic dialogues. The reason they turn up from time to time is that Plato is indeed prepared to abandon the primordial thinking in favor of the later so-called "metaphysics," but precisely this incipient metaphysical thinking still has to preserve a recollection of the primordial thinking. Hence the story.

In dialogue with Glaucon Socrates tells the concluding myth. Socrates begins with the words (Politeia, X, 614b2) *Αλλ' οὐ μέντοι σοι, ἦν δ' εγώ, 'Αλκίνου γε ἀπόλογον ἐρῶ, ἀλλ' ἀλκίμου μὲν ἀνδρός, 'Ηρὸς τοῦ 'Αρμενίου, τὸ γένος Παμφύλου.* "But in the meantime I will not tell you the story selected for the entertainment of Alkinoos (the king of the Phaiecians) but an *ἀπόλογον,* an apology (defense) of a brave man, Er, Armenios's son, one of the tribe of Pamphyliers."

The play on words between *οὐ 'Αλκίνου γε ἀπόλογον* and *ἀλλ' ἀλκίμου μὲν ἀνδρός* cannot be rendered in the translation. This play on words introducing the μῦθος is not at all playful; it is supposed to indicate the essence of the λόγος about to be narrated, i.e., the essence of the μῦθος. This λόγος is called *ἀπόλογος. 'Απόλογος* is used here in an essentially ambiguous sense, and indeed in a different verbal construction each time: *'Αλκίνου ἀπόλογον* and *ἀλκίμου ἀνδρὸς ἀπόλογον,* i.e., an *ἀπόλογος* "for" Alkinoos versus an *ἀπόλογος* told by a brave man. In the first case, according to the meaning of its root *ἀπολέγειν,* to assort, to select, *ἀπόλογος* means something chosen for the pleasure of Alkinoos. In the second case, where it is properly meant, the same word *ἀπόλογος* means the "apology" by which the brave man sets apart what he says from everything else that is told and thus preserves it in its special truth. The words that follow do not abandon what they say, do not squander anything in the looseness of mere entertainment and non-committal chatter. The words that follow are protective words resisting the importunity of ordinary explanation and, strictly taken, may be said and heard only in their properly essential form. This already establishes decisively that our "reference" to the μῦθος, as a mere reference, is questionable on many grounds.

"Er," the son of Armenios, had once in battle completed his life: *ὅς ποτε ἐν πολέμῳ τελευτήσας.* When, ten days afterwards, they collected the dead, who were already decomposed, Er was taken up as non-decomposed and brought home where he would be buried on the twelfth day. Lying on the funeral pyre, he came back to life and, as one who had come back, reported what he had seen "there." He said (614b9-c1):

ἐπειδὴ οὗ ἐκβῆναι, τὴν ψυχὴν πορεύεσθαι μετὰ πολλῶν, καὶ ἀφικνεῖσθαι σφᾶς εἰς τόπον τινὰ δαιμόνιον,

his "soul," after it was elevated from the here, went with many (others) on a journey, and they arrived then at some kind of—as we say— "demonic" place; and there were two chasms (*χάσματα—χάος*, openings) in the earth next to one another, and there were also two others (openings) in the sky opposite to each other. *Δικασταί* were pointing toward order but were sitting between these gaping openings in the earth and in heaven. To Er, the brave warrior, the pointing ones gave the task to become *ἄγγελον ἀνθρώποις γενέσθαι τῶν ἐκεῖ* (614d2), a messenger to men about "the there." Hence it was necessary for him *ἀκούειν τε καὶ θεᾶσθαι πάντα τὰ ἐν τῷ τόπῳ* (614d3)—to hear as well as to see everything in that place, a place said to be *δαιμόνιος*.

d) *Ψυχή*: the ground of a relation to beings. The thinker's knowledge of the daimonia. Reference to Aristotle and Hegel. *Δαιμόνιον*: the presence of the uncanny, the extraordinary, in the ordinary. The *δαίμονες*, the ones who point to and indicate what is ordinary.

Here we need to clarify what *ψυχή* means and what *δαιμόνιον* means. *Ψυχή* is the "soul"—that is the correct translation, just as we translate *ἀλήθεια* by "truth" and *ψεῦδος* by "falsity." But in fact the word *ψυχή* cannot be translated. If we try to clarify it by saying it means the essence of what is alive, the question immediately arises as to how the essence of "life" in the Greek sense is to be thought. *Ψυχή* refers to the ground and mode of a relation to beings. A relation of the living thing to beings, and thereby also a relation to itself, can exist: in that case the living thing must have the word—*λόγον ἔχον*—because Being only reveals itself in the word. It is also possible for the relation of something alive to beings not to exist: the *ζῷον*, the living thing, is alive nevertheless, but it is then *ζῷον ἄλογον*, a living thing without the word: e.g., an animal or a plant. The way a living thing is posited in relation to beings and therewith also in relation to itself, the being-posited, thus understood, into the unconcealed, the position in Being of a living thing, that is the essence of the "soul"; it has arrived at a *τόπος τις δαιμόνιος*.

If we render *δαιμόνιος* as "demonic," we obviously remain close to the word and apparently do not translate at all. In truth, it is precisely a "translation" when we "transport" the Greek *δαιμόνιον* into an undetermined or half-determined representation of the "demonic." "Demons" are for us "evil spirits"—in Christian thought, "the devil" and his cohorts. The demonic is then equivalent to the devilish in the sense of the Christian belief in, and profession of, the devil, or, on the other hand, in the correlated sense of an enlightened morality, where the "devilish" is understood as evil and evil is a violation of the principles of good citizenship. Such conceptions of the "demonic" will never touch the essence or the essential compass of the Greek δαιμόνιον. But as soon as we try to approach the essential realm of the "demonic" as it is experienced by the Greeks we must engage ourselves in a meditation which, from a pedagogical point of view, will again draw us away from the so-called theme of our lectures.

Aristotle, Plato's disciple, relates at one place (Nicomachean Ethics, Z 7, 1141b 7ff.) the basic conception determining the Greek view on the essence of the thinker: καὶ περιττὰ μὲν καὶ θαυμαστὰ χαλεπὰ δαιμόνια εἰδέναι αὐτοὺς φάσιν, ἄχρηστα δ' ὅτι οὐ τὰ ἀνθρώπινα ἀγαθὰ ζητοῦσιν. "It is said they (the thinkers) indeed know things that are excessive, and thus astounding, and thereby difficult, and hence in general 'demonic'—but also useless, for they are not seeking what is, according to straightforward popular opinion, good for man."

The Greeks, to whom we owe the essence and name of "philosophy" and of the "philosopher," already knew quite well that thinkers are not "close to life." But only the Greeks concluded from this lack of closeness to life that the thinkers are then the most necessary—precisely in view of the essential misery of man. The Germans would not have had to be the people of thinkers if their thinkers had not known the same thing. Hegel says in the preface to the first edition of his *Logic* in 1812, ". . . *a civilized people without metaphysics*" is like an "otherwise copiously decorated temple without the Holy of Holies."[1]

The thesis quoted from Aristotle says the thinkers know δαιμόνια, "the demonic." But how are "the philosophers," these harmless eccentrics who occupy themselves with "abstract" matters, supposed to have a knowledge of "the demonic"? Δαιμόνια is used here as an all-encompassing word for what is, from the point of view of the ordinary busy man, "excessive," "astounding," and at the same time "difficult." On the contrary, what is current, what a man is doing and what he pursues, is for the most part without difficulty for him because he can always find, going from one being to the next, a way of escape from difficulty and an explanation. The many and all too many pursue only the beings that are current; for them, these are real, if not precisely "the" reality. But in mentioning "reality," the throng attests that, besides what is currently real, it has something else in view, which, to be sure, it does not clearly see. The essence of the πολλοί, the many, does not consist in their number and mass, but in the way "the many" comport themselves toward beings. They could never be busy with beings without having Being in view. Thus "the many" see Being and yet do not see it. But because they always have Being in view, although not in

---

1. Hegel, WW (*Verein von Freunden*) Bd. 3, p. 4.

focus, and only deal with, and calculate, and organize, beings, they ever find their way within beings and are there "at home" and in their element. Within the limits of beings, of the real, of the "facts," so highly acclaimed, everything is normal and ordinary.

But where, on the contrary, Being comes into focus, there the extra-ordinary announces itself, the excessive that strays "beyond" the ordinary, that which is not to be explained by explanations on the basis of beings. This is the uncanny, literally understood and not in the otherwise usual sense according to which it rather means the immense and what has never yet been. For the uncanny, correctly understood, is neither immense nor tiny, since it is not to be measured at all with the measure of a so-called "standard." The uncanny is also not what has never yet been present; it is what comes into presence always already and in advance prior to all "uncanninesses." The uncanny, as the Being that shines into everything ordinary, i.e., into beings, and that in its shining often grazes beings like the shadow of a cloud silently passing, has nothing in common with the monstrous or the alarming. The uncanny is the simple, the insignificant, ungraspable by the fangs of the will, withdrawing itself from all artifices of calculation, because it surpasses all planning.[1] The emergence and the concealment that dwell in all emerging beings, i.e., Being itself, must therefore be astonishing to common experience within the everyday dealing with beings, if this does manage to get Being actually in focus, though it always has some view of it. The astounding is for the Greeks the simple, the insignificant, Being itself. The astounding, visible in the astonishing, is the uncanny, and it pertains so immediately to the ordinary that it can never be explained on the basis of the ordinary.

Perhaps, after this exposition, we may translate τὸ δαιμόνιον ("the demonic") by "the uncanny." We may indeed do so, provided we think the uncanny, the extraordinary, and what cannot be explained on the basis of the ordinary, as the *result* of the δαιμόνιον, and thus acknowledge that the δαιμόνιον is not the demonic because it is the uncanny, but that it is the uncanny precisely because it possesses the essence of the δαιμόνιον. The δαιμόνιον is not identical in essence with the uncanny in the sense just delimited, and moreover the uncanny is not the *ground* of essence of the δαιμόνιον. What then is the δαιμόνιον itself?

We may call the δαιμόνιον the uncanny, or the extraordinary, because it surrounds, and insofar as it everywhere surrounds, the present ordinary state of things and presents itself in everything ordinary, though without being the ordinary. The uncanny understood in this way is, with regard to what is ordinary or natural, not the exception but the

---

1. Cf. *Grundbegriffe, Gesamtausgabe* Bd. 51.

"most natural," in the sense of "nature" as thought by the Greeks, i.e., in the sense of φύσις. The uncanny is that out of which all that is ordinary emerges, that in which all that is ordinary is suspended without surmising it ever in the least, and that into which everything ordinary falls back. Τὸ δαιμόνιον is the essence and essential ground of the uncanny. It is what presents itself in the ordinary and takes up its abode therein. To present oneself in the sense of pointing and showing is in Greek δαίω (δαίοντες—δαίμονες).

These are not "demons" conceived as evil spirits fluttering about; instead, they determine in advance what is ordinary, without deriving from the ordinary itself. They indicate the ordinary and point toward it. Τὸ δαιμόνιον is what shows itself in pointing at what is ordinary and in a certain way therefore what is also present everywhere as the perfectly ordinary, though nevertheless never the merely ordinary. For those who came later and for us, to whom the primordial Greek experience of Being is denied, the uncanny has to be the exception, in principle explainable, to the ordinary; we put the uncanny next to the ordinary, but, to be sure, only as the extraordinary. For us it is difficult to attain the fundamental Greek experience, whereby the ordinary itself, and only insofar as it is the ordinary, is the uncanny. The uncanny appears "only" in the form of the ordinary, because the uncanny makes allusion to the ordinary and is in the ordinary that which alludes and points and has, as it were, the same character as the ordinary itself.

It is only with difficulty that we attain this simple essence of the δαιμόνιον, since we do not experience the essence of ἀλήθεια. For the δαίμονες, the self-showing ones, the pointing ones, are who they are and are the way they are *only* in the essential domain of disclosure and of the self-disclosing of Being itself. Night and day take their essence from what conceals and discloses itself and is self-lighting. That which is lighted, however, is not only what is visible and seeable, but prior to that—as the emerging—it is what surveys everything that comes into the light and stays in it and lies in it, i.e., everything normal and ordinary, and it is what gazes into everything ordinary, indeed in such a way that it precisely appears in the ordinary itself and only in it and out of it.

e) The looking (θεάω) that offers the sight of Being. The outward look (sight) of Being (εἶδος). The Greek god (δαίμων) that in looking presents itself in unconcealedness. What looks into the ordinary: the extraordinary, the uncanny. The appearance of the uncanny in human looking.

"To look" is in Greek θεάω. Remarkably (or should we say amazingly?) only the medial form θεάομαι is known, translated as "contemplate" or "spectate;" whence we speak of the θέατρον, the place of the spectacle, the "theater." Thought in the Greek manner, however, θεάομαι means to provide oneself with the look, i.e., θέα, in the sense of the sight in which something shows itself and presents itself. Θεάω, "looking," therefore in no way means "seeing" in the sense of representational looking upon and looking at, by which man turns toward beings as "objects" and grasps them. Θεάω is rather the looking in which the one who looks shows himself, appears, and "is there." Θεάω is the fundamental way the one who looks presents (δαίω) himself in the sight of his essence, i.e., emerges, as unconcealed, into the unconcealed. Looking, even human looking, is, originally experienced, not the grasping of something but the self-showing in view of which there first becomes possible a looking that grasps something. If man experiences looking only in terms of himself and understands looking precisely "out of himself" as Ego and subject, then looking is a "subjective" activity directed to objects. If, however, man does not experience his own looking, i.e., the human look, in "reflection" on himself as the one who represents himself as looking, but if instead man experiences the look, in unreflected letting-be-encountered, as the looking at him of the person who is encountering him, then the look of the encountering person shows itself as that in which someone awaits the other as counter, i.e., appears to the other and is. The looking that awaits the other and the human look thus experienced disclose the encountering person himself in the ground of his essence.

We moderns, or, to speak more broadly, all post-Greek humanity, have for a long time been so deflected that we understand looking exclusively as man's representational self-direction toward beings. But in this way looking does not at all come into sight; instead it is understood only as a self-accomplished "activity," i.e., an act of re-presenting. To re-present means here to present before oneself, to bring before oneself and to master, to attack things. The Greeks experience looking at first and properly as the way man emerges and comes into presence, with other beings, but as man *in his essence*. Thinking as moderns and therefore insufficiently, but for us surely more understandably, we can say in short: the look, θέα, is not looking as activity and act of the "subject" but is sight as the emerging of the "object" and its coming to our encounter. Looking is self-showing and indeed that self-showing in which the essence of the encountering person has gathered itself and in which the encountering person "emerges" in the double sense that his essence is collected in the look, as the sum of his existence, and that this collectedness and simple totality of his essence opens itself to the look—opens itself at any rate in order to let come into presence in the unconcealed at the same time the concealment and the abyss of his essence.

(Looking, ϑεᾶον, is: to provide sight, namely the sight of the Being of beings, which are the looking ones themselves. Through such looking, man is distinguished, and he can be distinguished by it only because the looking which shows Being itself is not something human but belongs to the essence of Being itself as belonging to appearance in the unconcealed.)

Consequently, only if we already think, or at least seek to experience, the fact that "essence" and Being have for the Greeks the basic feature of self-disclosing, only if we think ἀλήϑεια, are we capable of thinking the ϑεάω, the look, as the basic mode of the self-showing appearance and essence that present themselves in what is ordinary. Only if we experience these simple essential states of affairs do we understand what otherwise is completely incomprehensible, that still at the end of the Greek world, namely with Plato, Being was thought in terms of the "sight" and the "look" in which something shows itself, in terms of the "countenance" that at any time "a thing" or, in general, a being "takes on." The "countenances" things take on, their "outward look," is in Greek εἶδος or ἰδέα. Being—ἰδέα—is what in all beings shows itself and what looks out through them, the precise reason man can grasp beings as beings at all. That which looks into all that is ordinary, the uncanny as showing itself in advance, is the originally looking one in the eminent sense: τὸ ϑεᾶον, i.e., τὸ ϑεῖον. We translate "correctly," though without thinking in the Greek manner, "the divine." Οἱ ϑεοί, the so-called gods, the ones who look into the ordinary and who everywhere look into the ordinary, are οἱ δαίμονες, the ones who point and give signs.

Because the god is, as god, the one who looks and who looks as the one emerging into presence, ϑεάων, the god is the δαίων-δαίμων that in the look presents himself as the unconcealed. The one who presents himself in looking is a god, because the ground of the uncanny, Being itself, possesses the essence of self-disclosing appearance. But the uncanny appears in the ordinary and as the ordinary. The looking one appears in the sight and "outward look" of the ordinary, of beings. That which within the ordinary comes to presence by his own look is man. Therefore the sight of the god must gather itself within the ordinary, in the ambit of the essence of this human look, and must therein have its figure set up. Man himself is that being that has the distinctive characteristic of being addressed by Being itself, in such a way that in the self-showing of man, in his looking and in his sight, the uncanny itself, god, appears.

Recapitulation

2) The undemonic of the δαίμονες. The disclosing emergence of
Being: the self-clearing. Looking (perceiving), the primordial
mode of the emergence into the light. The intermediate position of
the animal (Nietzsche, Spengler). Man: the looked upon. Θέα and
θεά: the same word. Reference to Heraclitus, Fragment 48.
Insufficient elucidation of the Greek divinities. The look as what
is decisive for the appearance of the uncanny within the ordinary.
The uncanny as showing itself within the ordinary, and its
relation, founded on Being, to the divinities.

The myth that concludes Plato's dialogue on the essence of the πόλις,
and that also, in another sense, first opens up the dialogue, itself concludes with an account of the essence of λήθη, the counter-essence
to ἀλήθεια. This account is the story of the warrior "Er." Having completed in battle his life "here," he began "there," with many others,
the passage which must be undergone before a human being, after a
new decision, begins again a new course "here." The warrior is given
the task of looking at the route "there" and at the places traveled
through, and as a messenger (ἄγγελος) he is then to report to men
"here."

The essence of the places, their co-appurtenance and their sequence
in the "there," i.e., the entire district of the "there," is a τόπος
δαιμόνιος. Now since, as will be shown, λήθη is the most extreme
and the ultimate place in this "demonic" district, we have to arrive
at a clear understanding of what is meant by δαιμόνιον in Greek
thought both in this case and in general in order to grasp the all-
determining locational character of λήθη. Our common, confused, and
murky representations of the "demonic" do not at all help clarify the
essence of the δαιμόνιον. On the other hand, our exposition has to
remain within the limits of a mere allusion. It will therefore not be
successful in obviating all misunderstandings.

By way of preparation, we note that the uncanny, or the extraordinary, shines throughout the familiar ambit of the beings we deal with
and know, beings we call ordinary. Thereby we understand "the uncanny" altogether "literally." We are divesting from the word any representation of the gigantic, the overpowering, the exaggerated, the weird.
Of course, the uncanny can also, in its excessiveness, hide behind such
figures. But it itself in its essence is the inconspicuous, the simple, the
insignificant, which nevertheless shines in all beings. If we conceive
the uncanny as the simple which shines into the ordinary, and which

does not stem from the ordinary, but which nevertheless appears in advance in all that is ordinary, shining through it and around it, then it is clear that the word "uncanny," as used here, has nothing at all in common with its banal sense as "impressive" and "moving." In the present context, the uncanny is to be thought as bearing no trace of the word's other meanings.

Yet what we are calling the "uncanny" we still grasp on the basis of the ordinary. What the so-called uncanny is *in itself* and what first admits of the character of the uncanny as its consequence, that is based on the shining into beings, on self-presentation, in Greek: δαίω.

What shines into beings, though can never be explained on the basis of beings nor constructed out of beings, is Being itself. And Being, shining into beings, is τὸ δαῖον—δαῖμον. Descending from Being into beings, and thus pointing into beings, are the δαίοντες—δαίμονες. The "demons," so understood, are altogether "undemonic": that is, judged in terms of our usual murky representation of the "demonic." But these undemonic δαίμονες are anything but "harmless" and "incidental." They are not casual additions to beings, which man could bypass with no loss of his own essence and could leave aside and could consider solely according to his whims and needs. In consequence of this inconspicuous unsurpassability, the δαίμονες are more "demonic" than "demons" in the usual sense could ever be. The δαίμονες are more essential than any being. They not only dispose the "demonic demons" into the disposition of the horrible and frightful, but they determine every essential affective disposition from respect and joy to mourning and terror. Here, to be sure, these "affective dispositions" are not to be understood in the modern subjective sense as "psychic states" but are to be thought more originarily as the attunements to which the silent voice of the word attunes the essence of man in its relation to Being.

We who have come so late, however, can only experience the essence of the δαίμονες as shining into the ordinary and presenting themselves in beings and in that way pointing beings toward Being, on the condition that we attain at least an incipient relation to the essence of ἀλή-θεια, and thereby recognize that, for the Greeks, disclosure and emergence prevail in the essence of every originarily emergent being. Insofar as Being comes into presence out of ἀλήθεια, there belongs to it self-disclosing emergence. We name this the self-opening and the clearing (cf. *Being and Time*). These names originate indeed from an experience of primordial thinking, for which ἀλήθεια must be thought according to its own properly perceived "truth." These other names, which here come to words unwittingly, as it were, do not consist in a mere substitution of designations for something that remains thought in the same way. What is cleared shows itself originally in the transparency of the diaphanous, i.e., as the bright and the clear. Only insofar as ἀλήθεια abides, does it bring the clearing into the unconcealed. Because the clearing occurs in the concealed essence of ἀλήθεια, we experience emergence and presence, i.e., Being, "in the light" of the bright and of the "light." Luminous self-disclosure shows itself as the shining. (The sun shines.) What shines is what shows itself to a looking. What appears to the looking is the sight that solicits man and addresses him, the look. The looking performed by man in relation to the appearing look is already a response to the original look, which first elevates human looking into its essence. Thus as a consequence of the abiding of ἀλήθεια, and only because of it, looking is the primordial way of emergence into the light and coming into the light, i.e., shining into the unconcealed. To be sure, we must understand looking in the original Greek manner as the way a man encounters us by looking at us and, in looking, gathers himself into this self-opening emergence, and therein, without holding back a remainder, presents his essence and lets it "emerge."

This looking, which first makes presence possible, is therefore more original than the presence of things, because the self-disclosing look, according to the full essence of disclosure, at the same time shelters and hides something undisclosed. The thing, on the contrary, lacking the look, appears only in such a way that it stands in the unconcealed but itself has nothing to disclose and consequently also nothing to hide.

Here the animal has a peculiar intermediate position. Animals are said to "watch" us. But animals do not look. The "peering," or "glaring," or "gawking" and "gaping" of an animal is never a self-disclosure of Being, and, in its so-called looking, the animal never produces a self-emergence in a being that is disclosed to it. We are always the ones who first take up into the unconcealed such "looking" and who, on our own, interpret the way animals "watch" us as a looking. On the other hand, where man only experiences Being and the unconcealed sketchily, the animal's "look" can concentrate in itself a special power of encounter. Looking, in the original sense of emergent self-presenting, i.e., determined from ἀλήθεια, is in Greek θεάω. On the other hand, looking in the sense of grasping, which is understood on the basis of the grasped and lets the encountering look come to itself and accepts it—this grasping look is expressed through the medial form θεάω in the word θεάομαι, to let the encountering look come to itself, i.e., to behold. The Greeks were acquainted with the grasping look, just as, conversely, in addition to such looking as an act of subjective representation, we also know the look of encounter. But the question is not whether both these essential forms of looking, the encountering and the grasping, are known or not. The issue is which one, the look of emerging into presence or the look of grasping, has the essential priority in the interpretation of appearances and on what basis this rank is determined. According to the priority of subjectivity in the modern period, looking as an act of the subject is decisive. Insofar as, in Nietzsche's terms, man is the animal identified as the superman, the animal that has its essence in the will to power, the look of the subject is the look of a being that advances by calculating, i.e., by conquering, outwitting, and attacking. The look of the modern subject is, as Spengler said, following Nietzsche, the look of the predatory animal: glaring.

The Greeks too experienced the look as an activity of man. But the basic feature of this grasping look is not glaring, by means of which beings are, so to say, impaled and become in this way first and foremost objects of conquest. For the Greeks, looking is the "perception" ["*Vernehmen*"] of beings on the basis of a primordial consent [*Einvernehmen*] given to Being, which is why the Greeks do not even know the concept of object and never think Being as objectivity. The Greeks experience the grasping look as perception, because this look is determined originally on the basis of the encountering look. Within the domain of the essence of ἀλήθεια, this latter has the priority. In the ambit of this primordial look, man is "only" the looked upon. This "only," however, is so essential that man, precisely as the looked upon, is first received and taken up into the relation of Being to himself and is thus led to perception. What looks is what looks into unconcealedness: τὸ θεᾶον is τὸ θεῖον. We translate the latter correctly but thoughtlessly, and presumptuously though emptily, as "the divine." Θεάοντες are the ones who look into the unconcealed. Θέα, the look, as the essence of emergent existence, and θεά, goddess, are one and the same "word," considering the Greeks did not use accent marks in their writing and, above all, recognizing the original attentiveness the Greeks displayed for the essential homophony of words and hence for the hidden ambiguity of their expression. In this regard, think, for example, of Heraclitus, Fragment 48:

τῷ οὖν τόξῳ ὄνονα βῖος ἔργον δὲ θάνατος.

"The proper name for bow is βιὄς"—the bow means and "is" in Greek existence (the) "life" (not as "biological" but as fateful life-course); what it produces, however, is "death." Βίος is ambiguous. From the bow there emerges and arises the flight and the course of the arrow. But the "bow," which thus lets arise, may also bring down. Ὄνομα is the name, the word that expresses, not mere noise and sound. The word βιος is in itself ambiguous and expresses in such ambiguity precisely the essence of death-bringing life. The Greeks hear θέα—θεά just as they hear βίος—βιός. Θεοί, so-called "gods," as the ones who look into the unconcealed and thereby give a sign, are θεάοντες, are by essence δαίοντες—δαίμονες, the uncanny ones who present themselves in the ordinary. Both words, θεάοντες and δαίοντες express the same thing, if thought of essentially. But the usual meaning of the names θεοί and δαίμονες ("gods and demons") no longer signifies the origin they express. Often what a word expresses is distorted and suppressed by its "meanings."

The ones who shine into the ordinary appear in this ordinary as something ordinary. The looking ones are present as ones who look into the ordinary, i.e., as men in the form of men. In what is ordinary, man appears as one who is present by way of looking. The animal, too, in a certain sense appears that way, which is why at the outset the divine also has the form of the animal. But precisely this circumstance testifies that neither the "animal" as such nor the "man" as such, but instead their look, is what is decisive for the appearance of the uncanny. Thus the gods appear in the form of man not because they are thought of as "human" and are anthropomorphized, but because the Greeks experience man as the being whose Being is determined through a relation of self-disclosing Being itself to what, on the basis of this very relation, we call "man." Therefore the look of the god who stems from Being can emerge "in" man and can look out from the form of "man" as gathered in the look. Therefore men are often divinized and thought of according to a divine form, since gods and men receive their respective distinct essence from Being itself, i.e., from ἀλή-θεια.

The "anthropomorphic" and the "theomorphic" precepts of the modern "explanation" of the Greek gods are erroneous in every case. This "explanation," that the gods are deprived of divine attributes according to the measure of man, and that men are unhumanly divinized, is *essentially* erroneous, since it relates to a way of questioning that is mistaken already in the raising of the question and must wander around in error, for the essential domain of ἀλήθεια, which alone elucidates everything, is not acknowledged or experienced. It is not in the reign of the individual gods that the divinities of the Greeks display the astonishing and the demonic in the true sense, but that is grounded in the provenance of their essence.

It may indeed be obvious that the Greek gods, who are no more, remain experienceable on the basis of Being as thought by the Greeks. Yet we do not think the Being which is to be expressed here, and we do not in advance reflect on it, but instead, in our usual haste, according to our pleasure or fancy, or quite thoughtlessly, we presuppose some idea of Being that is not experienced in a decisive manner and is not correspondingly elucidated. In this way again and again the most facile precept imposes itself, that these divinities must be explained as a "product of man" or more particularly of "religious" man. As if this man, even for a moment, could have been man without the relation of these divinities to his own essence, i.e., without the abiding of this very relation in Being itself.

f) The difference between the Greek gods and the Christian God. The word as naming Being in its looking-into, and myth as a mode of the relation to appearing Being. Man: the God-sayer. "Decline" of cultures (Nietzsche, Spengler). The basic character of the oblivion of being: A-theism.

The Greeks neither fashioned the gods in human form nor did they divinize man. The essence of the Greek gods cannot be explained as an "anthropomorphism," no more than the essence of Greek man can be thought as a "theomorphism." The Greeks neither humanized the gods nor divinized man; quite to the contrary, they experienced the gods and men in their distinct essence, and in their reciprocal relation, on the basis of the essence of Being in the sense of self-disclosing emergence, i.e., in the sense of looking and pointing. That is why only the Greeks have a clear knowledge of the essence of the "demigods," ἡμίθεοι, who dwell in the between, between the gods and men.

The "anthropomorphic" conception of the Greek gods and the "theomorphic" conception of Greek men, who have neither humanized nor anthropomorphized god nor divinized themselves into gods, are equally groundless answers to deficient questions. To ask whether the Greeks anthropomorphized the "divine persons" or divinized human personalities into divine persons is to inquire into the "person" and "personalities"—without having determined in advance, even provisionally, the essence of man and of the divinities as experienced by the Greeks and without giving a thought to what is in fact first, namely that for the Greeks no more than there are "subjects" are there "persons" and "personalities." And how could even the slightest thing about an "anthropo-morphy" or about a "theo-morphy" be determined without the foundation of the essence of μορφή as experienced by the Greeks and the essence of the Greek concepts of "forming," "becoming," and "being"? And how could that be gained unless, in advance of everything, the essence of ἀλήθεια were better known?

The fundamental essence of the Greek divinities, in distinction to all others, even the Christian God, consists in their origination out of the "presence" of "present" Being. And that is also the reason why the strife between the "new," i.e., the Olympic, gods and the "old" ones is the battle, occurring in the essence of Being, that determines the upsurge of Being itself into the emergence of its essence. This essential nexus is the reason the Greek gods, just like men, are powerless before destiny and against it. Μοῖρα holds sway over the gods and men, whereas in Christian thought, e.g., all destiny is the work of the divine "providence" of the creator and redeemer, who as creator also dominates and calculates all beings as the created. And so Leibniz can still say: *cum Deus calculat, fit mundus*—"because and while God calculates, the world arises." The Greek gods are not "personalities" or "persons" that dominate Being; they are Being itself as looking into beings. But because Being always and everywhere infinitely exceeds all beings and juts forth in beings, therefore where the essence of Being has come originarily into the unconcealed, as is the case with the Greeks, the gods are more "excessive" or, spoken in the Christian and modern way, more "ethereal" and more "spiritual," despite their "human qualities." Precisely because the "gods" are δαίμονες—θεάοντες and appear along with the appearance of the familiar and ordinary, their uncanniness is so pure in measure and in mildness that when they appear αἰδώς and χάρις—awe and favor of Being—shine everywhere in advance, pointing while shining, and attuning while pointing. Although we are thinking the essence of the Greek gods more originarily if we call them the attuning ones, we should indeed name them this way since awe and favor and brilliance of mildness belong to Being, and these are experienced poetically in αἰδώς and χάρις and thoughtfully in θαυμαστόν and δαιμόνιον. From this attuning and pointing light stems the brilliance of θεῖον, the shining. Precisely this brilliance secured for the Greeks at the same time an experience of the dark and of the empty and of the gaping. Whereas the low-German word "*Got*" signifies, according to its Indo-European root, a being man invokes and hence is the invoked one, the Greek names for what we call "God" [*Gott*] express something essentially different: θεός—θεάων and δαίμων—δαίων mean the self-emergent looking one and Being as entering into beings. Here God and the gods, already by the very name, are not seen from the standpoint of man, as invoked by man. And when the gods are in fact invoked, e.g., in the ancient formulas of oaths, there they are called συνίστορες, the ones who "see" and have seen and as such have beings in unconcealedness and can therefore point to them. But συνίστορες are not "witnesses," since bearing witness, as long as we do not understand it originarily as bringing about (the look), is already founded on the having seen of the seer. The gods, as θεάοντες, are necessarily ἵστορες. Ἱστορία means "to bring into view" (from the stem *fid; videre, visio*), to place in the light, in the brightness. It is therefore that the ἱστορεῖν claims, properly and first, the ray of light. See Aeschylus, *Agamemnon*, 676, where it is said of Menelaus: εἰ γοῦν τις ἀκτὶς ἡλίου νιν ἱστορεῖ—if still any ray of the sun has him in sight, i.e., lets him be visible and stand in the light.

Yet the name and the designation of the divinity (θεῖον) as the looking one and the one who shines into (θεάον) is not a mere vocal expression.

The name as the first word lets what is designated appear in its primordial presence. The essence of man, as experienced by the Greeks, is determined on the basis of his relation to self-emergent Being, so that man is the one who has the word. And the word is in essence the letting appear of Being by naming. Man is the ζῷον λόγον ἔχον—the being that emerges by naming and saying and that in saying maintains its essence. The word as the naming of Being, the μῦθος, names Being in its primordial looking-into and shining—names τὸ θεῖον, i.e., the gods. Since τὸ θεῖον and τὸ δαιμόνιον (the divine) are the uncanny that look into the unconcealed and present themselves in the ordinary, therefore μῦθος is the only appropriate mode of the relation to appearing Being, since the essence of μῦθος is determined, just as essentially as are θεῖον and δαιμόνιον, on the basis of disclosedness. It is therefore that the divine, as the appearing and as what is perceived in the appearing, is that which is to be said, and is what is said in legend. And it is therefore that the divine is the "mythical." And it is therefore that the legend of the gods is "myth." And it is therefore that man in the Greek experience, and only he, is in his essence and according to the essence of ἀλήθεια the god-sayer. Why this holds can only be understood and thought on the basis of the essence of ἀλήθεια, insofar as the latter prevails in advance throughout the essence of Being itself, throughout the essence of divinity and the essence of humanity, and throughout the essence of the relation of Being to man and of man to beings.

But what if precisely this essence of ἀλήθεια, and with it the primordial self-manifesting essence of Being, are distorted by transformations and because of such distortion are ultimately prey to concealment in the sense of oblivion? What if the essence of Being and the essence of truth are forgotten? What if the *oblivion of Being* invisibly and signlessly surrounds with error the history of historical humanity? If the originary divinity emerges on the basis of the essence of Being, should the oblivion of Being not be the ground for the fact that the origin of the truth of Being has withdrawn itself into concealedness ever since, and no god could then appear emerging out of Being itself?

"A-theism," correctly understood as the absence of the gods, has been, since the decline of the Greek world, the oblivion of Being that has overpowered the history of the West as the basic feature of this history itself. "A-theism," understood in the sense of essential history, is by no means, as people like to think, a product of freethinkers gone berserk. "A-theism" is not the "standpoint" of "philosophers" in their proud posturing. Furthermore, "a-theism" is not the lamentable product of the machinations of "freemasons." "Atheists" of such a kind are themselves already the last dregs of the absence of the gods.

But how is an appearance of the divine at all supposed to be able to find the region of its essence, i.e., its unconcealedness, if, and as long as, the essence of Being is forgotten and, on the basis of this forgottenness, the unacknowledged oblivion of Being is elevated to a principle of explanation for every being, as occurs in all metaphysics?

Only when Being and the essence of truth come into recollection out of oblivion will Western man secure the most preliminary precondition for what is the most preliminary of all that is preliminary: that is, an experience of the essence of Being as the domain in which a decision about the gods or the absence of the gods can first be prepared. But we will not recollect Being itself and its essence as long as we do not experience the history of the essence of truth as the basic feature of our history, as long as we calculate history only "historiographically." For it is also a historiographical calculation when we come to know the Greek world as something of the past and establish that it has "declined," a constatation mostly made in the "historiographical" form of saying that Hellenism would contain for us "eternal values." As if essential history could be something allowing itself to be exploited for values! The obeisance before the "eternal values" of past cultures is the basic form in which historiographers take leave of history without experiencing it at all and destroy all sense for tradition and dialogue.

But if we continue to speak of peoples who have "declined" and the "declined" Greek world, what then do we know of the essence of historical decline? What if the decline of the Greek world were that event by which the primordial essence of Being and of truth would be secured back in its own concealedness and thereby first become futural? What if "decline" would not be end but beginning? Every Greek tragedy narrates the decline. Every one of these declines is a beginning and dawning of the essential. When Spengler, wholly on the heels of Nietzsche's metaphysics and coarsening it everywhere and leveling it down, speaks of the "decline of the West," he is not at all speaking of history. For he has already in advance devalued history to a "biological process" and made out of history a greenhouse of "cultures" that grow and fade away like plants. Spengler thinks history, if he thinks at all, in a history-less way. He understands "decline" in the sense of mere coming to an end, i.e., as biologically represented perishing. Animals "decline," they perish. History declines insofar as it falls back into the concealedness of its beginning—i.e., it does not decline in the sense of perish, because it can never "decline" *that way.* If, in order to elucidate the δαιμόνιον, we point here at the essence of the Greek divinities, then we have in mind not antiquated things, or the objects of historiography, but history. And history is the event of the essential decision about the essence of truth, which event is always a coming one and never something past. In forgetting, however, we are subservient to the past in the most dire way.

g) The divine as it enters into the unconcealed. The daimonion:
the look in its silent reception into the appurtenance to Being. The
disclosive domain of the word. The "correspondence" of the divine
and legend-ary (τὸ θεῖον and ὁ μῦθος). The setting into work (art)
of unconcealedness and its medium of word and myth.
Εὐδαιμονία and δαιμόνιος τόπος.

If we leave behind the oblivion of Being, insofar as we can now do
so and insofar as we can at all do so by our own initiative, and if
we think the primordial essence of Being, i.e., ἀλήθεια, and if we think
of ἀλήθεια in such a way that we are thinking its essence still more
primordially, then we will experience the demonic in the sense of the
Greek δαιμόνιον.

The δαιμόνιον is the essential character of the θεῖον, which, as the
looking one, looks into what is normal and ordinary, i.e., appears in
it. This appearing is in itself δαῖον, the divine as entering into the unconcealed. What enters into the unconcealed and appears there has as basic
modes of appearance looking and saying, whereby we must note that
the essence of saying does not consist in vocal sound but in the voice
[*Stimme*] in the sense of soundless attuning [*Stimmenden*], signaling,
and bringing the essence of man to itself, bringing it, namely, into its
historical destiny [*Bestimmung*]: in its way of being the "there," i.e.,
as the ecstatic clearing of Being (see *Being and Time*, §§ 28ff.). The
look in its silent reception into the self-perceiving-gathering appurtenance to Being is the δαιμόνιον. This "claim" of the divine, grounded
in Being itself, is taken up by man into dictum and legend, because
the disclosure of the unconcealed and the securing of the disclosed takes
place first, and only, in speech.

Sight into the unconcealed transpires first, and only, in the disclosive
word. Sight looks, and is the appearing self-showing that it is, only
in the disclosive domain of the word and of telling perception. Only
if we recognize the original relation between the word and the essence
of Being will we be capable of grasping why, for the Greeks and only
for them, to the divine (τὸ θεῖον) must correspond the legendary (ὁ
μῦθος). This correspondence is indeed the primordial essence of all
analogy (homology), the word "ana-logy" taken essentially and literally. Insight into this analogy, in which a dictum, a word, a legend,
corresponds to Being, i.e., discloses it by speaking of it as the same
in a comparison, puts us into a position to finally provide the answer
to an earlier question.

In our first elucidation of the essence of μῦθος as the disclosive legend
in which and for which Being appears, we asserted that, in accord with
the essential dignity of the word, poetizing and thinking had the highest
rank for the Greeks. This claim was bound to provoke an objection,

and the foregoing elucidations of δαιμόνιον and θεῖον have lent it still more significance. For the Greeks, beings appear in their Being and in their "essence" not only in the "word" but equally in sculpture. If indeed the divine in the Greek sense, τὸ θεῖον, is precisely Being itself looking into the ordinary, and if the divine essence appears precisely for the Greeks in the architecture of their temples and in the sculpture of their statues, what happens then to the asserted priority of the word and accordingly to the priority of poetizing and thinking? For the Greeks, are not architecture and sculpture, exactly with regard to the divine, of a higher rank, or at least of the same rank, as poetry and thinking? Is there not a well-justified ground to our readily-adopted procedure of forming our standard "historiographical picture" of the essence of the Greek world on the basis of architecture and sculpture? Here we will only be able to raise and clarify these far-reaching questions within the limits drawn by our meditation on the essence of the δαιμόνιον.

It is easy to see that at issue here are the relations among the "classes of art" and their rank: architecture, sculpture, poetry. We are thinking of the *essence* of art here, and indeed not in general and vaguely, and to be sure not as an "expression" of culture or as a "witness" to the creative potential of man. Our focus is how the work of art itself lets Being appear and brings Being into unconcealedness. This kind of questioning is far removed from metaphysical thinking about art, for the latter thinks "aesthetically." That means the work is considered with regard to its effect on man and on his lived experience. To the extent that the work itself comes to be considered, it is looked upon as the product of a creating, a "creating" which again expresses a "lived urge." Thus even if the work of art is considered for itself, it is taken as the "object" or "product" of a creative or imitative lived experience; that is to say, it is conceived constantly on the basis of human subjective perception (αἴσθησις). The aesthetic consideration of art and of the work of art commences precisely (by essential necessity) with the inception of metaphysics. That means the aesthetic attitude toward art begins at the moment the essence of ἀλήθεια is transformed into ὁμοίωσις, into the conformity and correctness of perceiving, presenting, and representing. This transformation starts in Plato's metaphysics. In the time before Plato, for essential reasons, a consideration "of" art did not exist, and so in general all Western considerations of art and all explications of art and historiography of art from Plato to Nietzsche are "aesthetic." This metaphysical basic fact of the unbroken domination of aesthetics is not changed at all, provided we keep the metaphysical in mind, if instead of a so-called cultivated and snobbish "aesthete," we have, e.g., a peasant, with his "natural" instinct, "experience" a nude in an art exhibit. The peasant, too, is an "aesthete."

Thinking about this unshakable fact, the suspicion must arise in us, after all we have been saying, that in our present desire to determine something about the art of the Greeks the obviousness of the aesthetic mode of consideration might in advance be burdening our approach with improper and distorting points of view.

According to the usual opinion, there are different "classes" of art. Art itself is the forming and shaping and "creating" of a work out of some matter. Architecture and sculpture use stone, wood, steel, paint; music uses tones, poetry words. One might agree that for the Greeks the poetic presentation of the essence of the gods and of their dominion was certainly essential; yet no less essential and in fact more "impressive," because of its visibility, would be the presentation of the gods immediately in statues and temples. Architecture and sculpture use as their matter the relatively stable material of wood, stone, steel. They are independent of the fleeting breath of the quickly fading and, moreover, ambiguous word. Hence through these classes of art, architecture, sculpture, and painting, essential limits are set for poetry. The former do not need the word, while the latter does.

Now, this view is quite erroneous. Indeed architecture and sculpture do not use the word as their matter. But how could there ever be temples or statues, existing for what they are, without the word? Certainly these works have no need for the descriptions of the historiography of art. The Greeks were fortunate in not yet needing historiographers of art, or of literature, music, and philosophy, and their written history is essentially different from modern "historiography." The Greeks had more than enough just with the tasks given them by poetry, thinking, building, and sculpturing.

But the circumstance that in a temple or in a statue of Apollo there are no words as material to be worked upon and "formed" by no means proves that these "works," in what they are and how they are, do not still need the word in an essential way. The essence of the word does not at all consist in its vocal sound, nor in loquacity and noise, and not in its merely technical function in the communication of information. The statue and the temple stand in silent dialogue with man in the unconcealed. If there were not the *silent word*, then the looking god as sight of the statue and of the features of its figure could never appear. And a temple could never, without standing in the disclosive domain of the word, present itself as the house of a god. The fact that the Greeks did not describe and talk about their "works of art" "aesthetically" bears witness to the fact that these works stood well secured in the clarity of the word, without which a column would not be a column, a tympanum a tympanum, a frieze a frieze.

In an essentially unique way, through their poetizing and thinking, the Greeks experience Being in the disclosiveness of legend and word.

And only therefore do their architecture and sculpture display the nobility of the built and the shaped. These "works" *exist* only in the medium of the word, i.e., in the medium of the essentially telling word, in the realm of the legendary, in the realm of "myth."

It is *therefore* that poetizing and thinking have a priority, one which to be sure is not grasped if we represent it "aesthetically" as a priority of one class of art over others. Similarly, in general art is not the object of a "cultural" or lived drive but is the setting into work of the unconcealedness of Being out of the holding sway of Being itself.

In μῦθος the δαιμόνιον appears. Just as the word and "having the word" sustain the essence of man, i.e., the relation of Being to man, so in the same range of essence, i.e., in relation to the whole of beings, the δαιμόνιον determines the basic relation of Being to man. Therefore in later Greek antiquity, with Plato and Aristotle, a word was still essential, one that named this relation of Being to man. That word is εὐδαιμονία.

Through the Roman-Christian translation as *beatitudo* (i.e., the state of the *beatus*, the blessed one) εὐδαιμονία was, of course, transformed into a mere quality of the human soul, "happiness." But εὐδαιμονία means the holding sway in the appropriate measure of the "εὐ"—the appearing and coming into presence of the δαιμόνιον.

This is not a "spirit" dwelling somewhere within the breast. The Socratic-Platonic talk of the δαιμόνιον as an inner voice signifies only that its attuning and determining do not come from the outside, i.e., from some being at hand, but from invisible and ungraspable Being itself, which is closer to man than any obtrusive manipulatable being.

Where the δαιμόνιον, the divine which enters into unconcealedness, the uncanny, must be said explicitly, there the saying is a legend, a μῦθος. The conclusion of the Platonic dialogue on the essence of the πόλις speaks of a δαιμόνιος τόπος. We now understand what this name means.

Τόπος is the Greek for "place," although not as mere position in a manifold of points, everywhere homogeneous. The essence of the place consists in holding gathered, as the present "where," the circumference of what is in its nexus, what pertains to it and is "of" it, of the place. The place is the originally gathering holding of what belongs together and is thus for the most part a manifold of places reciprocally related by belonging together, which we call a settlement or a district [*Ortschaft*]. In the extended domain of the district there are thus roads, passages, and paths. A δαιμόνιος τόπος is an "uncanny district." That now means: a "where" in whose squares and alleys the uncanny shines explicitly and the essence of Being comes to presence in an eminent sense.

§7. The Greeks' final word concerning the hidden counter-essence of ἀλήθεια, λήθη (II). The concluding myth of Plato's Politeia. The field of λήθη.

a) The district of the uncanny: the field of withdrawing concealment. The exclusiveness of the uncanny in the place of lethe. The sight of its emptiness, and the nothingness of the withdrawal. The uncontainable water of the river "Carefree" in the field of λήθη. The saving of the unconcealed by thoughtful thinking; the drink of the thinker.

The district mentioned in the concluding myth of Plato's Politeia is neither on "earth" nor in "heaven." Quite to the contrary, in this district there are such things, and only such things, which point to the subterrestrial, the supraterrestrial, and to what pertains to the earth. The subterrestrial and the supraterrestrial are the places whence the "demonic" shines up upon, or down upon, the earth. They are the places of the gods. In the district of the uncanny the ones who come from the subterrestrial and the supraterrestrial meet in order to wander through this δαιμόνιος τόπος before they again go through a new mortal course on earth. In wandering through the district of the uncanny, its places must be traversed according to explicitly delimited stops and times.

The last place within the district of the uncanny, consequently the one at which the wanderer must stop immediately prior to the transition to a new mortal course, is τὸ τῆς Λήθης πεδίον, the field of withdrawing concealment in the sense of oblivion. In this field of λήθη the whole wandering is gathered. Here the "demonic" of the entire locality dwells in the most extreme and highest sense. The warrior narrates that the way to the field of λήθη leads through a blaze consuming everything and through an air that asphyxiates everything; καὶ γὰρ εἶναι αὐτὸ (τὸ τῆς Λήθης πεδίον) κενὸν δένδρων τε καὶ ὅσα γῆ φύει (621a3f.). "Also, it (namely this field of withdrawing concealment) is itself bare of all that grows as well as completely void of everything the earth lets spring forth." This field of concealment is opposed to all φύσις. Λήθη does not admit any φύειν, any emerging and coming forth. Λήθη appears as the counter-essence to φύσις. If we understand φύσις as "nature," and λήθη as "forgetting," then we will never comprehend how φύσις and λήθη come to be opposites, why they stand in an emphatic relation to each other. But if we think of them in the Greek manner, then it becomes clear that λήθη as essential withdrawing and concealing never lets anything emerge, and hence it sets itself against all coming forth, i.e., against φύσις. The field of λήθη prevents every disclosure of beings, of the ordinary. In the essential place of λήθη everything disappears. Yet it is not only the completeness of the with-drawal or the presumed quantity of the concealment that distinguishes this place. The point is rather that the "away" of the withdrawn comes into presence itself in the essence of the withdrawal. The "away" of what is withdrawn and concealed is surely not "nothing," for the letting disappear that withdraws everything occurs in this place—in this place alone—and presents itself there. The place is void—there is nothing at all that is ordinary in it. But the void is precisely what remains and what comes into presence there. The barrenness of the void is the noth-ing of the withdrawal. The void of the place is the look that looks into it and "fills" it. The place of λήθη is that "where" in which the uncanny dwells in a peculiar exclusivity. The field of λήθη is, in a pre-eminent sense, "demonic."

But to the extent that this place, in its own domain, still allows some-thing to appear and come into presence, then as belonging to the field of λήθη this must itself partake of the essence of the field. All the wan-derers find in this place is a river. But already the name of the river indicates that it is appropriate to the place, i.e., it is in service to the essence of λήθη. The river in the field of λήθη is called Ἀμέλης, which means "Carefree." The warrior narrating the μῦθος of the δαιμόνιος τόπος says, (621a4ff.): σκηνᾶσθαι οὖν σφᾶς ἤδη ἑσπέρας γιγνομένης παρὰ τὸν Ἀμέλητα ποταμόν, οὗ τὸ ὕδωρ ἀγγεῖον οὐδὲν στέγειν. "They pitched their tents after evening descended, near the river "Carefree," whose water no vessel could cover, i.e., contain" (στέγη: the roof, the cover). This water does not know care (μελέτη) concerning what is opposed to disappearance, to going away, and con-sequently to withdrawing concealment. This water, which cannot be contained in any vessel because it is the pure going away itself, does not know μελέτη τῆς ἀληθείας, care over unconcealedness, the care that beings be secured in the unconcealed and therein remain constant. "Care" in no way means here a kind of preoccupation or distress over some external state of the world and man. Instead, care is uniquely the care over unconcealedness and belongs in the domain of the δαιμόνιον. Care belongs to the event of the essence of disclosure and concealment. Accordingly, the corresponding "carefreeness" is neither an arbitrary freedom from preoccupation as regards some thing or other, nor is it only a property of man. It is solely the not caring about ἀλήθεια, because "carefreeness" *is* concerned with the dominion of λήθη and attends to the withdrawing concealment. Therefore this carefreeness too is a δαιμόνιον. Hence in the realm of essential thinking, where the essence of Being is thought, just as is unconcealedness, whenever the word "care" occurs, something else is intended than the regretful-ness of a human "subject" staggering around in the "nothing in itself," in a "lived experience" objectified into empty nothingness.

The water of the river flowing in the field of λήθη eludes all containment and itself effectuates only the one withdrawal letting everything escape and thus concealing everything. After passage through the δαιμόνιος τόπος, everyone who is to begin again a journey on the earth must first drink from the water of the river "Carefree," and precisely a certain amount: μέτρον μὲν οὖν τι τοῦ ὕδατος πᾶσιν ἀναγκαῖον εἶναι πιεῖν, "It is necessary for everyone to drink a certain amount of this water" (621a6f.). Everyone going through the mortal journey on earth is on the earth and in the midst of beings in such a way that on account of this drink there hold sway a concealment and a withdrawal of beings, so that a being only is insofar as at the same time and in opposition to this concealment and this withdrawal there also prevails an unconcealedness in which the unconcealed is conserved. By this drink, taken in measure, the man returning to earth carries an essential belongingness to the domain of the essence of concealment. All dwell to a certain degree within the essential region of concealment—τοὺς δὲ φρονήσει μὴ σῳζομένους πλέον πίνειν τοῦ μέτρου· "But the ones who were not saved by insight drank more than the measure" (621a7f.). Φρόνησις here means the insight of the intuition that looks into what is properly intuitable and unconcealed.

The look-into meant here is the looking of the gaze into the essence, i.e., the gaze of "philosophy." Φρόνησις here means the same as "philosophy," and that title means: to have sight for what is essential. He who can look in such a way is a σῳζόμενος, a saved one, "saved" namely in the relation of Being to man. The word σῴζειν, like φρόνησις and φιλοσοφία, is an essential word. The Greek thinkers speak of σῴζειν τὰ φαινόμενα—"to save what appears"; that means to conserve and to preserve in unconcealedness what shows itself as what shows itself and in the way it shows itself—that is, against the withdrawal into concealment and distortion. He who in this fashion saves (conserves and preserves) the appearing, saves it into the unconcealed, is himself saved for the unconcealed and conserved for it. The ones, however, who are not like that, who thus lack the gaze into the essence, are ἄνευ φιλοσοφίας, "without philosophy." "Philosophy" is accordingly not a mere dealing with universal concepts on the part of thinking, to which one can dedicate oneself or not without there occurring anything essential. Philosophy means to be addressed by Being itself. Philosophy is in itself the basic mode in which man comports himself to beings in the midst of beings. Men who lack philosophy are without insight. They deliver themselves over to what happens to appear and likewise to what happens to disappear. They are at the mercy of the withdrawal and the concealment of beings. They drink beyond the measure of the water of the river "Carefree." They are the careless ones, who feel content with the thoughtlessness that has withdrawn from every claim on the thinker. These careless ones are the ones who have become happy in putting behind themselves the care concomitant with belonging to a people of poets and thinkers. (In recent days it was publicly announced by the ministry of propaganda in a loud voice that the Germans no longer need "thinkers and poets" but "corn and oil.")

"Philosophy," as the heedfulness to the claim of Being on man, is first of all the care for Being and never a matter of "cultural formation" and knowledge. Therefore it is possible that many persons may possess a great amount of learned information about philosophical opinions without ever being "philosophical" and without "philosophizing." Then again, others may be touched by the claim of Being without knowing what it is and without responding to the claim of Being with appropriate thinking.

Of course a certain knowledge belongs to this thoughtful thinking and so does a carefulness in reflection and in the use of words, which essentially surpasses all demands of mere scientific accuracy. According to the experience of the Greek thinkers, this thinking always remains a saving of the unconcealed from concealment in the sense of veiling withdrawal. This latter is experienced more originally in thought than anywhere else. The thinker in particular must have drunk the just measure of water from the river "Carefree." "Seeing," in the sense of the gaze into the essence, the seeing of genuine thinking, does not come about by itself but is, in a different way than the usual "seeing" and "seeing-to," threatened on all sides by errors. But what about the one who not only drinks beyond the measure, but who drinks only this water?

Recapitulation

1) Field and lethe. The divine for the Greeks: the uncanny in the ordinary. The *θεῖον* in primordial *ἀλήθεια* and *λήθη*. *Ἀλήθεια* and *θεά* (Parmenides).

About the time that the Greeks departed from their essential history, they expressed once more the legend of the counter-essence of *ἀλήθεια*, the *μῦθος* of *λήθη*. This legend, which concludes Plato's dialogue "Politeia," ends with a tale about *λήθη*. This observation is correct, but in such a casual form it may easily occasion a misinterpretation of the essence of *λήθη*. In truth what is at issue here is *τὸ τῆς Λήθης πεδίον*—the field of withdrawing concealment. Plato does not say simply *τὸ πεδίον τῆς Λήθης*, but *τὸ τῆς Λήθης πεδίον*. Initially, the relation between the field and *λήθη* is left undetermined, because the linguistic expression, the genitive, can mean many different things: in the first place, it could mean that in the field λήθη occurs and appears. Taken in this way the field and λήθη are indifferent to one another. But the field can also be determined in its character as a field precisely on the basis of λήθη and become in that way a region appropriate to λήθη alone. Here field and λήθη are indeed still distinguished, but they are no longer indifferent to one another. Finally the field and its character as field can belong to λήθη itself. Now field and λήθη are not distinguished from each other, but λήθη itself is field. It is the place, the "where," in such a way that withdrawing concealment does not occur at some spot or other within the field but instead is itself the "where" for what must belong to it. Accordingly, what is to be thought is "the field of λήθη." This field belongs together with other places, and as a whole they make up a τόπος δαιμόνιος: a "demonic district."

The elucidation of the essence of the δαιμόνιον leads to a clarification of the essence of the θεῖον. Together, these provide an indication of the essence of the Greek divinities. This indication would certainly be very much misunderstood if it were to engender the view that henceforth "we" could straightaway be certain on our own of the essence of the Greek gods and therewith be assured of their proximity. The indication does not reach that far. It can only remind us that as long as the essence of ἀλήθεια is not completely disinterred, we will not have preserved the one thing by which we might endure the remoteness of the Greek gods, acknowledge this remoteness as an event of our history, and experience these gods as the ones they used to be. Instead of that, we are still in constant danger—from literary works, books, conferences, and feuilletons—of being talked into and persuaded of an immediate relation to the Greek gods. It makes no matter here whether this literature is professorially boring in the style of the historiography of religion or whether the results of the historiography of religion are elaborated and recounted more poetically. The way to these gods, even to their remoteness, certainly leads through the word. But this word cannot be "literature." (Experts know of course that the fine book of W. F. Otto, *Die Götter Griechenlands*, does not belong to this literature; but even here the step into the domain of ἀλήθεια is lacking.)

For the Greeks the divine is based immediately on the uncanny in the ordinary. It comes to light in the distinction of the one from the other. Nowhere do we find here a display of unusual beings, by means of which the divine would first have to be awakened and a sense for it first aroused. Therefore also the question of the so-called "Dionysian" must be unfolded first as a Greek question. For many reasons we may doubt whether the Nietzschean interpretation of the Dionysian can justly be maintained, or whether it is not a coarse interpreting back of an uncritical nineteenth century "biologism" into the Greek world.

Everywhere there holds sway in advance for the Greeks the simple clarity of Being which lets beings arise in a lustre and sink down into darkness.

Therefore what belongs to the appearance of Being is still of the type uncanny, so that there is no need to ascribe to Being a divine character subsequently and to demonstrate it afterward. If now, however, ἀλήθεια belongs to the essence of primordial Being and so does its counter-essence λήθη, then each of these is primordially a θεῖον. Therefore even for Plato λήθη is still essentially "demonic." Should we then be offended if in Parmenides' primordial thinking ἀλήθεια appears as θεά, as goddess? We would now be more surprised if that were not the case.

Λήθη, in Plato's "myth," is the δαιμόνιον of a field that resides not in the here but in the there. This field is the ultimate thoroughfare, where the wanderers must stop immediately prior to their transition out of the there into the here. It is said of the "field of λήθη": κενὸν δένδρων τε καὶ ὅσα γῆ φύει—"it is bare of all that grows as well as completely empty of everything that the earth allows to spring forth."

b) The measure of withdrawing concealment in unconcealedness. The countenance of the ἰδέα in Plato and the grounding of anamnesis (as well as forgetting) in unconcealedness. Λήθη: πεδίον. The interpretation of the beginning of Homer's poems and of Parmenides' utterance. The unforgetting of ἀλήθεια through the withdrawal of λήθη. The overcoming of experience since Plato through procedural operations (τέχνη). Reference to Homer, Iliad, XXIII, 358ff.

τόν δὲ ἀεὶ πιόντα πάντων ἐπιλανθάνεσθαι—"However, for one who would constantly drink (this water) his relation to beings as a whole and to himself would stand in the concealment that withdraws everything and does not leave anything preserved" (621a8f.). On such a one further words should not be wasted. He could not be on earth as a man, since all beings would be concealed to him and there would be nothing unconcealed at all, nothing to which he could relate disclosively, i.e., for the Greeks, in speech (μῦθος, λόγος), and thereby be a man. Complete, measureless oblivion, i.e., concealment, would exclude the least ground of the essence of man, because such oblivion would allow no disclosure and would deny unconcealedness its essential foundation. Conversely, we see from this that a measure of withdrawing concealment belongs to the possibility of unconcealedness. Λήθη, the concealment that does not allow anything to emerge but only withdraws, nevertheless prepares the ground of essence of disclosure and so holds sway in unconcealedness.

Man stems from the district of the uncanny divine place of withdraw-ing concealment. And since λήθη pertains to the essence of ἀλήθεια, un-concealedness itself cannot be the mere *elimination* of concealedness. The α in ἀ-λήθεια in no way means simply an undetermined universal "un-" and "not." Rather, the saving and conserving of the un-concealed is necessarily in relation to concealment, understood as the withdrawal of what appears in its appearing. The conserving is grounded in a per-petual saving and preserving. This preserving of the unconcealed comes to pass in its pure essence when man strives freely for the unconcealed and does so incessantly throughout his mortal course on earth. To strive for something freely and to think only of it is in Greek μνάομαι; the "perpetual" endurance on a path and a course is in Greek ἀνά—; the incessant thinking of something, the pure saving into unconcealedness of what is thought, is thus ἀνάμνησις. A self-manifesting being, having come into unconcealedness as such, is understood by Plato as that which steps into view and thus emerges in its look. The "look" in which something comes to presence as unconcealed, i.e., in which it *is*, is what is meant by εἶδος. The sight and the aspect something offers, through which it looks at man, is ἰδέα. Thought in Plato's sense, uncon-cealedness occurs as ἰδέα and εἶδος. In these and through these, beings, i.e., what is present, come to presence. The ἰδέα is the countenance by which at any time self-disclosive beings look at man. The ἰδέα is the presence of what is present: the Being of beings. But since ἀλήθεια is the overcoming of λήθη, what is unconcealed must be saved in un-concealedness and be secured in it. Thus man can comport himself to beings as unconcealed only if he perpetually directs his thinking to the unconcealedness of the unconcealed, i.e., to the ἰδέα and the εἶδος, and in that way saves beings from withdrawal into concealment.

In Plato's sense, i.e., thought in the Greek way, the relation to the Being of beings is therefore ἀνάμνησις. This word is usually translated as "memory" or perhaps "recollection." This translation transforms everything into the "psychological" and does not at all touch the essen-tial relation to ἰδέα. The translation of ἀνάμνησις by "recollection" im-plies it is a matter here only of something "forgotten" welling up in man once again. But we have learned in the meantime that the Greeks experience forgetting as the event of the concealment of beings; accord-ingly, so-called "memory" is actually based on unconcealedness and disclosedness.

Plato inaugurates, along with the transformation of the essence of ἀλήθεια into ὁμοίωσις, a transformation of λήθη and of the ἀνάμνησις opposing it. The event of the withdrawing concealment becomes trans-formed into the human comportment of forgetting. Similarly, what is opposed to λήθη becomes a fetching back again by man. As long as we think the Platonic ἀνάμνησις and ἐπιλανθάνεσθαι only on the basis of what came afterward, i.e., in modern terms, think them only in a "subjective" sense as "remembering" and "forgetting," we will not grasp their essential ground for the Greeks, which in the thinking of Plato and Aristotle radiates its light for the last time.

The tale of the water of the river "Carefree" is the last word the warrior pronounces regarding the δαιμόνιος τόπος. The μῦθος reaches its peak in the legend of the field of λήθη. The essential view of thinking, which gathers everything into itself and finds expression in this dialogue on the essence of the πόλις, is directed to the region of withdrawing concealment. This is the one and only thing necessary, since ἀ-λήθεια, which is what is to be experienced, is itself by essence founded on λήθη. Between these nothing mediates and there is no transition, because both in themselves pertain immediately to each other by their very essence. Whenever a belonging together is an essential one, the transition from one side to the other is "sudden;" it takes only a moment and is over in a trice. Therefore the warrior concludes his "narration" of the μῦθος with the following words (621b1ff.): ἐπειδὴ δὲ κοιμηναι καὶ ξέσας νύκτας γενέσθαι, βροντήν τε καὶ σεισμὸν γενέσθαι, καὶ ἐντεῦφεν ἐξαπίνης ἄλλον ἄλλη φέρεσθαι ἄνω εἰς τὴν γένεσιν, ᾂττοντας ὥσπερ ἀστέρας. "After they lay down to rest and midnight struck, a thunderstorm and an earthquake set in, and from there (from the field of λήθη) all of a sudden everyone else was carried away, going toward the emerging prominence (toward being on earth) like a flight of stars (shooting stars)." αὐτὸς δὲ τοῦ μὲν ὕδατος κωλυθῆναι πιεῖν. "He himself, however, was indeed prevented from drinking the water" (621b4f.).

That is decisive: the μῦθος does not tear away from concealment something unconcealed but speaks out of that region from which springs forth the original essential unity of the two, where the beginning is. ὅπῃ μέντοι καὶ ὅπως εἰς τὸ σῶμα ἀφίκοιτο, οὐκ εἰδέναι, ἀλλ' ἐξαίφνης ἀναβλέψας ἰδεῖν ἔωθεν αὐτὸν κείμενον ἐπὶ τῇ πυρᾷ. "In what way meanwhile and in what fashion he came into his 'bodily' presence he claimed not to know, but he did know that when he suddenly opened his eyes, he saw it was morning and he himself was lying on the pyre" (621b5ff.).

The looking up, the seeing of the ἰδέα, the dawning light, the morning, the fire and the pyre—all this expresses in such an essential way relations and features of Greek thinking that we are listening inappropriately to the concluding word of the μῦθος if we find in it merely a figurative ending to the narrative. Now is not the time to consider these relations. But neither may we close our ears to what Socrates, i.e., here, Plato himself, remarks concerning the μῦθος just told. Καὶ οὕτως, ὦ Γλαύκων, μῦθος ἐσώθη καὶ οὐκ ἀπώλετο, καὶ ἡμᾶς ἄν σώσειεν, ἂν πειθώμεθα αὐτῷ, καὶ τὸν τῆς Λήθης ποταμὸν εὖ διαβησόμεθα καὶ τὴν ψυχὴν οὐ μιανθησόμεθα. "And so, O Glaucon, a legend has been saved and did not get lost, and it could save us, too, if we would be obedient to it; and then we will fittingly traverse the river flowing in the field of λήθη and will not desecrate the 'soul,' i.e., the fundamental power to say beings" (621b8ff.).

Once again there is talk of σῴζειν, saving. What is preserved and secured is the legend of the essence of λήθη, the withdrawing conceal-ment. That the μῦθος as a whole is to secure in the unconcealed pre-cisely this closing expression of the essence of concealment can be rec-ognized from the fact that out of the rich content of the μῦθος Plato in the end once more mentions τὸν τῆς Λήθης ποταμόν, the river flowing in the field of λήθη. A superficial reading of this passage had already in antiquity led to the false notion of a "river Lethe," as if λήθη itself were the river. But λήθη is neither the river itself, nor is it symbo-lized by the river. Λήθη is πεδίον, field, region, the essence of the place and of the sojourn from which there is a sudden transition to a place and a sojourn that, as the unconcealedness of beings, envelops the mor-tal course of man. In the emptiness and abandonment of the field of all-withdrawing concealment, what alone can exist is this river, because its water corresponds to the essence of the field in that this water with-draws from and eludes all containment and in that way carries the essence of the place of the withdrawing concealment everywhere it is taken as a drink. The place of λήθη is to be traversed only by travers-ing the single thing that exists at this place, namely the water of the river. If it were only a matter of *stepping* across, then the water would run past the ones who are crossing and would flow away and would not affect them in their essence. But the crossing must occur and does occur only by the water becoming a drink and thus entering into man and determining him from the very innermost of his essence. And thereby it also determines how man, destined to unconcealedness, will in the future stand in the unconcealed while retaining a relation to withdrawing concealment. The appropriate, i.e., the measured crossing of the river flowing through the place of λήθη consists in taking a drink of the water according to the fitting measure. Yet the *essence* of man, and not only the individual man in his destiny, is saved only when man, as the being he is, harkens to the legend of concealment. Only in that way can he follow what unconcealedness itself and the disclo-sure of the unconcealed demand in their essence.

Without insight into the δαιμόνιον of λήθη, we will never be able to appreciate the astonishing fact that the "mother of the muses," and consequently the essential *beginning* of poetry, is "Mnemosyne," i.e., the primordial free salvation and preservation of Being, without which poetizing would even lack what is to be poetized. If we look into this essential connection between Being and unconcealedness, between unconcealedness and salvation versus the concealed, between salvation and preservation, Being and word, word and saying, saying and poetizing, and poetizing and thinking, we will then perceive the first lines of Homer's poems quite differently than we used to:

ILIAD: *Μῆνιν ἄειδε, θεά, Πηληϊάδεω Ἀχιλῆος / οὐλομένην,*[1]
ODYSSEY: *Ἄνδρα μοι ἔννεπε, Μοῦσα, πολύτροπον, ὃς μάλα πολλὰ πλάγχθη,*[2]

Here the "goddess" and the "muse" are not simply "invoked" for the purpose of a solemn introduction, but these lines say that the utterance of the poetical word is the speaking and the song of Being itself, and the poet is merely the *ἑρμηνεύς*, the interpreter of the word. The poet does not invoke the goddess, but instead, even before saying his first word the poet is already invoked himself and already stands within the appeal of Being and as such is a savior of Being versus the "demonic" withdrawal of concealment.

If Parmenides names the goddess *Ἀλήθεια* at the very outset of his utterance, that is not, as philologists maintain, a kind of poetically fashionable introduction to his so-called "didactic poem," but instead it is the naming of the essential place, where the thinker as thinker dwells. The place is *δαιμόνιος τόπος*.

For us of today the *μῦθος* of *λήθη* at the conclusion of the dialogue on the *πόλις* is the last word of the Greeks on the hidden counter-essence to *ἀλήθεια*. This withdrawing counter-essence to disclosedness "withholds" unconcealedness but at the same time also holds in itself the essence of unconcealedness. What is counter to *ἀλήθεια* is neither simply the opposite, nor the bare lack, nor the rejection of it as mere denial. *Λήθη*, the oblivion of withdrawing concealment, is that withdrawal by means of which alone the essence of *ἀλήθεια* can be preserved and thus be and remain unforgotten. Thoughtless opinion maintains that something is preserved the soonest and is preservable the easiest when it is constantly at hand and graspable. But in truth, and that now means for us truth in the sense of the essence of unconcealedness, it is self-withdrawing concealment that in the highest way disposes human beings to preserving and to faithfulness. For the Greeks, the withdrawing and self-withdrawing concealment is the simplest of the simple, preserved for them in their experience of the unconcealed and therein allowed to come into presence. Therefore Plato could not invent

---

1. "O goddess, sing of the fatal vengeance of the Peleidian Achilles"—Tr.
2. "O muse, sing for me of that much-wandering and much-suffering man"—Tr.

the μῦθος of λήθη; no μῦθος is ever invented nor found by seeking. The legendary word is a response to the word of an appeal in which Being itself dispenses itself to man and therewith first indicates the paths a seeking might take within the sphere of what is disclosed in advance.

Certainly the time of Plato, four centuries later, is no longer the age of Homer. The ability, hence the inclination as well as the aptitude, to express the appeal of Being becomes more and more concerned with establishing something that has been attained in the meanwhile, namely a being-at-home in beings on the basis of what man has instituted by his own procedures. The legendary word is not weaker; but man's perception is more variegated and dispersed and hence too volatile to experience as present the simple, which comes into presence originarily and therefore constantly. In the final era of the completion of the Greek world, we recognize already the traces of the early form of that historical condition which then determines the epoch of modernity in the West. In this epoch, as a consequence of a peculiarly concealed incertitude, certitude in the sense of unconditional certainty counts as what is most valuable, and therefore ascertaining becomes the basic character of all comportment. Ascertaining is not a merely subsequent corroboration but is rather the aggressive making secure in advance for the sake of certitude. The content and the reality of everything objective has whatever validity it has as the inexhaustible occasion for objectivization in the sense of the certification of the content of world and "life." Procedural processes (τέχνη) and their modes dominate experience. A river no longer flows in the mysterious course of its windings and turnings along banks it itself has carved out, but it now only pushes its water to an "end" predirected to it without detours, between the uniform rails of cement walls, which are in no way banks. The fact that precisely at the time of Socrates and Plato the word τέχνη, which there surely still means something essentially different from technique in the sense of modern technology, is often used, and is already thought of, is a sign that procedural processes are lording it over experience. The ability to listen to legend becomes weaker and more withdrawn from its essence.

The legendary word of Homer has not faded away. The otherwise silent μῦθος of λήθη exists. Therefore even the Platonic μῦθος of λήθη is a remembering of, not merely a thinking "about," the λήθη Pindar and Hesiod mention. This remembering utterance of the μῦθος preserves the primordial unveiling of the essence of λήθη and at the same time helps us to think more attentively the domain in which Homer already mentions the counter-word to λήθη, ἀλήθεια.

In the penultimate book Ψ (XXIII) of the Iliad there is in verse 358ff. a passage referred to at the conclusion of the consideration of the oppositional character of the essence of ἀλήθεια. This song poetizes the death, the ritual burning, and the funeral of Achilles' fallen friend Patroclos, and it poetizes the war games instituted in honor of Achilles. The first of the games is to be the contest of the chariots. After Achilles drew lots determining the order of the warriors,

> σήμηνε δὲ τέρματ᾽ Ἀχιλλεὺς
> τηλόθεν ἐν λείῳ πεδίῳ παρὰ δὲ σκοπὸν εἶσεν
> ἀντίθεον Φοίνικα, ὀπάονα πατρὸς ἑοῖο,
> ὡς μεμνέῳτο δρόμους καὶ ἀληθείην ἀποείποι.

"Achilles indicates the turn (of the course),
(letting it appear) farther in broad space, and next to the end of the course he places
the divine Phoenix, the war companion of his father,
so that he might keep the course in view and accordingly bring to word what is unconcealed."

ὡς μεμνέῳτο δρόμους—so that he might keep, i.e., so that he will not let fall away into concealment the outcome of the battle of the chariots. Here ἀλήθεια, the unconcealedness of the battle, i.e., the battle as it appears in its presence, is founded unequivocally on a μεμνέῳτο— we would say on a "not forgetting," though in that way we would falsify the matter. Indeed in the Greek language μιμνῄσκειν and μέμνημαι surely express the counter-essence to ἐπιλανθάνεσθαι. But the latter is determined on the basis of its relation to λήθη. Accordingly, in the original understanding of μιμνῄσκειν there lies the sense of keep-ing, and precisely the holding of the unconcealed as such. This holding is, however, not a mere be-holding or taking notice but is letting oneself be held by unconcealedness, dwelling in it as that which secures the unconcealed against the withdrawal of concealment.

Recapitulation

2) The origination of man out of the uncanny district of withdrawing concealment. The inception of the transformation of man's basic position. The coming to presence together of ἀλήθεια and μέμνημαι.
Reference to Homer, Iliad, XXIII, 358ff.

Plato's myth at the conclusion of the Politeia says that man stems from the uncanny district of withdrawing concealment and in the "here" traverses a mortal course through beings in the midst of beings as a whole. Therefore, in opposition to the concealment he bears with him as the legacy of that district, when man returns to the "here," he must first freely pursue (μνάομαι) beings. He does so by removing the concealment and thus letting the un-concealed show itself. Beings show themselves first by being un-concealed, because concealedness surrounds those who have been transposed back into the here, as a consequence of the draught they had to take from the river in the λήθη-place. The μῦθος understands the necessity of ἀλήθεια and its essential relatedness to λήθη, as the ground preceding it, on the basis of the essential provenance and destiny of man. This emphatic reference to man already indicates a transformation of the basic position of thinking among the Greeks. This transformation signifies the inception of metaphysics. The history of the Greeks thus heads toward the completion of its essential possibility. Λήθη will no longer be experienced as a pure event but will be thought on the basis of the comportment of man in the sense of the later "forgetting."

But if λήθη, no matter how conceived, is originally the counteressence to ἀλήθεια, and if to λήθη as withdrawing concealment there corresponds a losing in the sense of forgetting, then a keeping and preserving must also originally stand in a correspondence to ἀλήθεια. Where ἀλήθεια comes to presence there holds sway a keeping of that which is saved from loss. Unconcealedness and keeping, ἀλήθεια and μέμνημαι, come to presence together. And this original belonging together of both, precisely as primordial, must also possess the inconspicuous character of what, like a source, comes to presence out of itself in its essence. Indeed there is testimony to this. We have in mind a place in Homer, Iliad, XXIII, 358ff. Achilles orders Phoenix, at the battle of the chariots, ὡς μεμνέῳτο δρόμους καὶ ἀληθείην ἀποείποι, "to keep the course in view and accordingly to bring to word the unconcealed."

Let it be noted parenthetically that ἀλήθεια and ἔπος—unconcealedness and word—are again mentioned together.

Part Two

The Fourth Directive from the Translating Word *ΑΛΗΘΕΙΑ*. The Open and Free Space of the Clearing of Being. The Goddess "Truth."

§8. The fuller significance of dis-closure. The transition to subjectivity. The fourth directive: the open, the free. The event of ἀλήθεια in the West. The groundlessness of the open. The alienation of man.

a) Preparation for the fourth directive. The insufficiency of "unconcealedness" as the translation used up to now. The ambiguity of the word "dis-closure" and its fuller significance. The conflict in primordial ἀλήθεια. Proximity and beginning. Reference to Homer. The two senses of appearance: pure emergence and being-encountered. Egohood. Reference to Kant, Descartes, Herder, Nietzsche. The priority of selfhood since Plato and Aristotle (Περὶ υχῆς, 8, 431; Μετ α, 1).

Μέμνημαι and *ἀλήθεια* are linked together in the verse from the Iliad quoted above (verse 361) and, specifically, there unconcealedness is a consequence of a keeping. That means Homer experiences the essential relation between *ἀλήθεια* and *λήθη* in simple clarity and understands *ἀλήθεια* on the basis of its relation to the concealing withdrawal of *λήθη*. Voss's translation of the verse, "To take good notice of the course and to proclaim everything precisely," bears not the slightest trace of what the Greek is saying. 'Αληθές has become "precise" and *μέμνημαι* mere "taking notice." The intrusion of "subjectivity" and of "subjective comportment" into the essential relation between *ἀλήθεια* and *μέμνημαι* is obvious.

In this passage, unconcealedness and the keeping that for us counts as a counter-comportment to "forgetting" are mentioned as it were spontaneously and for the Greeks in a "natural" way in their essential relationship. But it would be erroneous to claim, solely on the basis of this passage, that unconcealedness corresponds to not-forgetting and that the ἀληθές, the unconcealed, is precisely what is not-forgotten. It *is* so, by all means, but only under the presupposition that we think of forgetting in terms of ἀλήθεια and not substitute for the essence of λήθη the "forgetting" which is later understood as inadvertence, a kind of psychic-subjective comportment.

Yet the "unconcealed" cannot simply be identified with the unforgotten, because the "unforgotten" may be something false and untrue and consequently is not by necessity something true, ἀληθές. But does this not also apply to the unconcealed as much as to the unforgotten, namely that it can be something false as well as something true? Besides, the so-called "false" must surely be something unconcealed and therefore would be true. The "unconcealed" also appears in the guise of mere semblance. What then distinguishes that unconcealed we call "the true"?

Hereby we are directing our gaze onto nexuses and abysses Greek thinking did not avoid, though we ourselves can hardly still surmise them, for we unwittingly mix into these necessary questions our ordinary understanding of the essence of truth, i.e., truth in the sense of "correctness" and "certitude." We can now see only this much, that mere unconcealedness, in which even something "false" may stand, does not exhaust the essence of ἀλήθεια; spoken more prudently, up to now we have not thought the essence of ἀλήθεια exhaustively. In fact through what we have just observed, i.e., in view of the essential relation of ἀλήθεια to λήθη (withdrawing concealment), a primordial essential moment of ἀλήθεια manifests itself, one that we have not yet mentioned and that is by no means expressed in the translation "unconcealedness," at all events not as long as we think "unconcealedness" in a careless and indeterminate way simply as the absence and elimination of concealedness.

The unconcealed is originally what is saved from withdrawing concealment and hence is secured in dis-closure and as such is uneluded. The unconcealed does not come into presence indeterminately, as if the veil of concealment had simply been lifted. The unconcealed is the un-absent, over which a withdrawing concealment no longer holds sway. The coming into presence is itself an emerging, that is, a coming forth into unconcealedness, in such a way that the emerged and the unconcealed are assumed into unconcealedness, saved by it and secured in it. "'Αληθές," the "unconcealed," reveals its essence to us now more clearly precisely from its relation to λήθη. The unconcealed is what has entered into the tranquility of pure self-appearance and of the "look." The unconcealed is what is secured thereby. The clarification of the essence of the counter-essence, λήθη as withdrawing concealment, first allows the essence of dis-closure to be brought into the light.

At the outset, "dis-closure" could only say as much as "un-veiling," the removal of the veiling and the concealment. But disclosure or dis-concealment does not mean the mere removal and elimination of concealment. We must think dis-closure exactly the way we think of dis-charging (igniting) or dis-playing (unfolding). Discharging means to release the charge; displaying means to let play out the folds of the manifold in their multiplicity. Our first tendency is to understand dis-closure or disconcealing *in opposition* to concealing, just as disentangling is opposed to entangling. Disclosure, however, does not simply result in something disclosed as unclosed. Instead, the dis-closure [Ent-*bergen*] is at the same time an en-closure [*Ent*-bergen], just like dis-semination, which is not opposed to the seed, or like in-flaming [*Entflammen*], which does not eliminate the flame [*Flamme*] but brings it into its essence. Dis-closure [*Entbergung*] is equally for the sake of an en-closure as a sheltering [*Bergung*] of the unconcealed in the unconcealedness of presence, i.e., in Being. In such sheltering there first emerges the unconcealed as a being. Disclosure—that now means to bring into a sheltering enclosure: that is, to conserve the unconcealed in unconcealedness. The word "dis-closure," the appropriateness of which only a far-reaching meditation could reveal, contains in its full sense equally essentially this emphasized moment of shelter, whereas "unconcealedness" names only the removal of concealedness. The word "dis-closure" is essentially and advisedly ambiguous in that it expresses a two-fold with an intrinsic unity: on the one hand, as *dis*closure it is the removal of concealment and precisely a removal first of the withdrawing concealment ($\lambda\acute{\eta}\vartheta\eta$) and then also of distortion and displacement ($\psi\varepsilon\~{\upsilon}\delta o\varsigma$); on the other hand, however, as dis*closure* it is a sheltering en-closure, i.e., an assuming and preserving in unconcealedness.

"Disclosure," understood in its full essence, means the unveiling sheltering enclosure of the unveiled in unconcealedness. It itself is of a concealed essence. We see this first by looking upon $\lambda\acute{\eta}\vartheta\eta$ and its holding sway, which withdraws into absence and points to a falling away and a falling out.

The lesson to be drawn, therefore, from our meditation on the opposition holding sway in unconcealedness is not that besides distortion and falsity, i.e., in brief, besides untruth, there would still be another counter-essence to truth, namely $\lambda\acute{\eta}\vartheta\eta$. Rather, our reflection resulted in the far-reaching insight that out of this counter-essence to truth the only conflictual and primordial essence of $\dot{\alpha}\lambda\acute{\eta}\vartheta\varepsilon\iota\alpha$ itself reveals itself more originally. ᾽Aλήθεια is *against* concealing closure, and through this "against" it is *for* sheltering enclosure. ᾽Aλήθεια is against concealing *because* it comes to presence in the unconcealed for the sake of a sheltering.

This "for" and "against" of $\dot{\alpha}\lambda\acute{\eta}\vartheta\varepsilon\iota\alpha$ are in themselves not "ruptures" through which its essence falls apart and thereby falls out into the essential-less, but instead they mark the conflict out of which ἀλήθεια is unified in its essence, and out of which it begins. The conflictual unity of immanence in the primordial essence is inwardness.

Admittedly, the Greeks think and speak still less about this more primordial essence of ἀλήθεια than about the essence of λήθη, for ἀλήθεια is to them the simple beginning of all that comes into presence. The Greeks therefore feel no urgency and have no incentive to direct their poetizing, thinking, and saying back into or beyond this beginning. For the Greeks there emerges in this beginning itself enough of what is entrusted to the saying of their poetry and thought, to its setting-up and rearranging. For us who have come later, however, just to get some inkling of this most primordial beginning of the history of the West we must explicitly pay heed to it and follow the directives the word "unconcealedness" provides.

By following the third directive and thinking through the oppositional essence of "unconcealedness" beyond the limits of the usual opposition (truth-untruth), both of the first mentioned directives take on a clearer imprint. That "unconcealedness" is related to "concealedness and concealment" has meant for us more than a mere verbal analysis of "unconcealedness" could yield. Likewise, the "un" in "unconcealedness" has revealed an essential "oppositional" manifold and has given a clue to the conflictual essence of truth. But if now by focusing on λήθη we glimpse the basic feature of sheltering enclosure in the essence of disclosure, and if this shelter secures in unconcealedness what it has to secure and to save, then the question looms large as to what unconcealedness itself might be, such that it can hold sway as sheltering and saving.

Thus it becomes necessary to follow a fourth directive the translating word "unconcealedness" offers to our thoughtful attention. What this fourth and last directive brings to our attention, which we must gradually learn to experience, was mentioned by the Greeks even less, was less explicitly thought of, and was less explicitly founded, than the previously mentioned features of the essence of ἀλήθεια. Still it rests primordially in the same, as yet concealed, essence of unconcealedness. Let us see what we can see here, without first relating to the previous directives. In doing so, however, it will necessarily appear that we are now more than ever interpreting back into the essence of the Greek ἀλήθεια something that does not reside in it. Measured against the barriers of the horizon of historiography, and of what is historiographically ascertainable, and of the "facts," everywhere so cherished, what is said here about ἀλήθεια is "in fact" an interpretation read into it. But if, on the contrary, we do not force on history historiographical horizons and cover it with them, if we rather let the beginning be the beginning it is, then another law holds. According to this law, we cannot read enough into the beginning, or, better said, we cannot interpret enough out of it, so long as we merely pay heed to this beginning in the rigor of its essence and do not get caught up in our own arbitrariness. For the reflection that attempts to investigate the essence of "truth" by no means desires, in the self-satisfied zeal of erudition, simply to discover what was once meant or was not meant. That could only be a *preparation* for the essential truth, which is "more alive" than today's much-invoked "life" and concerns man's historical destiny, because this essence has come to presence for us already now long ago, without our thinking of it or making ourselves ready for it.

What we are presently trying to bring into essential focus, through the fourth directive, belongs even more primordially to the essence of ἀλήθεια than the counter-essence discussed up to now in all its multiplicity. Since our focus is to be directed to something that comes to presence more primordially in ἀλήθεια, therefore, along with ἀλήθεια and through it, it is disclosed prior to all else, and as unconcealed it is still closer to us than what is closest, i.e., closer than what otherwise stands out first in the essence of ἀλήθεια. What we are now to be directed toward is nearer to us than what is ordinarily and "at first" the closest, and therefore it is correspondingly more difficult to see. Thus in the zeal of the ordinary seeing of sense perception, we overlook what holds good and serves under visible things and between them and our vision, the closest of all, namely brightness and its own proper transparency, through which the impatience of our seeing hurries and must hurry. To experience the closest is the most difficult. In the course of our dealings and occupations it is passed over precisely as the easiest. Because the closest is the most familiar, it needs no special appropriation. We do not think about it. So it remains what is least worthy of thought. The closest appears therefore as if it were nothing. We see first, strictly speaking, never the closest but always what is next closest. The obtrusiveness and imperativeness of the next closest drives the closest and its closeness out of the domain of experience. This follows from the law of proximity.

This law of proximity is grounded in the law of the beginning. The beginning does not at first allow itself to emerge as beginning but instead retains in its own inwardness its beginning character. The beginning then first shows itself in the begun, but even there never immediately and as such. Even if the begun appears as the begun, its beginning and ultimately the entire "essence" of the beginning can still remain veiled. Therefore the beginning first unveils itself in what has already come forth from it. As it begins, the beginning leaves behind the proximity of its beginning essence and in that way conceals itself. Therefore an experience of what is at the beginning by no means guarantees the possibility of thinking the beginning itself in its essence. The first beginning is, to be sure, what is decisive for everything; still, it is not the primordial beginning, i.e., the beginning that simultaneously illuminates itself and its essential domain and in that way begins. This beginning of the primordial beginning comes to pass at the end. We know, however, neither the character nor the moment of the ultimate end of history and certainly not its primordial essence.

Therefore the completion of the history of the first beginning can be a historical sign of the proximity of the primordial beginning, which latter includes future history in its proximity. Following the law that rules the beginning in its beginning, even the Greeks therefore necessarily overlook what is closest in the essence of ἀλήθεια. This overlooking does not stem from a lack of attention; it is not the consequence of negligence or incapacity. On the contrary, it is due precisely to their faithfulness to the most primordial experience of the still withdrawing beginning that the Greeks overlook the primordiality of the beginning. But because, on the other hand, the closest, and it alone, already dwells in all that is close, what is closest in the essence of ἀλήθεια must then be expressed in the speech of the Greeks, even if only incidentally, i.e., in the sense of something vaguely glimpsed though not explicitly regarded.

The passage from the Iliad (B, 349ff.) elucidated earlier, where Nestor speaks of the return of the Greeks and of Zeus's lightning on the right, on the occasion of the Greeks' departure for Troy, revealed an inner connection between ψεῦδος, distortion, as a concealment but consequently also as a disclosure, and φαίνειν, showing as letting appear. The unconcealed, that which lies in the light of the day, is what appears from out of itself, in appearing shows itself, and in this self-showing comes to presence (i.e., for the Greeks, "is"). In this way Greek experience is a revelation of a more original relation between what is unconcealed and what appears. Both are in a certain sense the same, and yet again not the same; for in the essence of appearance there is hidden an ambiguity that can be decided in more than one way. Appearance is founded in a pure shining, which we understand as a radiating light. The same appearance, however, is also a self-showing that meets a reception and a perception. Perception can now grasp what shows itself merely as what is perceived in the perceiving and can overlook as something incidental, and ultimately forget, the appearance that dwells in the self-showing, i.e., appearance in the sense of pure shining and radiating. The unconcealed is thus experienced more and more only in its relation to man and in terms of man, i.e., in its character as something encountered. But it is not thereby necessary that man, even if he thinks the relation of Being to himself emphatically in terms of himself, should also posit himself as "subject" in the modern sense and declare Being to be his representation.

The selfhood of man includes, indeed by necessity, selfishness and egoism as its excess. These do not at all coincide with the Ego constituting the essence of "subjectivity," i.e., the rebellious sovereignty of modern man. But even the essence of the Ego does not consist in the self-isolating exclusion of the individual from the rest of beings (this exclusion is called "individualism"). Metaphysically thought, the essence of the Ego consists rather in its making every other being something standing over against it, its object, its over-and-against, its projected ob-ject. The essence of the Ego (the I) has its distinguishing mark in the experience of all beings as objective and as standing over and against its representations. Thereby the Ego proceeds to the totality of beings and presents this to itself as something to be mastered. Only in the reign of subjectivity does there become historically possible an epoch of cosmic discoveries and planetary conquests, for only subjectivity marks off the essential bounds of an unconditioned objectivity and does so ultimately as a claim of its will. The essence of subjectivity, namely the Ego of the *perceptio* and *representatio*, is so essentially distinct from the "egoism" of the individual I that, according to Kant, the essence of the Ego consists precisely in the holding sway of consciousness in general as the essence of a self-posited humanity. Selfhood, in the sense of subjectivity and Ego, unfolds itself later in many forms, which arise historically as nation and people. The concepts of "people" and "folk" are founded on the essence of subjectivity and Ego. Only when metaphysics, i.e., the truth of beings as a whole, has been founded on subjectivity and the Ego do the concepts of "nation" and "people" obtain that metaphysical foundation from which they might possibly have historical relevance. Without Descartes, i.e., without the metaphysical foundation of subjectivity, Herder, i.e., the foundation of the concept of a people, cannot be thought. Whether one can retrospectively establish historiographical relations between these two is a matter of indifference, since historiographical relations are always only the facade, and for the most part the concealing facade, of historical nexuses. As long as we know with insufficient clarity the proper essence of subjectivity as the modern form of selfhood, we are prey to the error of thinking that the elimination of individualism and of the domination of the individual is ipso facto an overcoming of subjectivity. In distinction to the "individualism" of the nineteenth century, which protected the pluralism and the "value" of the unique and had as its counter-essence the distinctionlessness of the herd, Nietzsche sees the emergence of a new form of humanity, characterized by the "typical."

In a note from the year 1888 (*Wille zur Macht*, 819) Nietzsche says:

"The feeling for and the pleasure in the *nuance* (—the proper modernity), in what is *not* general, goes counter to the drive that has its pleasure and power in the grasp of the *typical* . . ." Nietzsche understands by "type" the subjectivity that, on the basis of the will to power, is installed in unconditioned domination and is hardened in the sense of the "will." The "symptom of the strength" of this subjectivity, i.e., the sign of the drive toward the type, is "the *preference for questionable and frightening things* . . ." (*W.z.M.*, 852). Nietzsche is not "preaching" here an unbridled morality or a special "philosophy" for the Germans, but instead he is thinking, as the thinker he is, beings in their Being. He thinks what *is* in world history, what, because it already is, is only coming.[1] As soon as we cease to interpret Nietzsche's metaphysics according to the bourgeois ideas of the end of the nineteenth century, and instead conceive it within the historical nexus to which it belongs exclusively, i.e., on the basis of its relation to the metaphysics of "objective" idealism and to Western metaphysics as a whole, we recognize that Nietzsche's concept of the "superman" manifests the counter-essence to the "absolute consciousness" of Hegel's metaphysics. But we will understand neither if we have not adequately understood the essence of subjectivity.

The form of the essence of subjectivity includes in itself a mode of the selfhood of man. But not every way of being a self is necessarily subjectivity.[2] As long as we fail to see this, then every time a priority is accorded to the self we will run the risk of misinterpreting it as "subjectivity" or even "subjectivism." The usual presentation of Greek sophistry and Socratism also fell victim to this superficiality of historiographical comparison and amalgamation. Now, insofar as Plato's thinking, as well as Aristotle's metaphysics, already passed through a confrontation with sophistry and Socratism, the selfhood of man and consequently the ground of man's essence received a peculiar privilege at the beginning of metaphysics. This is immediately evident in the way beings, as what appears in unconcealedness, are exclusively determined in relation to perception (νοῦς) and to the ψυχή, the essence of "life." And that leads finally to the proposition asserted by Aristotle in his treatise Περὶ Ψυχῆς (Γ 8, 431b21): ἡ ψυχὴ τὰ ὄντα πώς ἐστι . . . "The soul (the essence of 'life') is in a certain way the beings . . ." That is, in a certain way the Being of beings, as the perceivedness of the perceived, is founded in the "soul." This sounds like a statement from Kant's *Critique of Pure Reason*, according to which the conditions of the possibility of experience are simultaneously the conditions of

---

1. Nietzsche, op. cit. XIV, *W.z.M.* n. 852.
2. See *Sein und Zeit*, § 64.

the possibility of the objects of experience. But Aristotle's thesis *only* sounds like that. Aristotle is not saying that the Being of beings would repose in and consist of representedness by a representing Ego, i.e., as subject of consciousness and of its self-certainty. Of course, the Being of beings, as the Being of what shows itself and appears, is unconcealedness, but unconcealedness still has its essence in *physis*.

Admittedly, Aristotle calls genuine being (Met. α 1) τὰ φανερώτατα πάντων, that which, of all things, is most apparent, in that it has already shown itself in advance in all things and everywhere. But τὰ φανερώτατα πάντων retains the distinguishing determination τὰ τῇ φύσει φανερώτατα πάντων (933b11), that which appears in such a way that its appearance is determined on the basis of self-emergence: φύσις.

Accordingly, at the beginning of metaphysics, both are retained: appearance in the sense of emergence and coming forth and also appearance in the sense of a self-showing to a perception or to a "soul." Here is hidden the reason for the peculiarly unsettling transitional character that marks metaphysics at its beginning and lets it become what it is: on the one hand, with respect to the beginning, the last light of the first beginning, and on the other hand, with respect to its continuation, the inception of the oblivion of the beginning and the start of its concealment. Because the subsequent time interprets Greek thought only in terms of later metaphysical positions, i.e., in the light of a Platonism or Aristoteleanism, and since it thereby interprets Plato as well as Aristotle either in a medieval way, or in a Leibnizian-Hegelian modern way, or even in a neo-Kantian way, therefore it is now nearly impossible to recall the primordial essence of appearance in the sense of emergence, i.e., to think the essence of *physis*. Accordingly, the essential relation between φύσις and ἀλήθεια also remains concealed. To the extent that it is ever referred to, it seems very strange. But if φύσις signifies a coming forth, an emergence, and nothing that one might mean by *ratio* or "nature," and if, then, φύσις is an equiprimordial word for what is named by ἀλήθεια, why then should not Parmenides' didactic poem on ἀλήθεια bear the title περὶ φύσεως, "On the Coming Forth into the Unconcealed"?

We of today only acknowledge slowly and with difficulty the distorting excessiveness of "nature" as a translation of φύσις. But even if we do succeed, we are still far from a transformation of experience and of thinking that might once more bring us into the proximity of the *first beginning*, in order to be closer to the beginning of the *approaching beginning*. Without having in view the essence of φύσις, we will not see what is closest in ἀλήθεια and toward which our thinking is now under way.

b) The fourth directive: the open as the primordial essence of unconcealedness. Reference to *Being and Time* and Sophocles, *Αἴας* V, 646f. Time as letting appear and concealing. Reference to Hölderlin. Time as "factor" in the modern period. The upsurge of the open into unconcealedness. The "identification" of openness and freedom. *'Aλήθεια* as the open of the clearing.

We shall conclude our elucidation of the essence of ἀλήθεια by attempting to follow a fourth directive provided by the translation of ἀλήθεια as "unconcealedness."

Thinking ahead, we can say that the *open* holds sway in the essence of unconcealedness. The word "open" makes us think first of what is not closed off, hence is dis-closed. Thought in this way the open proves to be a consequence of an opening up and a disclosing. For now, let us leave undecided whether or not the open must be the essential ground of disclosedness, providing the possibility of unconcealedness in the first place, rather than merely being its result. Prior to all that, we need to see that the Greeks did in fact experience within the realm of the essence of ἀλήθεια something that made it necessary for them to speak in some way of the open. But nowhere among the Greeks do we find the essential concept of the open. On the contrary, we encounter in the essential domain of ἀλήθεια, and of the Greek thinking of Being, words and names referring only approximately to what we are calling the open.

A simple dictum from Greek poetry may testify to this. In addition, it will again provide us with an opportunity to think in a mysteriously simple way the essential unity of the fundamental Greek words, a unity we have more than once considered in the course of our meditation. The dictum names the relation between concealment and disclosure, appearance and emergence. Thereby it immediately provides the directive that is to guide our present reflection. The dictum expresses simultaneously what could be called a foreword to the saying of the essence of Being.

The dictum deals with "time." In *Being and Time*, time is experienced and named as fore-word for the word "of" Being. The Greek dictum on time occurs in Sophocles' tragedy *Αἴας*, (V, 646f.), and is as follows:

ἅπανθ' ὁ μακρὸς ἀναρίθμητος χρόνος
φύει τ' ἄδηλα καὶ φανέντα κρύπτεται

"The broad, incalculable sweep of time lets emerge everything that is not open as well as concealing (again) in itself what has appeared."

Let us consider this dictum starting from the end. The last word is κρύπτεται. Κρύπτεσθαι means to take back into oneself, to hide back and conceal in oneself. This is the way χρόνος, "time," conceals. "Time" is primordially for the Greeks in every case only the "right" or "wrong" time, the appropriate or inappropriate time. That means each being has *its* time. "Time" is in every case the "time in which" this or that occurs; i.e., it is the "time point," which does not mean the "punctual now" but "point" in the sense of the place, the locality, to which an appearance in its appearing belongs temporally at any "time." "Time" is here not a "series" or "sequence" of indifferent "now-points." Instead, time is something that in its way bears beings, releasing them and taking them back.

"Time" understood in the Greek manner, χρόνος, corresponds in essence to τόπος, which we erroneously translate as "space." *Τόπος* is place, and specifically that place to which something appertains, e.g., fire and flame and air up, water and earth below. Just as τόπος orders the appurtenance of a being to its dwelling place, so χρόνος regulates the appurtenance of the appearing and disappearing to their destined "then" and "when." Therefore time is called μαχρός, "broad," in view of its capacity, indeterminable by man and always given the stamp of the current time, to release beings into appearance or hold them back. Since time has its essence in this letting appear and taking back, number has no power in relation to it. That which dispenses to all beings their time of appearance and disappearance withdraws essentially from all calculation.

The fact that the Greek god who is older than the highest of the Olympic gods, the "ancient father" of Zeus, is called "Kronos," "time," can be appreciated by us only if we realize that the Greek divinities consist in general in a looking and appearing and that "time" is what lets appear and conceals. In the securing essence of the immemorial god "Kronos" repose the "ancient friends" from whom "all power arises" (Hölderlin, "Nature and art, or Saturn and Jupiter," IV, 47).[1] So the primordial essence of time is essentially remote from number, from calculation, and from all "artifices": ἀναρίθμητος.

Admittedly, already among the Greeks, in Aristotle's *Physics*, the essence of time was understood precisely on the basis of "number." That is certainly food for thought, above all because the Aristotelian determination of the essence of χρόνος has dominated the Western understanding of time ever since. Not only in the mathematical formulae of modern physics but in general in all human comportment towards time, time becomes a "factor," i.e., a "worker," that "works" either "against" or "for" man, namely "against" or in "favor" of the calculation by means of which man makes plans to master beings and secure himself in them. In modern terms, time is something man takes into account, and pre-

---

1. Hölderlin WW (Hellingrath), IV, p. 47.

cisely as the empty frame of the progression of occurrences one after the other. Everywhere, not only in physics, time is the "parameter," i.e., the coordinates along which runs (παρά) all measurement (μέτρον) and calculation. Man uses and consumes time like a "factor." As a consequence of this disposition, which consumes and uses up, man constantly has less and less time in spite of all his time-saving, and that is why the saving and economy of time are necessary in even the tiniest procedures of technology. Modern man, the subject to whom the "world" has become a uniquely uniform "object," consumes even time. Modern man therefore always "has" less and less time, because he has taken possession of time in advance only as calculable and has made time something of which he is obsessed, though he is presumably the ruler whose rule masters time. For primordial Greek thinking, on the contrary, time, always as dispensing and dispensed time, takes man and all beings essentially into its ordering and in every case orders the appearance and disappearance of beings. Time discloses and conceals.

Thus time can κρύπτεσθαι, hide back into itself, only what has appeared: φανέντα. Beings, coming into presence and becoming concealed in absence by the "sweep" of time, are understood here in terms of appearance. What appears, however, is what it is only insofar as it comes forth and emerges. Something must therefore be present letting the appearance emerge. Φύσις, φύειν (see above λήθη—myth) is said of the earth, ἡ γῆ φύει—the earth lets come forth. We often, and even correctly, translate φύειν as "growing," but in doing so we must not forget to think this "becoming" and "growing" in the Greek manner as a coming forth, out of concealedness, of the germ and the root from the darkness of the earth into the light of the day. Even now we still say, though to be sure only as a figure of speech: time will bring it out into the light of day; everything needs (in order to come forth) its time. The φύειν of φύσις, the letting come forth and the emergence, lets what emerges appear in the unconcealed.

Admittedly, Sophocles does not use the word ἀλήθεια—unconcealedness—in his dictum about time, the time that hides (κρύπτεσθαι) and lets come forth (φύει). Nor does he say that time lets the concealed come forth, φύει τὰ λαθόντα, but instead he says φύει τὰ ἄδηλα—time lets come forth into appearance that which is determined to appear but is not yet δῆλον: ἄ-δηλον, the un-open. Corresponding to the unopen, as the concealed, is the un-concealed, the openly revealed, i.e., what came forth into the open and appeared in the open. The open dwells in unconcealedness. The open is that closest that we co-intend in the essence of unconcealedness, though without explicitly heeding it or genuinely considering it, let alone grasping its essence in advance so that the presence of this open could order and guide all our experience of beings. We already know the unconcealed and the disclosing (ἀληϑές) have an eminent relation to ἔπος, μῦθος, λόγος, i.e., to the word. Saying and legend are essentially related to φαινόμενον, to that which shows itself in unconcealedness. The disclosive utterance in an assertion is therefore still for Aristotle ἀποφαίνεσθαι—a bringing into appearance. Instead of ἀποφαίνεσθαι Aristotle often says, as did Plato and the earlier philosophers, δηλοῦν—to place into the open.[1] In speaking of unconcealedness (ἀλήθεια), φύσις (emergence into the un-concealed), φαίνεσθαι (appearing and letting appear), κρύπτεσθαι (concealing), and λανθάνειν (being-hidden), what is always named, though for the most part only incidentally, is τὸ δῆλον, that which stands out into the open and therefore is the open.

The essence of unconcealedness provides a directive toward the open and openness. But what are these? Here the Greeks are silent. We find ourselves without support or assistance when it becomes necessary to reflect on the essence of the open pervading ἀλήθεια. This reflection will seem strange to the ordinary view, especially because it shows that the open is by no means first and only a result or consequence of disclo-sure but is itself the ground and the essential beginning of unconcealed-ness. For, to disclose, i.e., to let appear in the open, can only be accom-plished by what gives in advance this open and thus is in itself self-opening and thereby is essentially open, or as we may also say, is of itself already "free." The still concealed essence of the open as the primordial self-opening is "freedom."

By identifying openness with freedom we are linking it with some-thing familiar and thus seem to be making the essence of the open comprehensible. But in fact this is mere semblance, and is even doubly so, insofar as the "identification" of openness and freedom, correctly thought of, grounds a still obscure openness in the essence of freedom, the origin of which is in turn equally obscure. In all metaphysics, the essence of "freedom" is understood in essential relation to the "will," and the freedom of the will is understood as the distinguishing mark of a power of the soul, i.e., understood in terms of human comport-ment. But for us now it is a question of thinking the essence of freedom in essential unity with the most primordial concept of ἀλήθεια, and indeed with a view to elucidating the essence of the open. Thereby we might grasp the freedom man must first attain, in accord with his essence, if he is to be able to let beings be in the open what they are as beings.

The free is the guarantee, the sheltering place, for the Being of beings. The open, as the free, shelters and salvages Being. We ordinarily think of the open, the free, and the vast as conditions of scattering, dispersion, and distraction. The open and its extension into the vastness of the

---

1. Cf. *Sein und Zeit*, §7, which has to be thought in conjunction with §44.

unlimited and limitless are zones without stopping places, where every sojourn loses itself in instability. The open provides no shelter or security. The open is rather the place where what is still undetermined and unresolved plays out, and therefore it is an occasion for erring and going astray. Thus with regard to the open two questions immediately arise. In the first place, as originating in primordial freedom, how is the open supposed to be the originary essence of unconcealedness? Secondly, how can the open be essentially sheltering?

It cannot be denied that the primordial essence of truth, ἀλήθεια, refers to the essence of the open and of openness. Although the Greeks did not explicitly think through and name the open as the essence of ἀλήθεια, yet they experienced it constantly in one regard, namely in the essential form of the lighted and the lighting, and this in turn in the shining of the light that provides brightness. We had incidentally mentioned the open as the lighted when we characterized the δαίμονες and the θεάοντες as ones who look and appear in the light, and we already indicated the connection between clearing and light. The light is the determining radiance, the shining and appearing. "The" light in the eminent sense shines as the light of the sun. On the basis of Plato's "cave allegory" we can immediately gather the connection between sun, light, unconcealedness, and unveiling on the one hand, and between darkness, shadow, concealedness, veiling, and cave on the other.

This reference to the essence of ἀλήθεια in the sense of the open of the clearing and of the light will serve to conclude our elucidation of the Greek experience of the essence of truth. Apparently, then, we need only take a few more steps in order to "explain" this essence of truth in a way that might satisfy even ordinary, i.e., modern, thinking and its demands.

c) Light and looking. The "natural" explanation of truth as lighting in terms of the "visual" Greeks, versus the disclosing look. The perceptual look. Ἀλήθεια: the event in the landscape of the evening that conceals the morning. Θεᾶν-ὁρᾶν and theory.

The light, understood as brightness, first bestows the possibility of the look and therewith the possibility of the encountering look as well as the grasping look. Looking is an act of seeing. Seeing is a power of the eye. Herewith we seem to reach a point that could entirely explain ἀλήθεια as the essence of truth for the Greeks, i.e., lighting and the open as the essence of truth. The Greeks were, as we say, "visual." They grasped the world primarily by the eye, and therefore they "naturally" paid attention to looking and the look. So they had to consider light and brightness. From the lighting and brightness and transparency (διαφανές) of the light there is only a small step to the lighted and the clearing, i.e., precisely to the open and then to the unconcealed as the essential. If we remember the Greeks were visual, and if we think of unconcealedness as openness and clearing, then the essential priority of ἀλήθεια becomes understandable at one stroke. This reference to the basic characteristic of the open in the essence of ἀλήθεια puts us on the path of the "most natural" explanation of ἀλήθεια.

The Greek essence of truth, unconcealedness, the open, the lighted, the clear, is thus explained by the fact that the Greeks were "visual." With this "explanation" we could conclude our discussion of the essence of ἀλήθεια as experienced by the Greeks. Nevertheless, in order to conclude a little more tidily, we must eliminate a minor disturbing moment. It is said that the Greeks were visual, and therefore their interpretation of the world was focused on seeing, on the countenance, and on the light. But why were the Greeks visual? Are not all people visual? Certainly they are, insofar as they have eyes and see. But the familiar characterization of the Greeks is supposed to indicate that for them the eye played a special role. Again we come back to the question, why? One might answer: because there in Greece the light is particularly impressive. But then it would not be the eye as eye but the light that predominates and determines the priority of lighting. Besides, the power of the light is no less dominating in the land of the Egyptians and to a certain degree in the land of the Romans. And there we do not find anything resembling the essence of truth in the sense of ἀλήθεια. But precisely this, one could counter, demonstrates that the Greeks were visual to a special degree. It is simply a given fact. It is something "ultimate" and, as it were, the "substance" of this humanity. Now, it is not at all our intention to deny the "fact" that the Greeks were visual or that in their world the light and seeing played a preeminent role. Yet the question remains, and in spite of all the "facts" is once more to be raised, whether the reference to these facts in the least "explains" the essence of ἀλήθεια and whether such an essence at all allows of being "explained" by "facts" or anything derived from "facts." We might even question still further whether "explaining," with regard to what is essential, brings us at all, and ever could, into a relation with what is essential in the essence. We are hereby approaching the question of the character and the very sense of the meditation we have been pursuing on the essence of ἀλήθεια.

That the Greeks were visual, that they were "eye-people," what does this contribute to an elucidation of the essence of truth as unconcealedness, openness, and clearing? It does not contribute anything, because it cannot have the least significance. That fact can not mean anything, because the factual functioning of the eyes does not give any information, and *cannot* give any information, about the relation of man to beings. What is just an "eye" without the ability to see? We do not

see *because* we have eyes, but we have eyes because we can "see."
But what does it mean to "see"? We understand it, in a very broad
sense, as the foundation for all physical, physiological, and aesthetic
"optics": namely, it is what allows for an immediate encounter with
beings, things, animals, and other people, in the light. Of what help,
however, would any light be, no matter how luminous, and what could
any optical instrument do, no matter how refined and accommodating,
if the power to see did not itself in advance get a being in sight by
means of the visual sense and the medium of the light? Just as the
eye without the ability to see is nothing, so the ability to see, for its
part, remains an "inability" if it does not come into play in an already
established relation of man to visible beings. And how could beings
be supposed to appear to man, if man did not already relate in his
essence to beings as beings? And how could such a relation of man
to beings as such hold sway if man did not stand in a relation to Being?
If man did not already have Being in view, then he could not even
think the nothing, let alone experience beings. And how is man supposed to stand in this relation to Being if Being itself does not address
man and claim his essence for the relation to Being? But what else
is this relation of Being to the essence of man than the clearing and
the open which has lighted itself for the unconcealed? If such clearing
did not come into play as the open of Being itself, then a human eye
could never become and be what it is, namely the way man looks at
the demeanor of the encountering being, the demeanor as a look in
which the being is revealed. Since the primordial essence of truth is
"unconcealedness" (ἀ-λήθεια), and since ἀλήθεια is already in the concealed the open and the self-luminous, therefore the clearing and its
transparency can altogether appear in the form of the lighting of brightness and of its transparency. Only because the essence of Being is ἀλήθεια can the light of the lighting achieve a priority. That is why the
emergence into the open has the character of shining and appearing.
And that is why the perception of what emerges and is unconcealed
is a perception of something shining in the light, i.e., it is seeing and
looking. Only because looking is claimed in this way can the "eye"
receive a priority. It is not because the eye is "sun-like," but it is because
the sun as what is radiant itself is of the light and is of the essence
of ἀλήθεια, that the eye of man can "look" and can become a sign
for the relation of man to the unconcealed in general. Because the essence of truth and of Being is ἀλήθεια, the open, the Greeks could
use the eye to characterize the essential relation of man to beings (i.e.,
ψυχή, the soul) and could speak of the ὄμμα τῆς ψυχῆς, the "eye
of the soul."

The Greeks also speak of a conversation of "the soul" with itself
(λόγος), and the essence of man would consist in the λόγον ἔχειν. If,

consequently, the essence of the "soul" is determined by λόγος, and indeed in a way that is no less essential than the determination by the perceptual look, and if the latter occurs in the lighting of ἀλήθεια, then the λέγειν of the human soul must also be founded by the λόγος which in its essence is nothing else than ἀλήθεια.[1]

The primordial essence of truth is ἀλήθεια not because the Greeks were visual, but instead the Greeks could only be visual because it is ἀλήθεια that determines the relation of their humanity to Being. This and only this, namely that the essence of truth originates as ἀλήθεια, but precisely in such a way as to conceal itself forthwith, is *the event* of the history of the Occident.

According to this essential origination of ἀλήθεια, the Occident [*Abendland*] is the not yet decided or delimited landscape of the earth upon which an evening [*Abend*] is descending, which as evening essentially takes its beginning from the dawn and therefore harbors in itself the morning of this landscape. Because the essence of truth holds sway as ἀλήθεια, the open and lighted determines what appears therein and makes it comply with the essential form of the look that looks into the light. In correspondence to this appearing look, the disclosing perception and grasp of beings, i.e., knowledge, is conceived as a looking and a seeing.

The look of Being, which looks into beings, is in Greek θέα. The grasping look in the sense of seeing is in Greek ὁράω. To see the encountering look, in Greek θεᾶν-ὁρᾶν, is θεοράω—θεωρεῖν, θεωρία. The word "theory" means, conceived simply, the perceptual relation of man to Being, a relation man does not produce, but rather a relation into which Being itself first posits man.

To be sure, when later ages and we of today say "theory" and "theoretical," everything primordial has been forgotten. The "theoretical" is a product of the human representational subject. The "theoretical" is the "merely" theoretical. The "theoretical" must, in order to justify its "truth claims" first prove itself by "praxis." Without such proof a relation to "reality" is denied it. Even where, within certain limits, a significance proper to the theoretical is acknowledged, one is calculating that a day will arrive in which it could be applied "practically," a view of its usefulness that subsequently justifies the prior "merely" theoretical comportment as unavoidable. But it is the practical, i.e., success and performance, that is the standard and the justification of the theoretical. Already four decades ago the Americans established this doctrine as the philosophy of "pragmatism." By this "philosophy" the Occident will neither be redeemed nor saved. The Greeks, however, who alone

---

1. On the Logos of Heraclitus, see *Gesamtausgabe Bd.* 55, pp. 185-402, as well as the epilogue of the editor, II, p. 405.

are the custodians of the beginning of the Occident, experienced immediately in θεωρία an essential relation to the θεάοντες, to the θεῖον, and to the δαιμόνιον. Therefore the Greeks do not first need to impute to θεωρία a practical "value" in order to justify its "truth claims" or in order to justify it over and against the suspicion that it is something "merely" theoretical, devalued as something "merely" abstract running about like some horror. With such a removal of the "theoretical," as the "abstract," from θέα, from the look of Being, can we then be surprised at "atheism," which circulates not only among "freethinkers" and within the "atheistic movement"?

That the basic Greek experience of Being is θεωρία does not testify first and foremost to the priority of seeing and looking but testifies above all to the primordial holding sway of the essence of ἀλήθεια, in which there dwells something like the clearing, the lighted, and the open. Insofar as we follow this directive from the essence of unconcealedness and think the open, our meditation on the essence of ἀλήθεια is indeed not at its end but is only now first brought to its beginning.

d) The open at the beginning of the meditation on the word
ἀλήθεια. Essential thinking: the leap into Being. Unconcealed
beings in the security of the groundlessness of the open (the free)
of Being. The concealment of the decision of the bestowal on man
of unconcealedness in the securing open. The entitlement, through
the bestowal of Being, to see the open: a historical beginning. The
alienation of man from the open.

The beginning requires of us, whose history has proceeded from the beginning, a reflection on the essence of the "open." In naming "the open" and using the word "openness," we seem to be representing something known and understandable. But, on the contrary, everything is blurred in the indeterminate—that is, unless we now take the word "open" seriously and think it exclusively within the essential nexus our meditation on the essence of ἀλήθεια has brought closer to us. We shall thus use the locution "the open" only in its indissoluble essential unity with ἀλήθεια and with the essence of ἀλήθεια as primordially experienced.

In this context, the open is the light of the self-luminous. We name it "the free" and its essence "freedom." "Freedom" has a primordial sense here, alien to metaphysical thinking. We might be inclined to elucidate the essence of freedom, thought here as the essence of the open, on the basis of the traditional delimitation of the various concepts of freedom. For we would be tempted to draw closer to the essence of what we are calling "the open" by approaching it gradually through our ordinary representations.

A way that is open we call free. Entrance and passage are granted. These show themselves as spaciousness. What can be traversed is known to us as the spaciousness of spaces, as their dimensional essence, an essence we also ascribe to time—by speaking of a "span of time" for instance. This represents what we presumably first encounter in naming the "open": an unclosed and unoccupied extension prepared for the reception and distribution of objects.

Yet the open in the sense of the essence of ἀλήθεια does not mean either space or time as usually intended, nor their unity, space-time, because all that already had to borrow its openness from the openness holding sway in the essence of disclosedness. Similarly, everywhere that something is "free of . . ." in the sense of "exempt from . . .," or is "free for . . ." in the sense of "ready to . . .," a freedom already comes to presence out of the freedom that first releases even space-time as an "open," traversable, extension and spread. The "free of" and the "free for" already require a clearing in which a detachment and a dona- tion constitute a more original freedom that cannot be grounded on the freedom of human comportment.

Hence we will never arrive at the open, as the essence of *aletheia*, simply by stretching the open in the sense of the "extended" or in the sense of the "free" as commonly understood, stretching it into a gigantic container encompassing everything. Strictly speaking, the essence of the open reveals itself only to a thinking that attempts to think Being itself in the way that it is presaged to our destiny in the history of the West as what is to be thought in the name and essence of ἀλήθεια. Every person in history knows Being immediately, though without ac- knowledging it as such. But as undeniable as is the immediacy of this knowledge of Being, that is also how rarely the thinking of Being suc- ceeds or even commences. It is not that this thinking is difficult and would require special arrangements in order to be carried out. If we may speak of a difficulty here, it consists in the fact that to think Being is very simple, but that the simple is for us the most arduous.

To think Being does not require a solemn approach and the preten- sion of arcane erudition, nor the display of rare and exceptional states as in mystical raptures, reveries, and swoonings. All that is needed is simple wakefulness in the proximity of any random unobtrusive being, an awakening that all of a sudden sees that the being "is."

The awakening for this "it is" of a being, and above all the remaining awake for the "it is," and the watching over the clearing of beings—that constitutes the essence of essential thinking. The "it is" of beings, Being, shows itself, if it does show itself, in each case only "suddenly"—in Greek ἐξαίφνης, i.e., ἐξαφανής, the way that something irrupts into appearance, from non-appearance. To this essentially unmediated and immediate irruption of Being into beings, which in turn only then appear as beings, there corresponds on the part of man a comportment that no longer adverts to beings but suddenly thinks Being. To think Being requires in each instance a leap, a leap into the groundless from the habitual ground upon which for us beings always rest. It is as the groundless that the free comes to light, and that is how we name it, provided we think nothing more of a being than its "it is."

This genuine thinking occurs "by leaps," for it ignores the bridges and railings and ladders of explanation, which always only derives beings from beings, since it remains on the "soil" of "facts." This ground is full of cracks. It never bears. For every being to which we adhere to the exclusion of all else bears only as a consequence of an oblivion of Being, wherein nevertheless the being is present. Being, however, is not a ground but is the groundless. It is called such because it is primordially detached from a "soil" and "ground" and does not require them. Being, the "it is" of a being, is never autochthonous in beings, as if Being could be extracted from beings and then stood upon them as on its ground. It is only beings in relation to beings that are autochthonous. Being, the never autochthonous, is the groundless. This seems to be a lack, though only if calculated in terms of beings, and it appears as an abyss in which we founder without support in our relentless pursuit of beings. In fact we surely fall into the abyss, we find no ground, as long as we know and seek a ground only in the form of a being and hence never carry out the leap into Being or leave the familiar landscape of the oblivion of Being. This leap requires no digressions or formalities. For everywhere and always and in the closest proximity to the most inconspicuous beings there already dwells the openness of the possibility of explicitly thinking the "it is" of beings as the free, in the clearing of which beings appear as unconcealed. The open, to which every being is liberated as if to its freedom, is Being itself. Everything unconcealed is as such secured in the open of Being, i.e., in the groundless.

The groundless, originally freed from every ground and its cracks, is what secures primordially; though to be sure it does not secure in the sense of a sanctuary man might hunt out somewhere within beings and arrange for himself. The security of the open does not provide a place of refuge through which man could acquit himself of his essence. The open itself secures the essential abode of man, provided man and only he is that being to whom Being illuminates itself. Being, as the open, secures in itself every kind of unconcealedness of beings. Hence, in securing, the secure open also conceals the primordial decision by which Being bestows on man unconcealedness, i.e., the truth of beings as a whole. The character of this bestowal hides and secures the way historical man belongs within the bestowal of Being, i.e., the way this order entitles him to acknowledge Being and to be the only being among all beings to see the open. A decision on this entitlement is rarely made. It is made every time the essence of truth, the openness of the open, is determined primordially. And that is a beginning of history. Indeed, historical man, insofar as he is, always belongs within the bestowal of Being. Man, and only he, constantly sees into the open, in the sense of the free, by which the "it is" liberates each being to itself and on the basis of this liberation looks at man in his guardianship of the open. Although man and only he constantly sees into the open, i.e., encounters beings in the free of Being, in order to be struck by them, yet he is not thereby already entitled to bring Being itself explicitly into its ownmost, i.e., to bring it into the open (the free), i.e., to poetize Being, to think it, and to say it. Because only unconcealed beings can appear and do appear in the open of Being, man adheres, at first unwittingly and then constantly, to these beings. He forgets Being and in such forgetting learns nothing more than the overlooking of Being and alienation from the open.

e) The open in the form of the unrestrained progression of beings. The open: the free of the clearing. The "open" of the "creature" in Rilke's eighth Duino Elegy. Reference to Schopenhauer and Nietzsche. The exclusion of the animal from the strife between unconcealedness and concealedness. The excitability of what is alive.

Being, from whose bestowal man cannot withdraw, even in the most extreme oblivion of Being, does, however, flow away from man into the indeterminate totality of beings as a consequence of his alienation from ἀλήθεια. In this way Being is identified without distinction with beings or else is cast aside as an empty concept. The distinction of all distinctions and the beginning of all distinguishing, i.e., the distinction between Being and beings, is then completely effaced and with human assistance is rejected without misgivings into heedlessness through a disregard for what is properly to be thought, rejected in the uncanny manner of oblivion and thoughtlessness. But Being remains—in the hardly considered manner of beings as a whole—and obtains its sense from an interpretation based in every case, though in various ways, on the privileged domain of beings. "Being" becomes a mere word-sound concealing what has withdrawn and been closed off, whereas it is precisely the opening open.

Beings proceed from and into beings. Only this progression "is," but it "is" only with the oblivion of the "is" itself and its essence. This unlimited progression of beings, one after the other and one into the other, counts as "Being." This unlimited progression of beings into beings refers then to the "open," in the sense in which we speak of "open water" when we are on the high seas and all borders of land disappear.

This is how Rilke, in the eighth Duino elegy, understands "the open." The "open" is for him the constant progression by beings themselves, from beings to beings within beings. The open as the unlimited progression of beings remains bound to this and so is chained to the ground. The open of the unrestrained progression of beings never arrives at the free of Being, and it is precisely this free that the "creature" never sees; for the capacity to see it constitutes what is essentially distinct about man and consequently forms the unsurmountable essential boundary between animal and man. "The open" in the sense of the unceasing progression of beings into beings and "the open" in the sense of the free of the clearing of Being in distinction from all beings are verbally the same, but in what the words name they are so different that no oppositional formulation could suffice to indicate the gap between them. For oppositions, even the most extreme, still require one same domain in which to be posed against each other. Precisely this is missing here. The metaphysics lying at the foundation of the biologism of the nineteenth century and of psychoanalysis, namely the metaphysics of the complete oblivion of Being, is the source of an ignorance of all laws of Being, the ultimate consequence of which is an uncanny hominization of the "creature," i.e., the animal, and a corresponding animalization of man. This is an assertion about the metaphysical foundation of a poetizing, an assertion carried out from the standpoint of thinking.

It could then be objected that this is to hale poetry in an unauthorized way before the court of philosophy. If philosophy and poetry were simply two different human occupations, existing each in itself and distinct by their very essence, then what we have been saying could be condemned as nonsense. But what if the essence of thinking and the essence of poetizing were to receive again their originary entitlements! And what if this could only occur insofar as the binding character of the word and of speech had to be decided primordially and had to be taken into human care? Here our concern is only to block the danger of a thoughtless confusion of similar verbal sounds. The following remarks on Rilke's poetry must be understood within the limits of this intention.

What Rilke, especially in the eighth of his Duino elegies, calls "the open" has only the sound and the vocalization in common with what the thinking of the essence of ἀλήθεια conceives in the word "open." A brief elucidation of what Rilke says about the "open" can help us consider more steadfastly the "open" as thought within the essential domain of ἀλήθεια, by decisively setting it off against the words of Rilke. It will also serve to make our meditation on ἀλήθεια more precise.

Rilke speaks of the "open" especially in the eighth of his Duino elegies, dedicated, significantly, to Rudolf Kassner. It is not our intention to present a comprehensive interpretation of this elegy, for that is not necessary. What is necessary is only an unequivocal indication of how Rilke's word about the "open" is distinct in all respects from the "open" as essentially connected to ἀλήθεια and to thoughtful questioning. The eighth Duino elegy begins:

> With all eyes the creature sees
> the open. Only our eyes are
> reversed and placed wholly around creatures
> as traps, around their free exit.
> What *is* outside we know from the animal's
> visage alone . . .

The first verses of the elegy immediately say to whom it is given to see "the open" and to whom it is not. The eyes of the "creature" and "our" eyes, i.e., human eyes, are opposed in this respect. What then does "creature" mean here? *Creatura*, from *creare*, means "what is made." *Creator* is the maker. *Creatio*, creation, is a biblical-Christian fundamental determination of beings. *Omne ens est qua ens creatum,*[1] with the exception of the uncreated creator himself, the *summum ens.* *Creatura* in the sense of *ens creatum* therefore *includes* man. According to the biblical narrative of creation, man is the *creatura* formed last. Thus *creatura* means "creation," i.e., the created world as a whole, in which man is included as the "crown of creation." It is in this sense that the word *creatura* occurs in the famous medieval *sequentia, Dies irae, dies illa*, a poem written by Thomas of Celano in the first half of the thirteenth century. He is the one who also wrote the celebrated biography of St. Francis of Assisi.

The fourth strophe of the *Dies irae*, which perhaps some of you have heard in Verdi's composition, is as follows:

> *Mors stupebit et natura*
> *cum resurget creatura*
> *Iudicanti responsura.*

> Death benumbs all that emerges
> when creatures rise
> to answer to their judge.

Now if Rilke places "creatures" in opposition to man, and this opposition is the exclusive theme of the eighth elegy, then the word "creatures" cannot mean *creatura* in the sense of the whole of creation. The

---

1. "Every being, as a being, is something made."—Tr.

unambiguous delimitation of this word in Rilke's language demands an interpretation of the "Duino elegies" as unitary, and specifically in their connection with the "Sonnets to Orpheus," which often are still farther reaching. But now is not the occasion to attempt it, and, in addition, the "hermeneutic presuppositions" are still lacking, and they must be drawn from Rilke's poetry itself.

The word "creatures" in Rilke's poetry refers to creatures in the stricter sense, i.e., "living beings," excluding man. This use of the word "creature" and "created being" does not refer to the creation of the creator, in the manner of Christian faith, but instead "creature" and "created being" are names for the living beings that, in distinction from the living being endowed with reason, man, are peculiarly "helpless" and "wretched." The "creature" is above all the "animal."[1] Once more it should be emphasized that "creature" is not being distinguished here from the creator and therefore is not put into relation to God by means of such a distinction. Instead, the creature is the a-rational living being in distinction from the rational. But Rilke does not take the "a-rational creature" according to the usual view, as lower, i.e., less potent, compared to the higher, more potent, human being. Rilke inverts the relation of the power of man and of "creatures" (i.e., animals and plants). This inversion is what is poetically expressed by the elegy. The inversion of the relation in rank of man and animal is carried out with regard to that which both these "living beings" are respectively capable of in terms of the "open." The "open" is accordingly that which pervades both and all beings. Is it therefore Being itself? To be sure. So everything hinges on this, that we reflect on the "sense" in which the Being of beings is experienced and spoken of here. The "open" is not without relation to $\dot{\alpha}\lambda\dot{\eta}\vartheta\varepsilon\iota\alpha$, if this is the still hidden essence of Being. How could it be otherwise? Yet the "open" according to the word of Rilke and the "open" thought as the essence and truth of $\dot{\alpha}\lambda\dot{\eta}\vartheta\varepsilon\iota\alpha$ are distinct in the extreme, as far apart as the beginning of Western thought and the completion of Western metaphysics—and nevertheless they precisely belong together—the same.

---

1. See the "little" creature, the bug, and the "great" bird, the bat. See letter to L. Salome 1.III, 1912, from Duino: "animal" and "angel" (R. M. Rilke, *Briefe aus den Jahren 1907 zu 1914*. Ed. Ruth Sieber-Rilke and Carl Sieber, Leipzig 1933. Letter to Lou Andreas Salomé from Duino on March 1, 1912, p. 221ff., especially p. 212.)

For Rilke, human "consciousness," reason, $\lambda\acute{o}\gamma o\varsigma$, is precisely the limitation that makes man less potent than the animal. Are we then supposed to turn into "animals"? See letter from Muzot on August 11, 1924, p. 282: "Counterweights." See The Naming of the Birds, the Child, the Beloved. (Rainer Maria Rilke, *Briefe aus Muzot*. Ed. Ruth Sieber-Rilke and Carl Sieber. Leipzig 1935. Letter from Muzot to Nora Purtscher-Wydenbruk on August 11, 1924, p. 277ff.)

With all eyes the creature sees
the open. Only our eyes . . .

do not see the open, not immediately. Man sees the open so little that
he is in need of the animal in order to see it. The fifth and sixth verses
say clearly:

What *is* outside we know from the animal's
visage alone . . .

What Rilke means by the open cannot be understood or even properly questioned unless we see clearly that the poet is making a distinction between the animal or a-rational living being on the one side and
man on the other. Guardini, on the contrary, interprets this elegy as
if, on the basis of the relation of the "creature"—we should say *ens
creatum*—to the "open," the poem is a sort of proof for the existence
of a creating God.

The opposition of animal and man, a-rational and rational living
being, is a distinction whose primordial form is to be sought among
the Greeks. We are already familiar with this distinction from our previous remarks. Man is accordingly τὸ ζῷον λόγον ἔχον, that which
emerges out of itself and in this emerging, and for its relation to the
emerged, "has the word." The "animal," on the contrary, is that self-
emergent to which the word is denied—ζῷον ἄ-λογον. The essence
of speech, however, is for the Greeks and still for Plato and Aristotle
τὸ ἀποφαίνεσθαι—the letting appear of the unconcealed as such, which
both philosophers express as τὸ δηλοῦν, the revealing of the open. Because he has the word, man, and he alone, is the being that looks
into the open and sees the open in the sense of the ἀληθές. The animal,
on the contrary, does not see the open, never does, not with a single
one of all its eyes. Now the start of Rilke's eighth elegy says exactly
the opposite. Does Rilke thereby bring about a reversal of the Western
metaphysical determination of man and animal in their relation to the
open?

The problem is that, as a fundamental condition of the essence of
a reversal ("revolution"), whatever it is with respect to which the reversal takes place must remain the same and must be held fast as the
same. And in the present case this condition does not obtain. For the
open meant by Rilke is not the open in the sense of the unconcealed.
Rilke knows and suspects nothing of ἀλήθεια, no more than Nietzsche
does. Accordingly, Rilke is bound within the limits of the traditional
metaphysical determination of man and animal. Specifically, Rilke takes
over the form of this determination that arose in the modern age and

was solidified in the nineteenth and twentieth centuries: from the Greek ζῷον λόγον ἔχον to the *animal rationale*. This essential determination of man as the "rational living being" is just as distant from the Greek one as *veritas* and *certitudo* are from ἀλήθεια. As *animal rationale*, man is the "animal" that calculates, plans, turns to beings as objects, represents what is objective and orders it. Man comports himself everywhere to objects, i.e., to what stands over and against him. This implies man himself is the "subject," the being that, positing itself on itself, disposes of its objects and in that way secures them for itself. Rilke always thinks of man in this modern metaphysical sense. That current metaphysical conception of man is the presupposition for Rilke's poetic attempt to interpret the essence of man in the sense of modern biological metaphysics. Man is the living being that, by way of representation, fastens upon objects and thus looks upon what is objective, and, in looking, orders objects, and in this ordering posits back upon himself the ordered as something mastered, as his possession.

The concluding part of the elegy expresses all this unequivocally, and thereby attests that the distinction between man and animal, or more precisely the interpretation of the human being on the basis of the animal, is the all-encompassing theme of the poem:

> And we: spectators always and everywhere,
> to whom all is turned and never out there!
> We are flooded with it. We order it. It breaks down.
> We order it again and we break down ourselves.

The decisive words of these verses resound: ". . . and never out there!" —i.e., never into the "open" the "creatures" "see with all their eyes," for we can know about the "out there" and about what is "outside" "from the animal's visage alone." What does Rilke then mean by the "open"? According to the obvious meaning, when we think of the "open," we think of something opened versus something closed. And what is open and opened is "a space." The open refers to the essential domain of space even if we think of it as what has been brought into the light, in the sense of the disclosed and unconcealed. On the path of the thinking that thinks ἀλήθεια in its essence we will arrive at the point at which we will have to ask about the relation between the unconcealed and space. Must we think the unconcealed on the basis of the essence of what is spatial, or is what is spatial and all space founded in the essence of ἀλήθεια as primordially experienced? In any case, the open refers to what is spatial. Rilke's talk about the "never out there" and the "what is outside" also refers to this domain. Moreover, the elegy says:

We never have, not even for one single day,
the pure space before us in which the flowers
infinitely emerge.

"Infinitely" here means "endlessly," "without stopping at a limit," and also means "as a whole." "Emerge," of course, does not refer here to what the Greeks think by φύειν but means the "mergence" through which, for example by dissolving sugar in water, the emergent is merged and assumed up into the whole of the air and all cosmic relations. This e-merging is possible because there is nothing standing over and against the "living being" (plant or animal) as object, turning the living being back on itself and forcing it into re-flection. The all-determining and all-encompassing basic meaning of the word "open" for Rilke is the limitless, the infinite, wherein living beings breathe and unrestrainedly dissolve into the irresistible causal nexuses of nature, in order to float in this infinity. In accordance with that limitless realm, Rilke names the animal "the free animal." To what extent Rilke can say: "With all eyes the creature sees the open," and to what extent "the open" is "so deep in the face of the animal," that is what the poet must justify poetically.

We need to clarify first of all the meaning of "seeing" here. Rilke says of "our eyes" that they would be "reversed." They do not go away into the objectless domain, but instead, in the very representing of the object, they are doubled back by that object onto themselves in the opposite direction. If our eyes therefore look at a creature, it is caught as an object by our representing; the "free exit" of the look of the creature into the open is suspended and distorted by our objectification. Our eyes are "traps" for the look of the animal, traps which catch its look and hold it fast. These traps close, occlude, and debar the open, the meaning of which is expressed most readily in the term "open water." This is reached when all borders of land have disappeared. The open is the absence of borders and limits, the objectless, not thought as lack but as original whole of reality, in which the creature is immediately admitted and let free.

Man, on the contrary, is forced into a relation to objects, with himself as the subject, a relation that posits the whole of what Rilke calls the open and at the same time occludes it whenever this relation arises. According to Rilke the animal sees more than man does, for the animal's gaze is not trammeled by any objects but can go on infinitely, in some unknown way, into the objectless. The animal "has before itself" the limitless. It never encounters a limit on its path, hence not even death. The animal is "free from death" as it goes on into the limitless; its advance is never doubled back, as is the case with human representing, and it never sees what is behind itself. The limitless as a whole can also be called "God" in a loose way of speaking. So in this elegy Rilke says:

> the free animal
> has its perishing constantly behind itself,
> and in front of itself God, and when it moves it moves
> in eternity, just as wells do.

This all sounds very strange and yet is only a poetic form of the popular biological metaphysics of the end of the nineteenth century. There, and in fact ever since Descartes, man's representing is called a consciousness of objects, one that is conscious of itself and is reflected onto itself. And so the comportment of the animal is unselfconscious and in that sense is an unconscious pressing and driving of the instincts out into a direction not "objectively" determined.

The priority of the unconscious over consciousness corresponds to the priority of the free animal over the imprisoned essence of man. The spirit of Schopenhauer's philosophy, mediated by Nietzsche and the doctrines of psychoanalysis, looms behind this poetry. Although Nietzsche's metaphysics with regard to the doctrine of the will to power remains outside the compass of Rilke's poetry, there still holds sway the one decisive common element: the essence of man as conceived on the basis of the essence of the animal. Here it is poetized, there thought. From a purely metaphysical viewpoint, i.e., with regard to the interpretation of beings as rational or irrational, the domain of Rilke's basic poetic experience is not at all distinct from the basic position of Nietzsche's thinking. Both are as remote as possible from the essence of truth as ἀλήθεια, just as was the metaphysics of the modern and medieval periods. Yet modern metaphysics, in unity with medieval-Christian metaphysics, reposes on the same ground, namely the Roman transformation of the metaphysics of Plato and Aristotle, and so it is easy to see in Rilke's poetry the last offshoot of modern metaphysics, in the sense of a secularized Christianity, and to show that the secularized is precisely only an epiphenomenon of the original Christian phenomenon. Such an interpretation makes Rilke's poetry appear to be some sort of derailed Christianity, badly in need of succor, and such apologetics risks flying in the face of the expressed word and will of the poet.

Now, we could reply that we are not interested in a Christian apologetic exploitation of the poetry of Rilke. We also reject any attempt to apply to poetry the measuring rod of a "philosophy." We adhere only to the poetical-artistic word. This is certainly an authentic attitude and one that does justice to the poet. But it leaves one question unasked, namely, to what does the poetical word properly oblige us? This question has its ground in a still more essential question: which truth is proper to poetry as poetry? The mere appeal to personal lived experiences and impressions, which is implied in the appeal to the poet himself as the ultimate support of the validity of his word, is here too little, i.e., it is nothing at all in an age in which not only the being or nonbeing of a people is to be decided, but where, prior to that, the essence and the truth of being and nonbeing themselves, and nothing less, are at stake. In this way it could be more important, i.e., more objective, to insert Rilke's poetry into the tradition of Christian consciousness rather than deliver it over to the subjective "experiences" of a perplexed individual.

Our thinking would be too narrow and too oblique if we were to defend the view that by referring to the "open" in Rilke we are measuring his poetry against the yardstick of philosophical concepts, in order to judge it or even condemn it according to that measure. To be sure, Rilke's word about the "open" would then be brought into relation with the essential sphere of ἀλήθεια. The question is whether this is only a so-called philosophical concept or whether in the course of our reflection it has become clear that ἀλήθεια names an event in whose compass even Rilke's word about the "open" belongs, just as does every occidental word that speaks of Being and truth, a speaking that may still experience and know this event or long since have forgotten its last tremors.

There is, of course, a gaping abyss between what Rilke names the open and "the open" in the sense of the unconcealedness of beings. The "open" that dwells in ἀλήθεια first lets beings emerge and come to presence as beings. Man alone sees this open. More specifically, man gets a glimpse of this open while comporting himself, as he always does, to beings, whether these beings are understood in the Greek sense as what emerges and comes to presence, or in the Christian sense as *ens creatum*, or in the modern sense as objects. In his comportment to beings, man in advance sees the open by dwelling within the opening and opened project of Being. Without the open, which is how Being itself comes to presence, beings could be neither unconcealed nor concealed. Man and he alone sees into the open—though without beholding it. Only the essential sight of authentic thinking beholds Being itself. But even there the thinker can behold Being only because he as man has already glimpsed it.

The animal, on the contrary, does not glimpse or see into, and certainly does not behold, the open in the sense of the unconcealedness of the unconcealed. Therefore neither can an animal relate to the closed as such, no more than it can comport itself to the concealed. The animal is excluded from the essential domain of the strife between unconcealedness and concealedness. The sign of this essential exclusion is that no animal or plant "has the word."

This reference to the exclusion of the animal from the essential domain of unconcealedness introduces us to the enigmatic character of all living beings. For the animal is related to his circle of food, prey, and sex in a way essentially different from the way the stone is related to the earth upon which it lies. In those living things characterized as plant or animal we find the peculiar arousal of excitability, by which the living being is "excited," i.e., stirred to an emerging into a circle of stimulatability on the basis of which it draws other living things into the circle of its activity. No excitability or stimulatability of plants and animals ever brings them into the free in such a way that what is excited could ever let the exciting "be" what it is even merely as exciting, not to mention what it is before the excitation and without it. Plant and animal are suspended in something outside of themselves without ever being able to "see" either the outside or the inside, i.e., to have it stand as an aspect unconcealed in the free of Being. And never would it be possible for a stone, no more than for an airplane, to elevate itself toward the sun in jubilation and to move like a lark, which nevertheless does not see the open. What the lark "sees," and how it sees, and what it is we here call "seeing" on the basis of our observation that the lark has eyes, these questions remain to be asked. In fact, an original poetizing capacity would be needed to surmise what is concealed to the living being, a poetic capacity to which more and higher things are charged, and more essential things (since they are genuinely essential), versus a mere hominization of plants and animals. But in metaphysics man too is experienced as a living thing and as an "animal" in a larger sense, on the basis of reasons referring back to the way Being itself primordially reveals itself.

Since, in metaphysics, man is experienced and thought of as the rational animal, animality is then interpreted, against the measuring rod of rationality, as what is irrational and without reason, i.e., interpreted against human intellectuality as what is instinctual. In this way, in metaphysics and in its scientific repercussions, the mystery of the living being goes unheeded; for living beings are either exposed to the assault of chemistry or are transferred to the field of "psychology." Both presume to seek the riddle of life. They will never find it; not only because every science adheres only to the penultimate and must presuppose the ultimate as the first, but also because the riddle of life will never be found where the mystery of the living being has already been abandoned.

Since Rilke's poetry, too, neither experiences nor respects the essential limits between the mystery of the living being (plant or animal) and the mystery of the historical being, i.e., man, his poetical words never attain the mountain height of a historically foundational decision. It is almost as if in this poetry there is operative an unlimited and ground-less hominization of the animal, by which the animal, with respect to the original experience of beings as a whole, is even raised above man and becomes in a certain way a "super-man":

What *is* outside we know from the animal's
visage alone . . .

Who are they who speak here in the "we"? The "we" are moderns of modern metaphysics, a humanity that, as regards an essential experi-ence of Being, has erred into the dead end of the oblivion of Being.

Rilke's poetry often relates to contemporary man with much serious-ness and care, though with no less an amount of confusion, thoughtless-ness, and flight. Rilke relishes word-forms but does not consider *the* word. He talks thoughtlessly about the "open" and does not question what the significance might be of the openness of the open, whether it only refers to an endless progression of unlimited objects or whether in the word of the "open" unconcealedness is thought, the uncon-cealedness that first releases objects into an objectivity as the free, with-out which not even the nothing could rise up in its excessiveness and brandish its menace.

"What *is* outside" and what "*is*" at all, be it "outside" or "inside," or in no "space," we only know on the basis of a knowledge of Being, which itself comes to presence as the free, and in its clearing beings find an access to unconcealedness and thereby an elevation to appear-ance, and thereby the order of presencing.

§9 Θεά—'Αλήθεια. *The looking of Being into the open lighted by it. The directive within the reference to the word of Parmenides: the thinker's journey to the home of ἀλήθεια and his thinking out to-ward the beginning. The saying of the beginning in the language of the Occident.*

We might now perhaps be able to see some things more clearly. The open holding sway in the essence of ἀλήθεια is difficult to behold not only because it is the closest but because it illuminates and thereby first bestows the closest, all that is close, and the far as well.

But this difficulty in beholding the open is only a sign that what could come within our essential regard might also be deprived by us of its arrival, due to our lacking the entitlement for that which has already bestowed itself on us as Being itself but which thereby also withdraws ever anew, without our surmising that event.

Nevertheless, we can now perhaps think and retain this one simple thing, namely: ἀλήθεια is the looking of Being into the open that is lighted by it itself as it itself, the open for the unconcealedness of all appearance. Could what has such an essence be a mere "concept"? The endeavor of our entire foregoing reflection has been nothing else than to bring us to a thoughtful experience of this astonishing question.

'Αλήθεια is θεά, goddess—but indeed only for the Greeks and even then only for a few of their thinkers. The truth: a goddess for the Greeks in the Greek sense. Indeed.

But what is the essence of truth *for us*? We do not know, because we neither comprehend the essence of truth nor do we comprehend ourselves, and we do not know who we ourselves are. Perhaps this double ignorance about the truth and about ourselves is itself one and the same. But it is already good to know this ignorance, and precisely for the sake of Being, to which the reverence of thinking belongs. Thinking is not knowing, but perhaps it is more essential than knowing, because it is closer to Being in that closeness which is concealed from afar. We do not know the essence of truth. Therefore it is necessary for us to ask about it and to be pressed toward this question so as to experience the minimal condition that must be fulfilled if we set out to dignify the essence of truth with a question. This condition is that we take up thinking.

Our attempted reflection has been accompanied by *one* insight. It is this: we may think the essence of truth only if we tread upon the most extreme edges of beings as a whole. We thereby acknowledge that a moment of history is approaching, whose uniqueness is by no means determined simply, or at all, on the basis of the current situation of the world and of our own history in it. What is at stake is not simply the being and non-being of our historical people, nor the being and not-being of a "European culture," for in these instances what is at stake is only beings. In advance of all that, a primordial decision must be made concerning Being and not-being themselves, Being and not-being in their essence, in the truth of their essence. How are beings supposed to be saved and secured in the free of their essence, if the essence of Being is undecided, unquestioned, and even forgotten?

Without the truth of Being, beings are never steadfast; without the truth of Being and without the Being and essence of truth the very decision about the Being and non-being of a being remains without the openness of freedom, from which all history begins.

The question returns: what is the essence of truth for us? Our lectures were only supposed to refer to the region out of which the word of Parmenides speaks.

The directive within this reference pointed to the destination toward which the primordial thinker is under way, namely the home of the goddess 'Aλήθεια. This home also directs the course of the thinker's genuine experience. The home of the goddess is the first place of arrival on the journey of thinking and it is also the point of departure for the course of thinking that bears out all relations to beings. The essence of this home is wholly determined by the goddess. Her dwelling there first makes the home the home it is. And in dwelling the "essence" of the goddess is fulfilled. She is the self-presenting and hence indwelling look of the light into the darkness. 'Aλήθεια is the disclosedness that in itself shelters all emergence and all appearance and disappearance. 'Aλήθεια is the essence of the true: the truth. Truth dwells in everything that comes to presence; it is the essence of all essence: essentiality [*Diese west in allem Wesenden und ist das Wesen alles "Wesens": die Wesenheit*].

To experience this is the destiny of the primordial thinker. His thinking knows in essentiality the essence of truth (not just the essence of the true) as the truth of the essence.

As the essence of emergence (φύσις), ἀλήθεια is the beginning itself. The journey to the home of the goddess is a thinking out toward the beginning. The thinker thinks the beginning insofar as he thinks ἀλήθεια. Such recollection is thinking's single thought. This thought, as the dictum of the thinker, enters into the word and language of the Occident.

This language expresses the essence of history, and history, because it is the sending of Being and because Being only comes to light unexpectedly, is appropriated always in the unexpectedness of the primordiality of the beginning. The history attuned to the primordial essence of the clearing of Being destines beings ever again to the destiny of decline in long-enduring concealments. According to this destiny, decline now holds sway, the evening of what emerged primordially.

The land drawn into its space-time from this history and sheltered therein is the Occident [*Abend-land*, literally, "evening-land"] according to the primordial (i.e., in terms of the history of Being) meaning of this word.

The language of the Occident expresses the beginning, i.e., the still concealed essence of the truth of Being. The word of the language of the Occident preserves the appurtenance of Occidental humanity to the home region of the goddess ἀλήθεια.

ADDENDUM

[Heidegger prepared the following draft of a recapitulation of pages 77–79 but did not include it in his lectures.—Ed.]

Modern man has a "lived experience" of the world and thinks the world in those terms, i.e., in terms of himself as the being that, as ground, lies at the foundation of all explanation and ordering of beings as a whole. In the language of metaphysics what lies at the foundation is *subjectum*. Modern man is by essence the "subject." Only because he is the "subject" can his I or his Ego become essential. And the fact that a Thou is set in opposition to the I, thereby relegating the I to its limits and raising the I-Thou relation to prominence, and the fact that the place of the individual is then taken by the community, the nation, the people, the continent, and the planet, these in no way, metaphysically speaking, cancel out the subjectivity of modern man, but in fact for the first time lead it into its unconditioned state. "Anthropology," the Anglo-American form of which is "sociology," is supplanting essential thought. Only when man becomes the subject do non-human beings become objects. Only within the domain of subjectivity can a dispute arise over objectivity, over its validity, its profit and its loss, and over its advantages and disadvantages in any particular case.

Since the essence of man, for the Greeks, is not determined as subject, a knowledge of the historical beginning of the Occident is difficult and unsettling for modern "thought," assuming that modern "lived experience" is not simply interpreted back into the Greek world, as if modern man enjoyed a relation of personal intimacy with Hellenism for the simple reason that he organizes "Olympic games" periodically in the main cities of the planet. For here only the facade of the borrowed word is Greek. This is not in any way meant to be derogatory toward the Olympics themselves; it is only censorious of the mistaken opinion that they bear any relation to the Greek essence. And we must come to know this latter if we wish to learn the quite different essence of modern history, i.e., if we wish to experience our own destiny in its essential determination. This task, however, is too awesome and too serious for thoughtless opinion and chatter to be accorded even the slightest consideration. Whoever is receiving these lectures simply for what they pretend to be, namely a thoughtful word of attention and incipient heedfulness, will also in time learn to set aside the all too quickly advancing sentimental lamentations of a thoughtless and garru-

lous "position taking." Whoever is sitting here merely to snap up material for his political or anti-political, religious or anti-religious, scientific
or anti-scientific sentiments is wrong and is substituting what just happens to come to his mind on a particular afternoon for what has been
the task of thinking in the Occident for the last two and a half millennia,
ever since its historical beginning. To be sure, the stupidity in circulation
will not, for thoughtful ones, be a reason to abrogate the task of focusing
on the essential. The empty chatter cannot be stopped. But by the same
token the consideration of the level of ones who are too lazy to think
endangers essential thought.

Our discussions about "the Roman" are being interpreted as stemming from an anti-Christian hostility. Let us leave it for theology to
decide whether the meditation on the essence of truth we have attempted here could not, taken in context, be more fruitful for the preservation of Christianity than the aberrant desire to construct new "scien-
tifically" founded proofs for the existence of God and for the freedom
of the will on the basis of modern atomic physics.

Primordially, the emergent essence of Being disposes and determines
the mode of the sheltering of the unconcealed as the word. The essence
of the word disposes and first determines the essence of the humanity
corresponding to it and thereby relegates this essence into history, i.e.,
into the essential beginning and the transformation of the essence of
the truth of beings. But nowhere does there exist a humanity that forms
for itself a view of Being and then sets itself up with that view as if
Being and the view of it were like the horns that form on an ox, with
which it then vegetates. Only because Being and the truth of Being
are essentially beyond all men and humanities, can, and therefore must,
the "Being" or "non-being" of man be at stake where man as historical
is determined to the preservation of the truth of Being. A decline is
never overcome by simply being stopped or reined in or led in progress
to better times. All progress might be a mere stepping away from—from
the essential domain of the beginning. Only in view of the beginning
can a decline be thought and experienced. The decline can only be
surmounted when the beginning is saved, but then it is already surmounted. And the beginning can only be saved when it is allowed
to be the beginning it is. The beginning is primordial only when thinking is primordial and when man in his essence thinks primordially.
This does not refer to the impossible task of repeating the first beginning
in the sense of a renewal of the Greek world and its transformation
into the here and now. On the contrary, it means to enter, by way
of primordial thought, into a confrontation and dialogue with the beginning in order to perceive the voice of the disposition and determination
of the future. This voice is only to be heard where experience is. And
experience is in essence the suffering in which the essential otherness

of beings reveals itself in opposition to the tried and usual. The highest form of suffering is dying one's death as a sacrifice for the preservation of the truth of Being. This sacrifice is the purest experience of the voice of Being. What if German humanity is that historical humanity which, like the Greek, is called upon to poetize and think, and what if this German humanity must first perceive the voice of Being! Then must not the sacrifices be as many as the causes immediately eliciting them, since the sacrifice has *in itself* an essence all its own and does not require goals and uses! Thus what if the voice of the beginning should announce itself in our historical destiny?

But what if the beginning has fallen into oblivion? Would we not then need to experience first of all that this oblivion is not mere negligence or dereliction on the part of man but is an event pertaining to the very essence of Being itself, i.e, to unconcealedness?

What if man had not only forgotten the essence of Being but if Being itself had forgotten man and had abandoned him to self-forgetfulness? Are we speaking of λήθη here only to appear erudite?

The Greeks are largely silent over λήθη. At times, however, they do speak of it. Hesiod mentions λήθη together with λιμός, the absence of food, as one of the daughters of the veiling night. Pindar also speaks of it and indicates the direction we need to follow in order to glimpse its hidden essence.

EDITOR'S AFTERWORD

The present volume 54 of Heidegger's *Gesamtausgabe* comprises the previously unpublished text of an hourly lecture course the philosopher conducted during the winter term 1942–43 at the University of Freiburg. The course was called "Parmenides and Heraclitus," but in view of the nearly exclusive occupation with Parmenides we have modified the title. The book is the eighteenth to appear in this series.

The editor had at his disposal author's manuscripts amounting to eighty-four numbered pages of lectures and thirty-four pages of recapitulations. Heidegger did not prepare a recapitulation for every lecture. The author himself indicated the pages where the recapitulations were to be inserted, but the choice of the exact place within those pages devolved upon the editor.

The manuscripts are in the folio format, and the writing is crosswise. The right halves of the pages contain numerous interpolations, enclosed within one another; Heidegger indicated their point of contact with the text in each case.

The "addendum" included herein is the text of a recapitulation referring to pages 77–79. It was not presented in the lectures and was described by Heidegger as a "mere draft."

The editor also had at his disposal typewritten copies of all the manuscripts mentioned above. They were checked twice against the originals. Some passages in the manuscripts, missing in the transcriptions, were inserted by the author himself at the proper place. Heidegger completely reviewed this transcript while he was preparing his lectures on the Logos of Heraclitus (cf. *Gesamtausgabe*, vol. 55). He supplemented the transcript on numerous occasions with some smaller and some larger interpolations. The editor deciphered these and without exception allowed for them in the present text.

The division into numbered paragraphs, the subdivisions, and the formulation of all the headings are the work of the editor. The latter adhere closely to the text of the lectures. In accord with Heidegger's wishes, an extensive table of contents precedes the work and this, together with the segmentation of the text, should make the overall structure of the lectures clearly visible.

In connection with the present volume, the reader is also referred to Heidegger's essay "Moira (Parmenides Fragment VIII, 34–41)" which appeared in his *Vorträge und Aufsätze*, first published in 1954.

The editor would like to express his sincere thanks for the assistance he received in his work from H. Heidegger, from H. Tietjen and W. Deyhle, who reviewed the typescript, and from F.-W. von Herrmann, who responded to questions concerning the deciphering of the interpolations. Likewise, thanks are due to Francis B. Vawter for technical help.

Manfred S. Frings
DePaul University